CAD AND RAPID PROTOTYPING
FOR PRODUCT DESIGN
DOUGLAS BRYDEN

Laurence King Publishing

Published in 2014 by
Laurence King Publishing Ltd
361–373 City Road
London EC1V 1LR
Tel: +44 20 7841 6900
Fax: +44 20 7841 6910
email: enquiries@laurenceking.com
www.laurenceking.com

A catalogue record for this book is available from the British
Library.

ISBN: 978 1 78067 342 4

Series and book design: Unlimited
Picture research: Douglas Bryden and Fredrika Lökholm

Printed in China

LAURENCE KING

CONTENTS

INTRODUCTION   6
    — Case Study Joris Laarman Lab (Bone Chair and Bone Chaise)   8

1 COMPUTER-AIDED DESIGN   10
What is Computer-Aided Design?   11
What is Computer-Aided Design Used For?   11
CAD Modelling Approaches   13
Drawings to 3D Models   15
    — Case Study Design Partners (G930 Wireless Gaming Headset)   20
    — Case Study DCA Design (Mylo Pushchair)   24
    — Case Study Therefore (VIA Personal Navigational Devices)   28
    — Case Study Tools Design (Lunchbox and Wine Catalyzer)   32
    — Case Study Factory Design (Superlight Aircraft Seating)   36
    — Case Study Studio Aisslinger (YILL Mobile Energy-Storage Unit)   38
Rendering   40
    — Case Study Stefano Giovannoni (AlessiPhone and AlessiTab)   50
    — Case Study Philips Design (DesignLine Television and Home Cinema System)   52
    — Case Study Priestmangoode (Moving Platforms)   54
Animation   56
CAD Software For Product Design   59

2 RAPID PROTOTYPING   66
What is Rapid Prototyping?   67
What is Rapid Prototyping Used For?   67
Rapid Prototyping Processes   67
Rapid Manufacturing and Additive Manufacturing   68
Subtractive RP   70
    — Case Study 2Form (Memento Rug)   76
    — Case Study Lauren Moriarty (Noodle Block Cube, Stitch Studies and Geometric Structure Cushion)   78
    — Case Study David Trubridge (Kina Light and Dream Space Gazebo)   80
    — Case Study Daniel Rohr (Colander Table)   84
    — Case Study Paul Loebach (Shelf Space)   86
Additive RP   88
    — Case Study Fuseproject (SAYL Office Chair)   100
    — Case Study Freedom Of Creation (Dahlia Wall Light, Palm Pendant Light, Macedonia Tray, Trabecula Tray, Punch Bag and V Bag)   102
    — Case Study Ryuji Nakamura & Associates (Insect Cage)   104
    — Case Study Michaella Janse van Vuuren (Chrysanthemum)   106

— Case Study WertelOberfell Platform (Fractal.MGX Table)   108
— Case Study Erich Ginder (Materialized Vase)   110
— Case Study Michael Eden (Wedgwoodn't Tureen, Vortex,   112
Maelstrom IV and Bloom)
— Case Study Bathsheba Grossman (Klein Bottle Opener)   116
Finishing Additive RP Models   118
Considerations For CAD Models Destined For RP   121

3 RESEARCH AND THE FUTURE OF CAD AND RAPID PROTOTYPING   128
Economics   129
Materials   131
The Environment   132
Consumers   134
Technology   135
Design   137
— Case Study RepRap (Self-Replicating Manufacturing Machines)   140
— Case Study Fab@Home (Open-Source 3D Printers)   142
— Case Study AM Research Group (Customized Sprinting Spikes)   144
— Case Study Growthobjects (Broccoli and Lily Lamp)   146
— Case Study Future Factories (Entropia Lamp)   148
— Case Study Bespoke Innovations (Bespoke Prostheses   150
Fairings)
— Case Study Exstent (ExoVasc Cardiovascular Device)   152
— Case Study Southampton University (Laser Sintered Aircraft)   154
— Case Study EADS (Airbike)   156
Conclusion   158

Glossary   164
3D Modelling, Rendering and Engineering Software   167
Common Types of 3D File   170
Further Reading   170
Internet Resources   171
Index   172
Picture Credits   175
Acknowledgements   176

INTRODUCTION

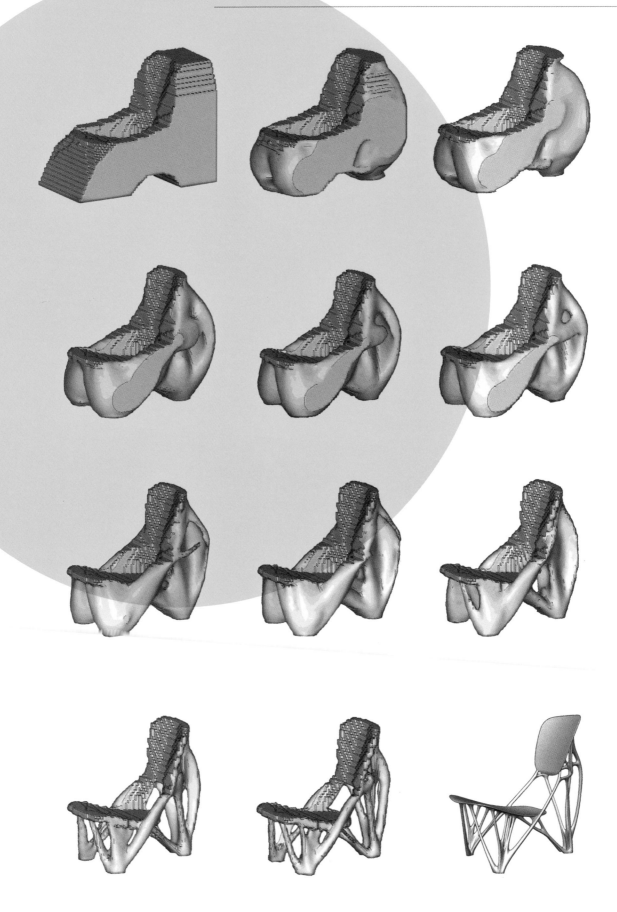

The impact of CAD and rapid prototyping

Computing technologies enable us to explore and define the world around us in an ever increasing number of ways, helping scientists, engineers, architects and designers to solve complex problems and define future directions for the man-made world in which we live. Product design involves an iterative process of research, analysis, thinking, conceptualizing, visualizing, model making, prototyping, testing and refining. As computing technologies evolve, they continue to influence this process. Computer-aided design (CAD) is a form of digital prototyping used within this product development process. Rapid prototyping (RP) refers to a set of computer-controlled machine processes used for prototyping and manufacturing parts from CAD files. CAD and RP are two sets of tools used by product designers in developing products from initial concept to manufactured product.

CAD and RP are embedded in product design, engineering and manufacturing. These technologies have greatly improved productivity by enabling designers and engineers to explore and to push the limits of product form and visual complexity, to evaluate better and to test more accurately their designs in ways not possible in the recent past, and to design products within ever shorter product development timescales. As advances in rapid prototyping technologies accelerate, these processes are increasingly used not only as a means to produce prototype parts but also to manufacture components and products, while at the same time they are freeing designers from many of the constraints placed on them by traditional manufacturing processes.

The computer is an invaluable tool in the design process, enabling designers to create and output virtual models as high-quality rapid prototyped models in order to evaluate their designs in the real world. CAD and RP now play a central role in design development and are a fundamental part of the professional practice of product design. It is therefore important for product design students to be aware of the range of CAD and RP processes used in industry, of how they are used and of the similarities and differences between different processes. This information can be difficult to find. This book aims to provide an informative, engaging and useful overview of the fundamental principles of computer-aided design and rapid prototyping and, through a variety of case studies, to reveal some of the processes by which these tools are being used by designers and researchers.

Organization of this book

Chapters 1 and 2 focus on the use of CAD and RP and include explanations of principles and processes, with the aid of screenshots, computer-generated images, photographs and illustrations. Chapter 3 focuses on research and discusses recent and speculative developments. Case studies of international product design consultancies, global manufacturing brands, leading product design practitioners and leading researchers are used throughout the book to provide a clear picture of current industry practice and research.

Case Study
Joris Laarman Lab

Products: Bone Chair, Bone Chaise
Client: Joris Laarman
Materials: Bone Chair: aluminium;
Bone Chaise: polyurethane
RP process: Bone Chaise: 3D printing
in ceramic (for mould creation)
Dimensions: Bone Chair: 750 x 760 x
350mm (29.53 x 29.92 x 13.78in); Bone
Chaise: 1470 x 770 x 850mm (57.87 x
30.31 x 33.46in)
Designer: Joris Laarman
Design to production: 2 years
Website: www.jorislaarman.com

Introduction

Following studies at the Design
Academy, Eindhoven, The
Netherlands, from which he graduated
in 2003, Joris Laarman established his
studio with film-maker Anita Star in
Amsterdam in 2004. Describing the
studio as a 'lab' and 'an experimental
playground set up to study and shape
the future,' their work focuses on
collaborations with craftsmen,
scientists and engineers to investigate
possibilities presented by emerging
technologies. In 2011 Laarman received
one of eight *Wall Street Journal*
Innovator of the Year awards and his
work forms part of the permanent
collections of several renowned
international museums, including the
Museum of Modern Art, New York, the
Victoria and Albert Museum, London,
Vitra Design Museum, Weil am Rhein,
Germany, the Pompidou Centre, Paris,
and the Rijksmuseum, Amsterdam.

Laarman recently worked with
Renny Ramakers of Dutch design
studio Droog and internet entrepreneur
Michiel Frackers on developing
Make-Me, an online platform for
open-source downloadable designs
and a virtual hub where designers can
be paired with manufacturers.

Approach

The bone furniture project started in
2004 when Laarman learnt of research

by German Professor of Biomechanics
Claus Mattheck and Lothar Hartzheim,
investigating the ways in which trees
and bones were constructed through
evolution. In 1998, Hartzheim, based at
the International Development Centre
at Opel, part of General Motors, had
worked with Professor Mattheck to
develop a new type of CAD software.
The software was used to model car
components based on natural
construction principles in order to
optimize their strength and reduce
their weight.

Amazed by the efficiency, beauty
and accuracy that this optimization
software could generate, and inspired
by the possibilities that the software
presented, Laarman wanted to use it
to optimize the design of furniture, the

same way it did for car parts, utilizing
material only where it was needed.

Process

Intending to use the software as
'a high-tech sculpting tool to create
elegant shapes', the project began
as an experiment. Working in
collaboration with the International
Development Centre at Opel, Laarman
determined that the unique software
could be adapted to produce a chair.

First, the required positions,
shapes and loading parameters for
the seat and back of the chair were
defined. Through a process of running
repeated generations of simulation,
similar to a speeded-up process of
evolution, the software then used an
algorithm to calculate the optimum size

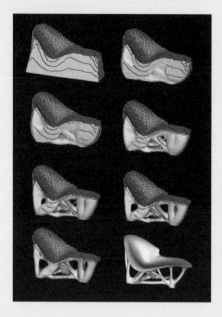

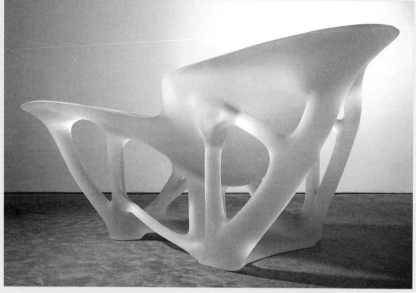

and shape of the supporting structure underneath the seat and back, removing any material not required for support and thickening areas bearing greater load. Material properties also determined the aesthetic of the products, with the stronger aluminium material specified for the chair resulting in a more slender structure than the chaise, for which polyurethane had been specified.

Laarman initially approached Clemens van Bliierswijk, a professor at the University of Twente in The Netherlands, with a speciality in live bone growth, to investigate the possibility of making the chair from actual bone, but this was found to be unfeasible. On receiving a commission from Droog and the Friedman Benda gallery in New York, Laarman reverted to more traditional forms of fabrication and selected casting to produce each of the two pieces in a limited-edition run of twelve.

To better evaluate the designs produced by the software, 1:1 scale polystyrene foam models of the two pieces were hand sculpted, closely referencing the designs the software had generated. Initially, Laarman wanted to create the chairs from paper using a somewhat dated rapid prototyping process named laminated object manufacturing (LOM). Two halves of the chair were fabricated on a LOM machine and glued together, but the final result proved to be too weak.

For each of the 12 chairs, which were gravity cast in molten aluminium, a disposable ceramic mould was created from several pieces, each of which had been created using three-dimensional printing (3DP). As this was a new and experimental technique, many tests were required to perfect it. To cast the chaises, a master pattern was first created from MDF using CNC machining. A reusable 30-piece epoxy resin mould was then made around the pattern at the workshop of designer and model maker Vincent de Rijk. Once the complex mould had been created, the master pattern was removed and a UV-resistant, clear polyurethane resin was used to cast each of the 12 chaises. Both the chair and the chaise were then polished to create the desired finish.

Laarman worked for three years in an attempt to make an economically viable, mass producible version of the Bone Chair, but the project was abandoned as it proved highly difficult and too expensive. Technological progress may one day make it accessible to a wider market.

Result

Completed in 2006, the Bone Chair and Bone Chaise now form part of an expanded collection of seven different designs, all produced from different materials and using a range of methods but following the same design principles.

There is a long tradition of mimicking nature in design, but the Bone Chair and Bone Chaise push beyond copying natural forms, instead utilizing mathematical code to reflect the code used by nature to create life. Laarman comments, 'ever since industrialization we have wanted to make objects inspired by nature, but our digital age makes it possible to use nature not just as a stylistic reference, but to borrow the underlying principles to generate shapes like an evolutionary process.'

Laarman has developed a unique way of creating furniture, questioning the design process and traditional thinking about designers' control over form giving. Instead of using the computer merely as a tool to enable the creation of a design vision, the computer becomes co-creator, anticipating a future in which designers and computers work together symbiotically to create products.

Fig. 1 (opposite)
Bone Chair.
Fig. 2
Development of the Bone Chair and Bone Chaise within the unique CAD software designed by Mattheck and Hartzheim.
Fig. 3
Bone Chaise.

COMPUTER-AIDED DESIGN

What is computer-aided design?

Computer-aided design (CAD) refers to the process of using computers and specialist software to create virtual three-dimensional models and two-dimensional drawings of products. Various different types of CAD software have been developed for use across a range of applications and industries. By using the computer in conjunction with paper and modelling by hand, product designers are able to develop their ideas more quickly, explore alternatives and, in conjunction with rapid prototyping, create accurate product prototypes.

What is computer-aided design used for?

CAD allows designers to explore multiple concepts in 3D more quickly, visualize more accurately and eliminate error from engineering drawings. Designers can ensure that separate components of a design fit together as intended and then create highly realistic images and animations of that design. CAD also allows for

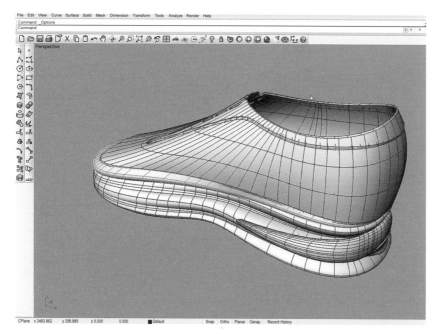

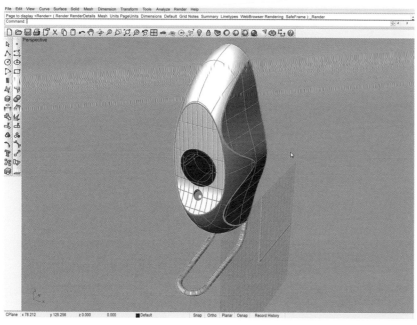

Fig. 1
A surface model of a casual athletic shoe concept (left) and a solid model of a design for an ophthalmic instrument (below).

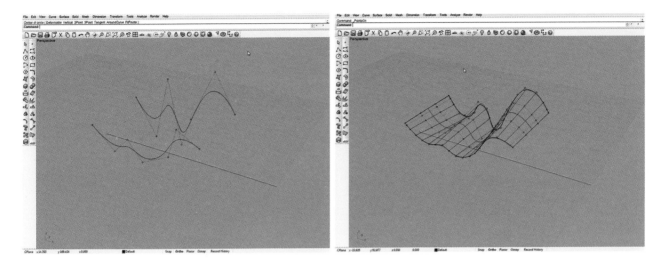

Fig. 2
Example of splines and a non-uniform rational
basis spline (NURBS) surface controlled by
control points.

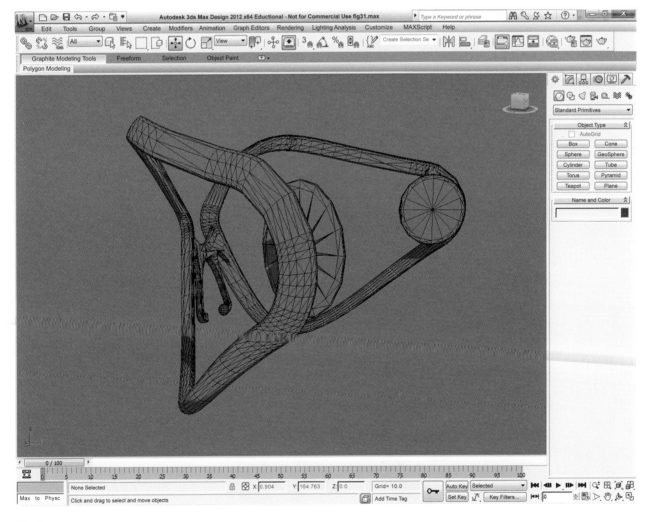

Fig. 3
A polygon mesh model of a pair of armless
sports glasses designed to stick to the wearer's
temples. By Ingo Aurin, the concept was chosen
for the Selected Excellent Works category, 2006
Charmant International Design competition.

more effective communication with engineers and manufacturers, providing the information necessary for the production and assembly of a product, and enabling engineers to perform complex calculations, such as stress testing. (Usefully, too, some CAD programs can be used to lock certain parts of models, preventing engineers from making unwanted changes to important visual aspects of a model.) By minimizing the opportunity for misinterpretation of design intent by engineers and manufacturers, CAD therefore increases the designer's control over the design process, although with this increased control comes increased accountability for the final product.

By providing a smooth transition between different phases of the design development process, as well as improved communication, CAD reduces both the time and cost of developing a design from sketch to manufactured product, enabling manufacturers to bring products to market more quickly.

CAD modelling approaches

CAD modelling can be divided into two fundamental techniques: surface modelling and solid modelling. Surface models can be thought of as consisting of skins of zero thickness, whereas solid models have thickness. Surface modelling techniques are used to create complex, free-form, curving surfaces, such as those required in the automotive and aerospace industries. Solid modelling techniques excel at the creation of mechanical, geometric-shaped components. Both of these techniques can be used to model consumer products.

Types of CAD modelling program
Historically, CAD modelling programs were divided into surface modellers and solid modellers, but today many programs are hybrids, used to create both surface models and solid models. Many programs enable the creation of geometry-driven models, whereby model dimensions can be adjusted to control the overall size and form of the model. The methods used to create models vary from program to program.

NURBS modellers
Non-uniform rational basis spline (NURBS) modellers are based on 'splines' – mathematically defined curves that have their shape controlled by control points sitting off the curves. The shapes of surfaces created in NURBS modellers are also controlled by control points sitting off the surface. The position of control points can be adjusted to change the shape of curves and surfaces, and the number of points can be increased to enable more specific manipulation. The smoothness of deformation during manipulation can be adjusted by changing a parameter known as the 'degree' of the curve or surface, with higher values of degree enabling smoother deformations. This form of surface editing is known as direct manipulation.

Polygon mesh modellers
Polygon mesh modellers are widely used in the gaming, animation, film and computer graphics industries for 3D visualization and effects – they allow intuitive sculpting of form as well as small file sizes, which enables quick rendering of frames and, in computer games, real-time visualization. In polygon mesh modelling, a group of triangular or four-sided quadrilateral (or quad) polygons (faces) are connected together to form an element, or mesh. Models of a given polygon mesh density can be subdivided into more refined polygon models through a process called 'subdivision', a method used to represent the required smooth surfaces while specifying a coarser, less refined and therefore less memory-intensive polygon mesh. The smooth surfaces are calculated from the coarse mesh by subdividing each polygonal face into smaller faces that better approximate a smooth surface.

Fig. 4
Example of a solid model.

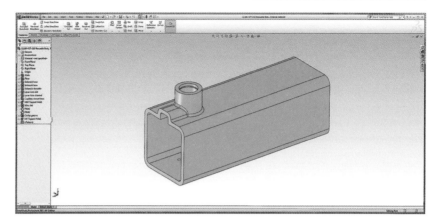

Fig. 5
Example of a solid model assembly.

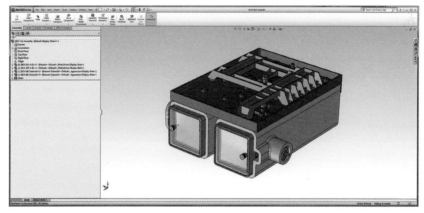

Although polygon mesh modellers can be used to create physical prototypes, they are not widely used in product design, where 3D surfaces need to be mathematically defined and physically prototyped. However, this is changing, with some NURBS surface modellers now including polygon mesh creation and editing tools, and with the emergence of software enabling translation between polygon meshes and NURBS surfaces.

Parametric modellers

In some CAD programs solid modelling is parametric, which means that models are driven by their dimensions (parameters). The process of creating a model in some solid modelling programs is recorded in a design history (sometimes referred to as a design tree or model tree), a list of the procedures, parameters and geometry used to create each solid object in the order they were created. CAD modelling programs with an integrated design history enable the dimensions and shape of a model and its features to be changed at any time during the modelling process, enabling continuous alterations and adjustments to the design. In solid model assemblies, where several part models are assembled together, changes to one part can 'trickle down' through the other parts in the assembly, saving the designer from having to painstakingly re-model each part. Accurate production drawings and bills of materials can also be created from solid component and assembly models, and an associative link can be created between a model and its drawings, meaning changes to the model trigger automatic updates to the drawings, and vice versa. Parametric modelling programs generally require a logic-oriented, planned approach to the modelling process and are less focused on free-form visual exploration than non-parametric modellers.

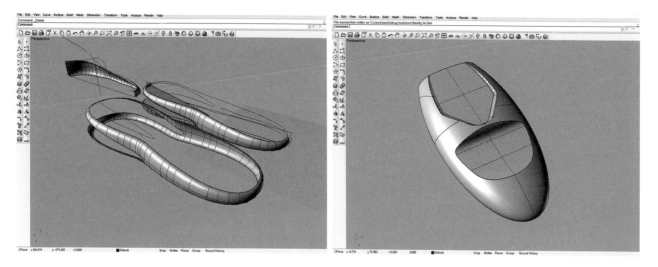

Drawings to 3D models

The process of moving from paper sketch to three-dimensional surface and solid in CAD involves a number of fundamental considerations, starting with the choice of whether to use surface or solid modelling techniques.

Surface modelling or solid modelling?

There are two main factors that affect this decision: the stage of the design process at which the model is being created, and the desired form of the model. In the early concept-exploration stages of the design process, specific dimensions and the number of parts may be undecided and less important than the ability to work quickly and intuitively, and to be able to manipulate the model to explore surface form and proportion. At this point, 3D software is a fundamental means of exploring options within the constraints of the brief, and surface modellers may be more useful, particularly for quickly exploring free-form, complex, curving surface form. At later stages in the design process, when design intent becomes more certain, requirements change. If accurate models with complex curving surfaces are required, capable CAD programs are used to create Class A surfaces (surfaces that the end user will see and touch and that have the mathematical definition, smoothness and high precision required for later use by manufacturing engineers). Solid modelling techniques are then used to transform the Class A surfaces into solids with thickness and volume.

    If geometric forms are desired from the outset, it makes greater sense to use solid modelling methods to create the CAD model. There is usually more than

Fig. 6
Early-stage surface model of a shoe sole and absorption system (left). Early-stage solid model of product designed to perform ultrasound analysis of heart valve prostheses for self-monitoring at home (right).

Fig. 7
How splines are used to generate a build.

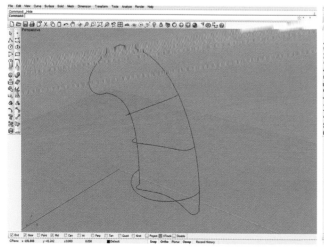

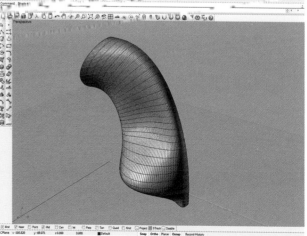

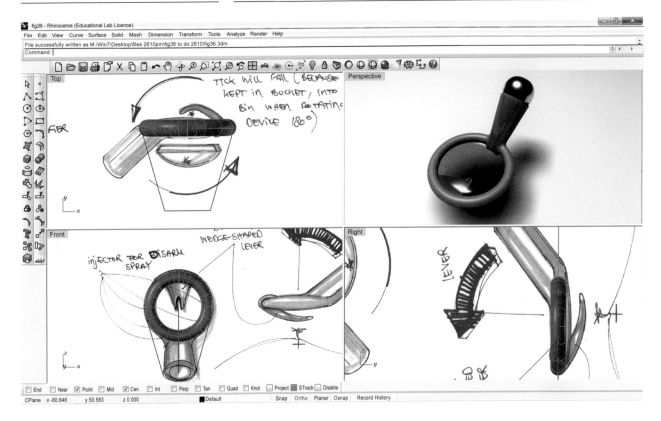

Fig. 8
A scanned sketch of a tick remover concept is used to aid the creation of a CAD model of the product in Rhinoceros 3D. The use of sketches as underlays on which to model helps translate a design from paper to CAD model.

one way to do this, so an understanding of a variety of different modelling techniques will help to select the fastest or most accurate way of achieving a particular form. Methods differ between different CAD programs but there are some similarities, and fundamental modelling concepts are largely the same.

Surface modelling

As explained earlier, in NURBS surface modelling, the process of modelling usually starts with drawing lines known as curves, or splines. Splines have no thickness and can exist on a single two-dimensional plane or as curves in three-dimensional space and form the edges, boundaries and/or cross-sections of the intended 3D surfaces. The splines are then used to generate the surfaces that give form to the 3D model. Splines are usually created by being drawn directly in the 3D CAD program, but they can also be imported from 2D CAD programs or 2D vector drawing programs. Imported splines will usually require rebuilding – an operation that simplifies their geometry to ensure better surface creation.

Types of surface

Splines are used to create open surfaces, closed surfaces, open polysurfaces and closed polysurfaces. (A polysurface consists of two or more surfaces joined together.) Open surfaces have zero thickness or volume and their shape can be edited using control points. Open polysurfaces also have zero thickness or volume. Closed surfaces and closed polysurfaces do have thickness and volume and are also known as solids. Because they consist of a single surface, closed surfaces can be edited using control points in the same way as open surfaces. Polysurfaces, whether open or closed, cannot be edited using control points.

Using sketches or photographs

Scans of hand-drawn design sketches showing plan and elevation views of a design or photographs of plan and elevation views of foam models can be imported into CAD programs and traced to create the profile curves required to generate surfaces. Creating a 3D model will typically involve creating several surfaces from splines that must then be merged/joined/knitted together so that no undesirable gaps are left at the juncture between the separate surfaces. This process is known as surface continuity, or geometric continuity.

Surface continuity

In order to achieve smooth outer surfaces on a product, in CAD it is important to be able to control the way that splines meet and flow into other splines, and therefore also the way in which surfaces meet and flow into other surfaces. There are four types of continuity that can be applied to splines and surfaces:

- Positional (G0)
- Tangential (G1)
- Curvature (G2)
- Acceleration (G3).

In G0 continuity, the curves or surfaces are coincidental to each other, but they may meet at an angle and therefore a crease/seam/kink may remain visible. In G1 continuity, the ends of curves and edges of surfaces become parallel to each

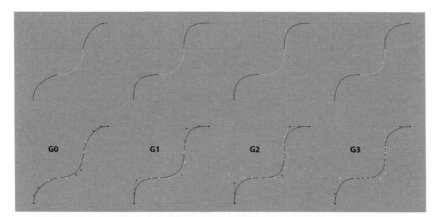

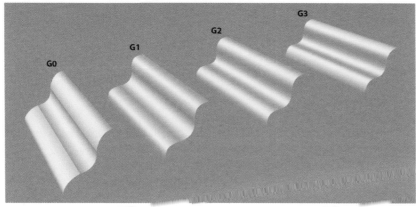

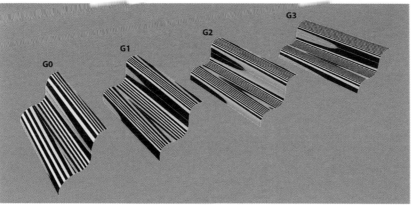

Fig. 9
Four versions of a similar form, each created from three separate curves and then extruded to create four surfaces. Note the variations in control point numbers, the alignment of highlighted control points, and the smoothness of each of the resulting surfaces.

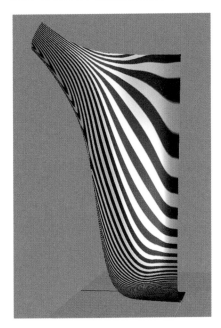

Fig. 10
Zebra Analysis of a surface.

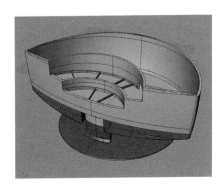

Fig. 11
A solid CAD model of an office desk tidy.

other, so a smooth transition between curves or surfaces is created. In G2 continuity, the curvature radius between two curves or surfaces becomes the same, so a smooth, seamless curve or surface is created. In G3 continuity, the rate of change of curvature between two curves or surfaces becomes the same, so a perfectly smooth curve or surface is created.

In models where smooth transitions between surfaces are desired, G1 (tangential) continuity may be sufficient, although depending on the shape of surfaces, the transition between surfaces can be more localized and therefore less smooth compared with G2 (curvature) and G3 (acceleration) continuity. Use of G2 and G3 continuity between surfaces is particularly important in the automotive industry, where continuous smooth reflections on car bodies are desired.

Analysing surface smoothness

Surface smoothness can be checked visually by applying a smooth and reflective material to a surface in CAD and adding sources of light into the scene to bounce off the surfaces. Many CAD programs include a surface analysis feature that allows an environment map (an image of an exterior or interior scene) to be mapped onto a surface, which then reflects the image. Continuity between surfaces can also be checked using a method known as Zebra Analysis, in which black and white stripes are created on the surfaces to provide a visual indication of their smoothness and that of the transitions between them. If the transitions are not smooth, this will be displayed as a sharp change in direction of the stripes at the points where the two surfaces meet. This technique mimics that used in the automotive industry, where neon ceiling lights are used to check the quality of reflections on the surfaces of prototype car bodies; however, it is an important consideration for any consumer product with glossy surfaces. Tools in some CAD programs also allow surfaces to be checked for their amount of curvature and their draft angle.

Solid modelling

A solid model in CAD is one that has thickness and encloses a volume. A solid model can be saved as a standard triangulation language (STL) file and sent to create a rapid prototyped physical model (see page 121). Solid models can be created using the primitive solid forms, such as spheres, boxes, cylinders, pyramids, cones and tori (singular: torus), found in most CAD programs. However, more commonly, and where more complex solid forms are required, the process of modelling begins with drawing construction curves, which are used to create the solids.

Once a drawing (or sketch) – or several – has been created, a 3D solid creation tool is used to transform it into a solid. Editing solid models is performed using a variety of tools. The fillet tool, for example, is used to place radii on the edges of solids. Faces of solids can be drawn on using drawing (sketching) tools to create shapes that can then be used to create holes, recesses or protrusions. As a general rule of thumb, solid-modelling editing tools can be used only on solid models and not on surface models, which are edited using separate surface editing tools. However, surface models can be transformed into solid models so that solid editing tools can be used and the model can be output as a rapid prototyped part.

Fully featured CAD programs include special integrated tools for adding assembly and structural features to solid models, such as screw holes, screw bosses and ribs that can be added to parts intended to be injection moulded, for example. Solid models can be assigned materials and imported into computer-aided engineering (CAE) software to allow engineering calculations to be performed. Data from solid models can be directly imported into computer-aided manufacture (CAM) and computer numerical control (CNC) software for quick and precise machining of moulds for injection moulding or die casting, or for the direct manufacture of parts.

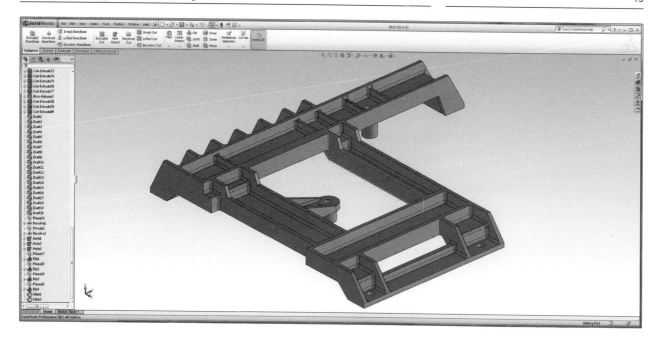

Modelling in parametric CAD programs

Whether modelling surfaces or solids, in parametric CAD programs, construction curves must be drawn on 2D construction planes. These curves control the dimensions of the surfaces, parts or features they are used to create. (In many parametric CAD programs, the term 'part' is used to describe a single solid model, while 'feature' – e.g. a hole or a radius on an edge – refers to any features and operations on that model.) Dimensions that control the shape and size of a part and its features are determined at the time of creation but can also be adjusted later. A geometric constraint engine is utilized within parametric CAD programs to manage associative relationships between component parts in product assemblies. Dimensional changes can therefore be made to component parts and to assemblies of parts to perform various 'what if?' scenarios.

As mentioned earlier (see page 14), when you create surfaces, parts and features in a parametric CAD program, the software records your actions to create a design history. This enables you to revisit and make changes to parts and features (e.g. the position of a hole) later in the modelling process, making some design alterations much easier than with those CAD programs that require you to start the modelling process all over again. Few non-parametric CAD programs include design history functionality.

Assemblies

Where a product consists of more than one part, you need to know how and if the parts will fit together when assembled. This requires a precise, logical, human way of working in CAD, where specific dimensions are known and can be checked, and parts are modelled separately and then brought together in a product assembly. The process of creating an assembly involves telling the CAD software how the separate parts relate to one another; it will also highlight any problems, such as wrongly sized or misaligned parts. In CAD programs that support assemblies, the separate components exist together in the virtual model space and can be saved together as an assembly file.

Fig. 12
A solid CAD model of a manifold bracket for a gas testing product, modelled in SolidWorks, a parametric CAD program. The model's design history (design tree) can be seen on the left of the screen.

Case Study
Design Partners

Product: G930 Wireless Gaming Headset

Client: Logitech

Material: ABS

Dimensions: 190 x 190 x 90mm (7.48 x 7.48 x 3.54in)

Designers: Eugene Canavan, Andreas Connellan and James Lynch (Design Partners); Melissa Yale and Alex Danielson (Logitech)

Design to production: 10 months

Modelling software: PTC Pro/Engineer (now Creo Parametric)

Visualization and rendering software: Adobe Photoshop, Autodesk Maya, Bunkspeed Shot, Maxon Cinema 4D, NewTek LightWave

Website: www.designpartners.com

Awards: CES Innovations (honoree) 2011, Good Design Award 2012, iF Product Design Award 2011, Red Dot Award 2011

Fig. 13
Photoshop and CAD renders were used for sales and marketing purposes. Renders of concepts were also used to gain input on design direction from Logitech's senior management.

Introduction

Design Partners are a multidisciplinary product design consultancy, comprising brand analysts, designers, engineers and digital media artists. The G930 Wireless Gaming Headset is one of a series of collaborations with Logitech on their G-series product line.

Approach

Feedback on previous G-series and competitor headsets was gathered from user group tests, and the key areas of concern that emerged were the function keys, adjustment usability and weight over prolonged usage periods. Although as a cordless product the G930 would require heavier internal components than previous Logitech headsets, the goal was to reduce weight as much as possible.

Process

Several early concepts were line drawn, scanned into Photoshop for rendering using a digital Wacom pen and tablet, then traced over to create 2D vector linework in Illustrator. The linework was then imported into Pro/Engineer to begin the process of CAD modelling. CAD models were quickly created and used to check whether the printed

circuit board (PCB) and battery would fit inside. The CAD models were used to create physical foam models on four- and five-axis CNC machines, and the foam models were then refined by hand, cutting, filling and sanding to create finished appearance models.

Once a concept had been selected, its revised foam model was used to generate a corresponding CAD model. A GOM Atos laser scanner captured the physical model and converted it into 3D point cloud data – a process known as 'reverse engineering', which allows an approach combining hand modelling with CAD modelling. A top-down methodology was used for the modelling process, whereby planes and pivot points were established and put into a master file that controlled the part files. When changes were made to the master, these trickled through and updated the associated part files.

During the subsequent development period, ergonomic data taken from the target market was used to check the size of the product. Usability issues, such as the numbers of buttons and controls, aesthetic considerations and mechanical feasibility were all tested, and internal components were modelled to ensure

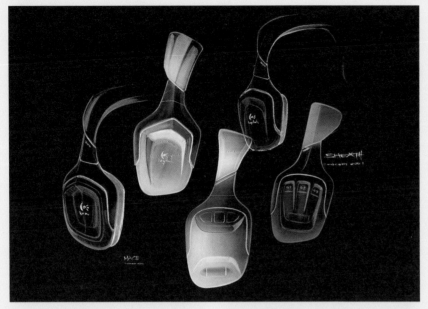

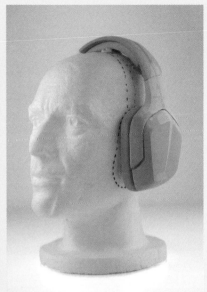

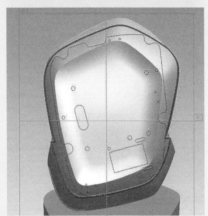

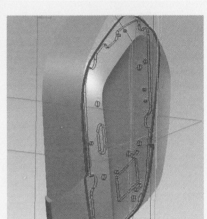

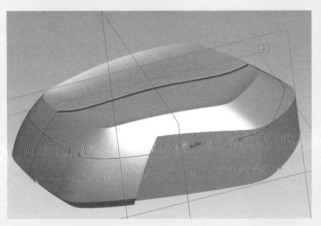

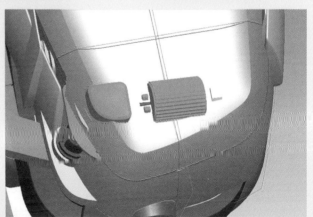

Fig. 14 (top left)
Early concept sketches.
Fig. 15 (top right)
Foam models were created from CAD data using four- and five-axis CNC machines, then refined by hand. These were later finished as appearance models to present to Logitech.

Fig. 16 (centre row and above)
Design Partners worked closely with Logitech's engineers, who provided information about internal components, which were then included within the CAD model. This enabled accurate positioning of such features as buttons. The model was adjusted to resolve any collisions between internal components and the surfaces of the concept model.

Case Study
Design Partners

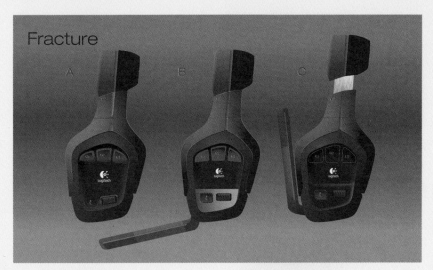

Fracture

that they fitted inside the product. Several colour, materials and finishes (CMF) proposals were also created.

The articulation and roll of the ear cups and adjustability of the headband were resolved in CAD, and the bending/clamping force and flexibility of various headband materials were tested using computer-aided engineering (CAE)/finite element analysis (FEA) software, PTC Pro/Mechanical (now Creo Simulate). The positioning of some of the split lines on the headband, where separate component parts met, was also revised, to avoid hair catching, possible prise points and potential creaking.

Result

The G930 has impressive virtual surround sound and voice access capability, and is 100g (3.5oz) lighter than its predecessor. The keys – angled towards the fingertips – are located in a recess to avoid accidental activation, while the feeling of the key press provides improved control. Simple intuitive adjustability and programmable controls allow gamers to tune the product to their individual preference.

Fig. 17 (above)
CMF options of chosen concept.

Fig. 18 (left)
Physical model of an early concept, with surfaces finished to appear as those on an end-use product. Appearance models such as this were presented to Logitech for feedback during the development of the design.

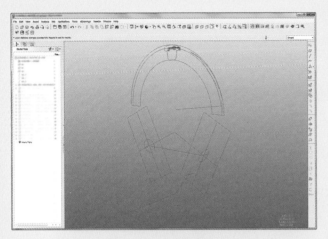

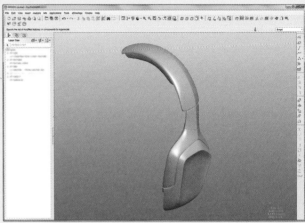

Fig. 19
Screen grabs showing the master file at several stages during the CAD modelling process. A top-down methodology was used; planes and pivot points were established in a master file, which controlled the part files. When changes were made to the master file, they were also applied to the associated part files. PTC Pro/Engineer CAD software was used for modelling, but Design Partners use a variety of software in their work, including Dassault Systèmes SolidWorks and CATIA.

Case Study
DCA Design

Product: Mylo Pushchair
Client: Mamas & Papas
Materials: aluminium, polypropylene, glass-filled nylon
Dimensions: 1100 x 600 x 1170mm (43.70 x 23.62 x 46.06in); folded: 220 x 600 x 75mm (8.66 x 23.62 x 2.95in)
Designers: DCA design team; Mamas & Papas' fabric and mechanical engineers
Design to production: 44 months
Modelling software: Dassault Systèmes SolidWorks and PTC Pro/Engineer (now Creo Parametric)
Visualization and rendering software: Adobe Illustrator, Adobe Photoshop, AutoDesk 3ds Max, Luxion KeyShot
Website: www.dca-design.com

Introduction

DCA specialize in delivering product design and innovation for larger organizations. Their team includes strategists, anthropologists, ethnographers, designers, ergonomists, engineers, technologists, project managers and prototype technicians. DCA first started working for Mamas & Papas in early 2007 on the design for a pushchair that functioned well and also looked different. DCA were responsible for user research, design strategy, industrial design and mechanical engineering.

Fig. 20
Mylo pushchair.

Approach

From the start, the needs of the end user were kept central to the design and development work. The concept progressed through many rigs, prototypes and visuals of increasing resolution, all allowing a growing panel of users to feed into the decision making. It rapidly became apparent that a pushchair is inherently a series of compromises and trade-offs, and that few products are required to do so much. DCA reached the conclusion that 'every pushchair has to decide what its agenda is and deliver on that, otherwise it won't deliver on anything.'

Process

DCA identified an often overlooked aspect of a pushchair: that it has two key users, parent and baby. Many pushchairs prioritize convenience for the parent and are designed around the frame. DCA shifted the balance from 'parent first' to 'parent and baby equal', placing the baby centre stage and designing from the seat out rather than the frame in. The twin goals were comfort for the baby and 'calm and simplicity' for the parent.

Fifty initial design concepts – divided between the frame and the seat, and in two streams of development, one mechanical and one visual – were eventually reduced to just two frame and two seat principles. Sketching and intensive scale model making progressed rapidly into rough, full-size mock-ups. Working in Pro/Engineer and SolidWorks, virtual models were created in parallel with the scale models and full-size test rigs.

Unable to use real babies in their test rigs, DCA utilized an ergonomist, applied anthropometric data and employed mannequins and CAD models of babies to ensure that designs fitted the required range from newborns up to three-year-olds.

Over 200 high-quality prototype parts were created during the design development, using a mixture of rapid prototyping processes. Large structural prototype components were created using selective laser sintering (SLS), and direct metal laser sintering (DMLS) was used for some small metal parts – both outsourced to prototyping bureaus. In-house, CNC machines were used to create aluminium and plastic parts, fused deposition modelling (FDM) machines were used to fabricate internal, non-visual parts, and test prototypes of the seat were made using a variety of fabrics.

Fig. 21 (top left)
Early concept sketches. Fifty initial design concepts were explored, divided between the frame and the seat.

Fig. 22 (top right)
The design team used intensive scale model making to explore concepts, moving quickly into rough full-size mock-ups.

Fig. 23 (above)
Concept rendering. At each monthly meeting, an improved mechanical solution and visual iteration were presented to Mamas & Papas.

Case Study
DCA Design

Result

The visual language of the Mylo Pushchair is the result of prioritizing the seat, simplifying the frame and creating innovative production techniques to move away from the ubiquitous crude 'Meccano' aesthetic. By using CAD as a tool – to explore, visualize, engineer and communicate with the client and manufacturer – but not relying solely on it, and by making quick, crude prototypes, which could be seen, touched and tested, early in the design process, DCA were able to identify the inevitable failures throughout the process.

Fig. 24 (above and right)
Test prototype.
Fig. 25 (below)
Component testing and analysis in CAE software.
Fig. 26 (opposite)
Refined concept renders.

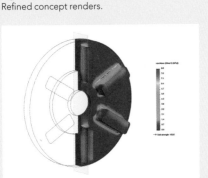

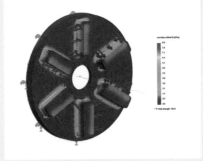

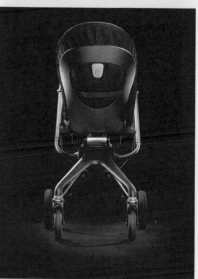

Case Study
Therefore

Product: VIA personal navigational devices
Client: TomTom
Materials: Main casing: PC/ABS; front bezel: PC/ABS and aluminium variant; mount: rubber over moulded glass-filled nylon
Dimensions: VIA 130: 4.3in screen, 119 x 85 x 19mm (4.69 x 3.35 x 0.75in); VIA 135: 5in screen, 134 x 95 x 20mm (5.28 x 3.74 x 0.79in)
Designers: Martin Riddiford (technical and product design) and Rachael Roberts (lead CAD engineer)
Design to production: 7 months
Modelling software: PTC Pro/Engineer (now Creo Parametric)
Visualization and rendering software: NewTek Lightwave and PTC Pro/Engineer
Website: www.therefore.co.uk
Awards: iF Product Design Award 2011

Fig. 27
TomTom VIA personal navigational device.

Introduction

TomTom required a new range of personal navigational devices (PNDs) to replace their existing mid-range product line. Therefore were asked to design and develop a family of three products, incorporating 3.5, 4.3 and 5in resistive LCD screens. These devices were to include new features, such as full voice control, hands-free calling, faster route calculation, an enhanced new user interface and advanced traffic information. They also needed to appeal to the current market, yet retain brand values.

Approach

Therefore were required to make the devices as slim as possible and to develop TomTom's integrated Easyport dashboard and windscreen mounting system. The design needed to be cost effective to manufacture without any compromise to quality or aesthetics. A palette of colours, materials and finishes was defined that would allow differentiation between the individual products, yet retain a cohesive family look and feel.

Process

TomTom provided Therefore with a package of components – including a resistive screen, speaker, battery and antennas – with which to develop the PNDs. The scheme was developed for a 3.5in PND and scaled up for the 4.3 and 5in versions. Using the ball of the mount as a reference point, internal components were positioned relative to this, enabling the same printed circuit board to be used in all sizes.

Sketches were initially used to flesh out internal component positions

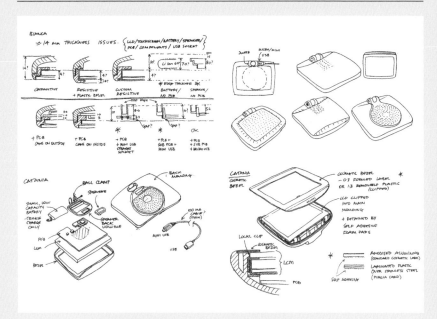

Fig. 28
Early concept and detail sketches.

Fig. 29
As the design solidified, internal parts were modelled and assembled in precise detail with full consideration for manufacture and assembly. The most challenging aspect of the development process for Therefore was that some internal components had not been determined at the outset of the project, and some were fully defined only at a late stage in the process.

and determine thicknesses, as well as establish a visual aesthetic. Simple handmade foam models were used to develop the 3D form and provide a physical reference, with sketches rendered in Illustrator and Photoshop to support the models. At this stage CAD was used to turn the concept into reality. A loose arrangement of the required elements started to define the overall dimensions of the casings. The approximate block models defining the covers then evolved into detailed parts with full consideration for manufacture and assembly. Internal components were modelled and assembled in CAD in precise detail. The process was top-down, with a master assembly file controlling each of the individual part files. Therefore explored two or three alternative internal build arrangements with different product-design form studies, alongside additional options for the mount, connectivity, screen type and battery size.

Rapid prototyping was then used to create models of the CAD, assessing size, aesthetics, usability and assembly. Stereolithography (SLA) and CNC milling were outsourced to a prototyping bureau, with finishing work on prototypes done in-house. Finally, a colour, materials and finishes exercise determined the finished look, initially using computer-generated images, then prototype models sprayed and finished to depict the final products accurately. LightWave was the preferred rendering software.

Case Study
Therefore

Result

The final product is robust, compact and retains the TomTom aesthetic. The front bezel subtly wraps to the rear moulding, blending the switch, speaker and mount areas on a simple 3D surface, and the various models are differentiated using painted and moulded details on the bezel. Tall components have been kept down the spine of the device so that its edges remain thin; the sides then pillow to reduce the overall visual volume. An integrated fold-flat mount rotates for either dash or windscreen mounting, making this a convenient and easy-to-use product.

Fig. 30
Therefore undertook a colour, materials and finishes exercise to determine how the final products would look and be distinguished from one another. Computer-generated images showed a range of colours and finishes, and eventually prototype models were sprayed and finished to depict the final products accurately. LightWave was the preferred rendering software.

Fig. 31
Packaging concepts explored in CAD.

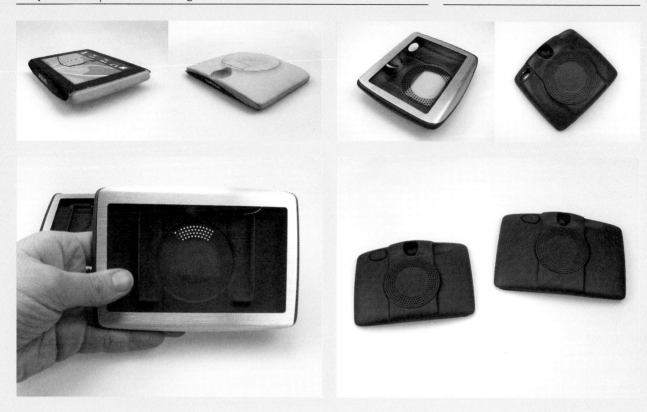

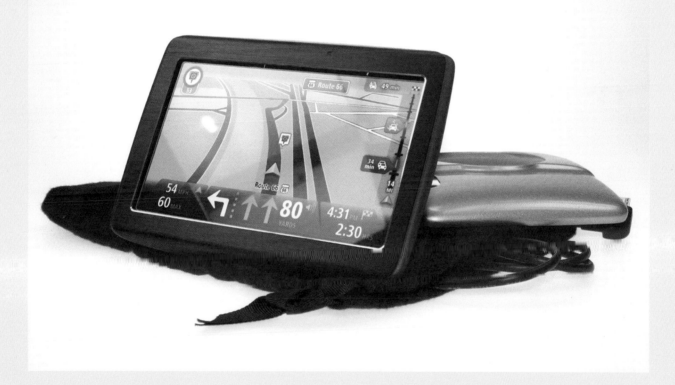

Fig. 32 (top)
Foam and rapid prototype development models.
Fig. 33 (above)
Final rapid prototyped appearance model with
applied finishes.

Case Study
Tools Design

Product: Lunchbox and Catalyzer
Client: Eva Solo
Materials: Lunchbox: polypropylene, TPE, stainless steel; Catalyzer: silicone rubber, stainless steel
Dimensions: Lunchbox: 15 x 15 x 84mm (0.59 x 0.59 x 3.31in); Catalyzer: 22 x 108mm (0.87 x 4.25in)
Designers: Claus Jensen and Henrik Holbæk
Design to production: Lunchbox: 24 months; Catalyzer: 20 months
Modelling software: Encore Software Shark FX
Visualization and rendering software: Next Limit Technologies Maxwell Render
Website: www.toolsdesign.com
Awards: Catalyzer: Red Dot Award 2011

Fig. 34
Eva Solo Lunchbox.
Fig. 35
CAD models exploring alternative geometries and concept renders.

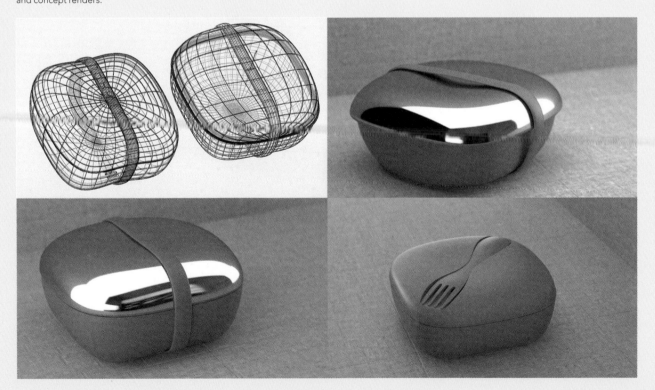

Introduction

Tools Design is an award-winning Danish design studio, based in Copenhagen with additional studios in France and Florida, USA. Their portfolio ranges from electronics and medical equipment to household products, and their output is often characterized by a simple approach: their design philosophy is to put 'something extra' into products.

Lunchbox Approach

In Denmark, schoolchildren and many workers bring their lunch to school or work. Traditionally, lunch consisted of sandwiches, but food choices have changed. Lunchboxes, however, have not evolved accordingly, so Danish homewares company Eva Solo approached Tools Design with the brief to design a lunchbox able to contain both 'dry' and 'wet' foods.

The Lunchbox started as a five-part construction: a stainless steel main container, a hard plastic lid with an integrated rubber gasket for airtightness, a 'spork' (spoon + fork),

a stainless steel 'plate' and a rubber band that wrapped around the whole box. However, the designers soon realized that they had started with the wrong design decision, which had resulted in a long line of 'repairs', and began a complete rethink.

Lunchbox Process

The concave sides that had been introduced to ensure a snug fit for the rubber band made it difficult to make the Lunchbox airtight. The vacuum inside the container also made it impossible to remove the tight-fitting lid without pressing the container against the body. After numerous attempts failed to solve the problem, the designers decided to replace the stainless steel container with polyethylene plastic, a slightly soft plastic often used for airtight food containers. The geometry was changed, retaining the concave near the bottom but adjusting the top edge to curve outwards. The lid was made from the same material and could be opened simply by grabbing a corner

and flexing it upwards. The 'spork' was the only part that remained unchanged throughout the project.

Fig. 36
Lunchbox development prototypes.

Case Study
Tools Design

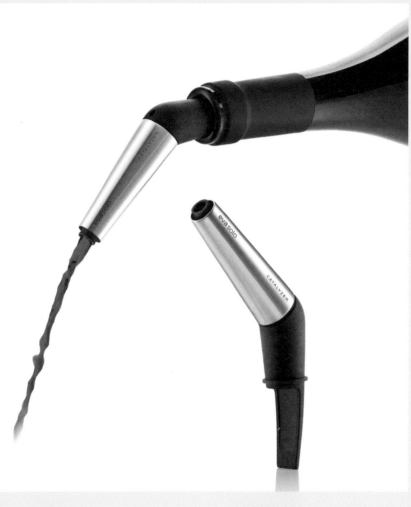

Catalyzer Approach

A Danish inventor had approached Eva Solo with the discovery that if you pour wine through a magnetic field it will improve the flavour of the wine. This proved especially noticeable with 'rough' or young wines. The inventor's homemade contraption – later named the 'Catalyzer' – featured a magnetic tube inside a larger tube; during pouring, the wine would surround the magnetic tube. Tools Design were asked to create a smooth-pouring device that would stand apart from other pourers. The primary challenge was to enable air to enter the bottle while the wine was being poured. If the entering air collided with the exiting wine, the result would be an uneven pour.

Catalyzer Process

Most quality wine pourers provide separate paths for the wine and air to travel, typically by allowing air to enter the bottle through a thin tube and the wine to exit through a wider tube. Once wine starts to travel through the bigger tube, incoming air keeps the thin tube clear of wine. The magnetic

Fig. 37 (above)
Eva Solo Catalyzer.
Fig. 38 (right)
A CAD model of the inner magnetic tube inside a larger, conical outer tube, with detailing to allow wine to be poured while simultaneously allowing air to enter the wine bottle.
Fig. 39 (opposite above)
Developmental renders were created using Next Limit Technologies' Maxwell Render software and presented to Eva Solo for feedback.
Fig. 40 (opposite below)
Development prototypes.

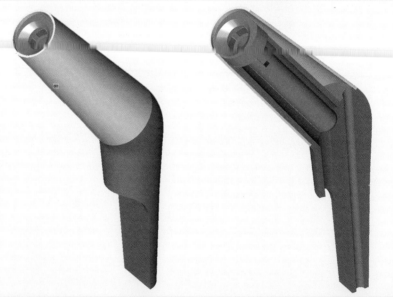

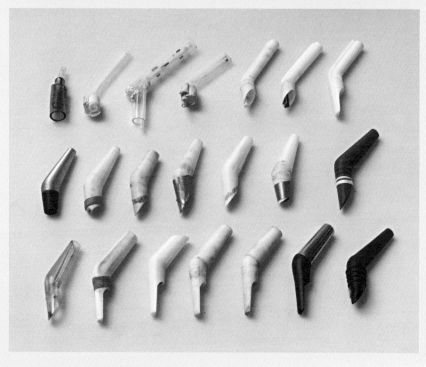

Results

The Lunchbox is a successful upgrade of the traditional plastic sandwich box and offers a much improved aesthetic to the airtight plastic kitchen-storage container, while the integrated spork solves the problem of forgotten cutlery. The tight-fitting lid ensures the product can be used for salads and food with sauces. The bottom part functions as a bowl and is microwave-safe, and the stainless steel lid also serves as a plate. The accompanying silicone band holds everything securely in place.

The gentle flow from the Catalyzer helps to protect wine, preserving its freshness, aroma and character. Its built-in magnet system treats a wine while it is poured, achieving a rounder, more balanced taste (confirmed in blind tastings with three of Denmark's leading sommeliers in 2010). The Catalyzer's magnetic field releases a wine's flavours by breaking the surface tension of the 'water barrier' encapsulating them, and releases the flavour-carrying oxygen in wine as it is poured. The Catalyzer also moderates tannins, which can account for a slightly bitter flavour in young wine. Tannins aggregate over the years, so they are neutralized in older wines; the Catalyzer accelerates this process.

tube took up valuable space in the middle of the wine tube, and also needed to be held in place. The extra components also added resistance to the wine flow – if the bottle was tilted too quickly, the wine would get 'confused' and flow out of the air intake tube.

Several CAD models and rapid prototypes, incorporating hand-moulded rubber parts, were created to simulate the final product and ensure the pourer located securely in the bottleneck during test pours. The process was a challenging one. Often, a rapid prototype would work

finish, although this off-tool sample would fail, proving that sometimes exact material characteristics are necessary in order to confirm product performance.

For both Lunchbox and Catalyzer, Tools Design used Shark FX for CAD modelling, while development prototypes were created in-house using a Dimension Elite 3D FDM rapid prototyping machine. Developmental and final renders were created using Maxwell Render.

Case Study
Factory Design

Product: Superlight aircraft seating
Client: Acro Aircraft Seating Ltd
Materials: aluminium, stainless steel, polyurethane foam, E-leather (reconstituted leather from off-cuts), Kydex thermoplastic
Designers: Adrian Berry and Adam White (creative directors), Matthew Fiddimore and Lee Bazalgette (associates), Peter Tennent (project management and strategy)
Design to production: 12 months
Modelling software: Dassault Systèmes SolidWorks
Visualization and rendering software: Autodesk 3ds Max, Adobe Illustrator, Adobe Photoshop
Website: www.factorydesign.co.uk
Awards: DBA Design Effectiveness Award 2011, Design Week Award 2011

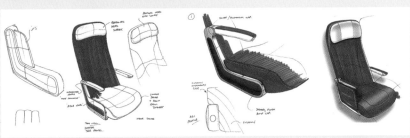

Fig. 41
Superlight aircraft seating.
Fig. 42
Concept sketches. Ideas were proposed to Acro Aircraft Seating every week, sometimes daily.

Introduction

Factory Design create consumer products, commercial goods, packaging, transportation and spaces. Acro Aircraft Seating were set up to produce a bespoke lightweight seat for low-cost airlines (weight having a significant effect on fuel consumption). Their brief for Factory Design was for a low-cost, lightweight seat that would not reduce – and would preferably enhance – the passenger experience. Acro also wanted a seat that could be manufactured in the UK without requiring specialist suppliers.

Approach

The design team at Factory Design comprised the creative directors, who provided overall direction for the project, a project manager, a designer and a CAD specialist, who built and managed the technical data. Acro had developed the initial engineering for an innovative single-spar support chassis geometry, which had the potential to be very light. The main design challenge was to achieve the weight and cost targets while still maintaining a product with quality and passenger appeal.

Process

Four general routes for design quickly became one preferred direction. From there, the design team concentrated on detail rather than fundamental construction changes. Graphic tablets were used in conjunction with Photoshop and Illustrator in the early stages of design sketching and visualization. A variety of scale and 1:1 model-making techniques were used to explore form and to test design ideas and mechanical principles, from card and hard foam styling models, to more robust test rigs and working mechanisms. In all, five 1:1 prototypes were created, amended and modified during the design process. Decisions about both appearance and comfort were made internally without input from focus groups.

Once a preferred approach to construction had been decided, work began in CAD using SolidWorks. CATIA CAE software was used to test and analyse the main chassis structure of the product. The entire assembly in CAD was controlled by Factory Design until it was handed over to Acro's engineering team. Anthropometrical data was used throughout the process to validate thinking but not in formal ergonomic trials; 3D CAD models of adults and infants were also used to validate design proposals.

Several colour, materials and finishes (CMF) options were created for the initial launch customer to choose from. For subsequent customers, many more trim and finish options have been developed. Factory Design used 3ds Max for their visualizations.

Result

At 31kg per triple, compared with a conventional 47kg, Acro's first production seat is the lightest in its class. On average, the reduced seating weight reduces the weight of an aircraft by 1 tonne, cutting both fuel consumption and CO_2 emissions.

The simplicity of the design and its fewer parts result in several advantages: product assembly time is reduced; fewer suppliers are required, which in turn means less administration and an easier-to-manage supply chain; and the low part count means fewer replacement parts to stock. Reduced

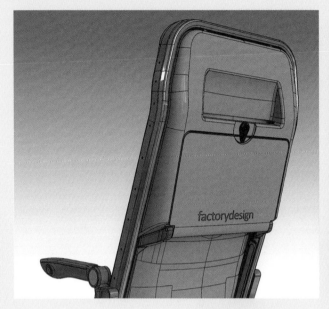

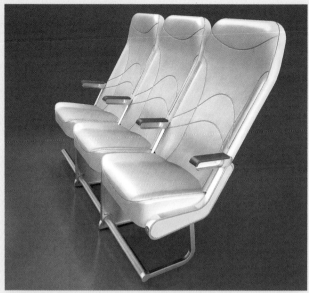

part complexity also enables local (rather than specialist) suppliers to be used, minimizing the carbon footprint, as well as increasing competitiveness for the supply of parts. Fewer, simpler parts and the elimination of trim panels mean the seats are robust and easy to maintain; any part of the seat can be replaced using a standard allen key in under two minutes.

Acro fulfilled their launch order and went on to secure further business without any advertising spend. From start-up to three years of trading, the company has grown solely from the sales of Superlight, and the product range is growing.

Clockwise from top left:
Fig. 43
Once a preferred approach to construction had been decided, CAD models were created using SolidWorks.
Fig. 44
One of several concepts exploring design, colour, material and finish options.
Fig. 45
CAD render of seating concept with integrated in-flight entertainment. Autodesk 3ds Max was used for visualizations.
Fig. 46
CAD render of the final seating concept. Several CMF options were created for the initial launch customer, Jet2.com, before they picked a scheme as part of their cabin 'refresh'.

Case Study
Studio Aisslinger

Product: YILL
Client: Younicos
Dimensions: 530 x 250mm
(20.87 x 9.84in)
Designer: Werner Aisslinger, Nicole Losos
Design to production: 12 months
Modelling software: Dassault Systèmes SolidWorks, PTC Pro/ Engineer
Visualization and rendering software: Adobe Photoshop, Luxion KeyShot
Website: www.aisslinger.de
Award: Red Dot Best of the Best 2011

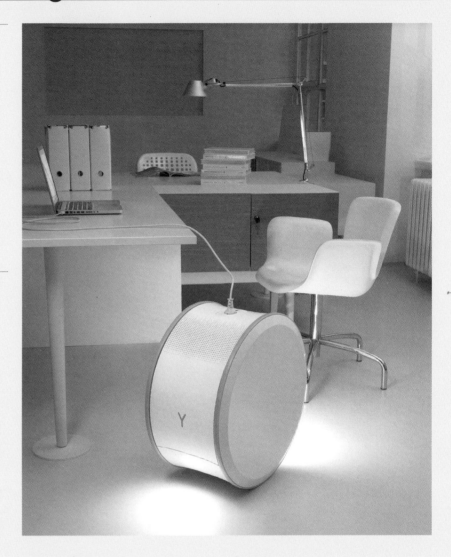

Fig. 47
YILL cordless mobile energy-storage unit.

Introduction

Werner Aisslinger's work covers a spectrum of experimental, artistic approaches, including industrial design and architecture. He has helped introduce new materials and techniques to the world of product design. Aisslinger has received numerous awards for his work, which features in the permanent collections of some of the major museums around the world. He works on product designs and architectural projects with a number of international brands, and has developed furniture with Cappellini, Zanotta, Magis, Porro and Vitra, among others.

Approach

Younicos, a company that develops storage systems and network solutions for safe, stable and cost-efficient electricity supply from regenerative energy sources, approached Studio Aisslinger to design a mobile energy charger. Designing a product often involves the reinterpretation of an existing archetypal product for a specific use; this, however, was an unknown product, which meant there was no design precedent to refer to. As part of a conceptual, environmental approach, the challenge was to design a brand new product that would become part of daily life in the future.

Process

Three initial concepts were presented to Younicos as paper and card models and computer renders made in SolidWorks. One concept was selected by Younicos for further development. Studio Aisslinger then created a refined model in SolidWorks, which was exported as IGES/STEP files for sharing with engineers at Younicos. The engineers used Pro/Engineer to create models with the forms, angles and radii specified by the designers, but which also included all of the internal components. The engineers and designers collaborated over the positioning of parting lines and

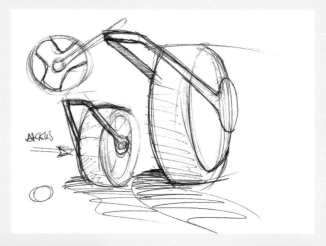

surface draft angles to ensure manufacturability of the parts while retaining design integrity. The aim was to design a product which, in addition to supplying energy, would provide illumination, interaction with the use of sound, would swing while standing and would move 'like a roly-poly'.

Result

YILL is a small, cordless mobile energy-storage unit, able to power a modern workstation for two to three days without cords or cables. It stores one kilowatt hour of energy, offering the ability to make a workstation's power source completely mobile. YILL thus has the potential to make elevated floors and socket banks things of the past. The product also enables a greater flexibility in the layout of workplaces, enabling teams to form quickly and easily where they are needed, even in older buildings.

YILL was designed to have long-lasting visual appeal and will hopefully become an everyday tool for handling energy in tomorrow's world.

Clockwise from top left:
Fig. 48
A retractable power cable allows for overnight recharge.
Fig. 49
Early concept sketches.
Fig. 50
Cardboard and foam mock-up modelling, vital for quick exploration of sketch concepts in 3D early in the design process.
Fig. 51
Development prototype with integral illumination and interface mock up.
Fig. 52
CAD model of final concept.
Fig. 53 (left)
An extendable handle and large wheels mean moving YILL around the home or office is easy.

Rendering

Rendering is the process of generating an image from a computer model, and is used by product designers to create realistic product visuals from 3D models. A large variety of renderers is available, some integrated within 3D modelling software, some available as plug-ins to 3D modellers and others as stand-alone programs. The process of creating a rendered image involves several steps:

– Adding a ground surface underneath the model to create a shadow
– Choosing a background colour or image
– Positioning the camera to create the desired view of the model
– Lighting the model and adjusting light and shadow settings
– Adding materials to the model
– Adjusting camera settings
– Adjusting anti-aliasing settings (see page 48) and specifying the size and resolution for the rendered image.

In recent years rendering programs have made significant advances, becoming much easier to use, faster and more capable, with less time and expertise now required to achieve photorealistic images. As a result, rendered images of 3D models are now used not only for communication with clients but also often on product packaging and for marketing and advertising purposes.

Fig. 54
Example of a large surface used as both the ground plane and the backdrop.

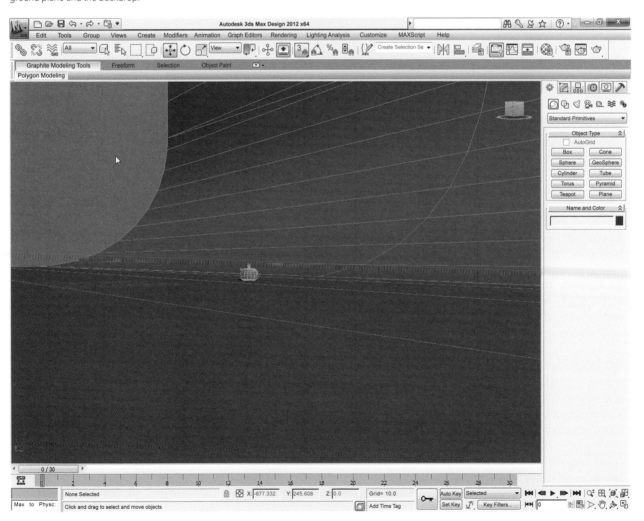

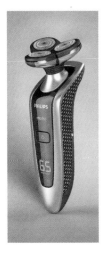  

Ground surface

A ground surface is a surface positioned under a 3D model to provide it with a shadow/reflection and prevent it from appearing to float in space, which would look unnatural for most products. To create a ground surface, either an infinitely large, flat ground surface can be specified and automatically added, or a surface can be created and sized so that its edges aren't visible in the render. With high camera positions, the ground surface is all that is seen behind the model; with low camera positions, both the ground surface and the background are seen, with a horizon line between the two. If a low camera position is desired but without the view of the horizon line and background, one option is to bend the ground surface upwards at some distance behind the model, as with the large paper backdrops studio photographers place behind their subjects. An alternative technique is to use a reflective material for the ground surface. This will reflect, and match, the background colour, and so have the effect of blending the ground surface into the background, making the horizon line much less noticeable.

Background

The background is the space that surrounds your model. The background colour affects the overall brightness of a scene and the colour and brightness of reflective surfaces in the scene. A background can be specified as a single colour, a gradient between two or more colours or a projection of an image of an interior or outdoor scene. In some rendering programs, a type of background known as an environment sphere or sky dome can provide illumination to your scene.

Fig. 55
High-realism renders of a CAD model of an electric shaver. Each render uses different background and camera lens settings.

Fig. 56
Two set-ups of a CAD model of a mobile phone in preparation for rendering, each using different camera positions and lens settings.

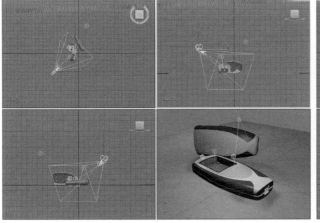 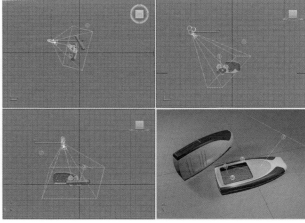

Camera

The position of the camera is the position of your view of the object in the perspective viewport. Lens length is an important camera setting to be aware of as it can significantly alter the dynamic of the render. Lower lens length settings make for a wider-angle view of the object, with settings below around 30mm significantly exaggerating perspective and increasing perceived depth in the scene. Higher lens length settings have the opposite effect, decreasing perspective and shortening perceived depth. Camera position and lens length determine the perceived scale of the object in the scene, with low camera positioning relative to the object (i.e. near the ground surface) and a low lens length setting giving the perception of objects of a larger size than with higher camera positioning and higher lens length settings. Focal distance and depth of field are settings that enable only a specific area of the model/scene to be in focus. For example, if you placed two copies of your product model into the scene, one in front of and one behind the original, you could adjust the focal distance and depth of field so that the model in the middle was in focus and the other two models were out of focus. This effect is often used in product photography. Experiment with different positions of view, lens length, focal distance and depth of field, as these can add visual interest and dynamism to the render.

Lighting

To recreate the way real products are photographed in professional studios, lights are placed into the model space to illuminate the model. Two types of light – spotlights and area lights – are normally used for this purpose. Spotlights produce a beam/cone of light, the diameter of which can be adjusted. Area lights can be thought of as being a bit like a light box or fluorescent ceiling panel, the size of which can be controlled. The larger the area light, the softer the illumination and shadows become. In some rendering programs, alternative shapes of area lights can be specified. An alternative to this technique, available in some renderers, is to use a skylight (or sky dome) to create natural-looking illumination across the entire scene and then supplement this with photometric area lights directed at the model, which are able to accurately match real-world luminance and colour values.

Fig. 57
Several types of light can be used to illuminate models prior to rendering. This example shows a typical set-up using spotlights. Note the placement of the lights in relation to one another, and in relation to the position of the camera.

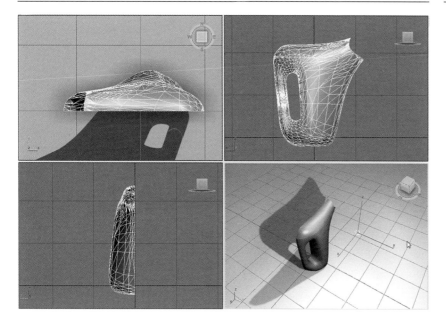

Lighting set-up

Lighting set-ups for studio shots in CAD/rendering programs can vary
substantially, but as a general rule, lighting is achieved with the use of three lights
positioned to direct light onto the model from different angles. A key light is the
main source of light, usually positioned around 30 degrees to the left or right of
the camera. A fill light is a secondary light, usually positioned around 30 degrees
to the other side of the camera from the key light. A back light (or rim light) is
usually positioned behind the object, pointing towards the camera. Additional
lights can be added if required to lighten or create highlights on specific areas of
the model. Lights are always placed according to the position of the camera, i.e.
the chosen point of view for the render. If another viewpoint of the model needs
to be rendered, you will need to rotate the model and, depending on the shape
of object, you may also need to adjust the position of lights and their settings.

Lighting settings

Lights have associated settings that can be adjusted to control the lighting in the
scene. Common settings are:

- Intensity
- Colour
- Decay
- Shadows.

Intensity controls the brightness of the light. Colour controls the hue of the light
Decay (or attenuation or distance fall off) refers to the way light becomes spread
out and therefore less intense over distance. Inverse Decay, a light setting found
in many renderers, is an accurate representation of the rate of decrease of light
intensity over distance. Shadows control the way shadows are created in the scene.

In some programs, any separate parts of a 3D model can be set to function
as a light source, which can be useful for renders of lighting products, and Inverse
Decay is a useful light setting to use in these situations. Some programs also
enable you to choose which objects in a scene you would like a particular light to
illuminate – useful for brightening certain parts of a model or scene without
affecting other parts.

Direct and ambient lighting

By default, some renderers use direct lighting (or infinite lighting) to illuminate 3D
models, casting light across the entire scene from a particular and constant

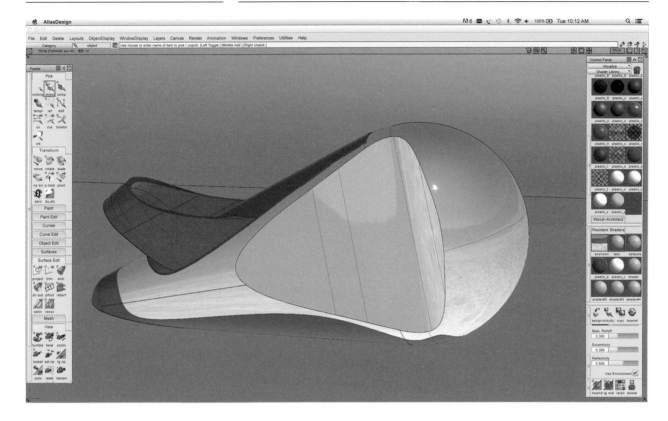

Fig. 59
Model of a concept for a tape dispenser being prepared for rendering in Alias Design software. An image is mapped onto the environment sphere enveloping the model in order to create realistic reflections in the surface of the model, and is also used to calculate illumination colour and intensity for the render.

Fig. 60
Render of a retinal imaging product designed by i4 Product Design for Optos. The render makes use of HDRI to recreate natural lighting for a model located in a context.

direction. Other renderers use ambient light (or global ambience) to evenly illuminate models. While direct and ambient lighting can be used to illuminate a model for a render, it is often insufficient for sophisticated rendered images of products.

Image-based lighting

When an image is mapped onto a background environment sphere, the colours in the image can be used to calculate both the illumination colour and the intensity of illumination in the scene. This is known as image-based lighting (IBL), a form of lighting gaining increasing popularity within rendering programs due to its simplicity and realism. IBL is a quick and effective way to illuminate a model to achieve a sophisticated render, and is useful for creating an image of a model located in a specific context. In addition to creating more natural lighting, IBL allows the image mapped onto the environment sphere to be used to create realistic reflections in reflective surfaces of the model. High dynamic range (HDR) images are now popular for use in IBL, as they allow greater levels of lighting contrast and better detail in bright and dark areas of reflection in the render. High dynamic range imaging (HDRI) or high dynamic range image-based lighting (HDRL) – also known as physically accurate, physically based and real-world lighting – is a way of illuminating a scene using a series of images and exposures of an environment (either interior or exterior) that are stitched together to create a 360-degree panoramic format image that can be mapped onto the environment sphere to envelop the model. HDR image files are used to illuminate and create reflections on your model and can also be used as the background in a rendered scene to show appropriate context for the product. IBL using HDR images is particularly popular in automotive visualization.

Global illumination

Some rendering programs support global illumination (GI), a type of illumination that recreates the way light bounces between surfaces in reality, creating additional indirect light and transferring colour between surfaces. Radiosity and photon mapping are two of the processes used by renderers to calculate and

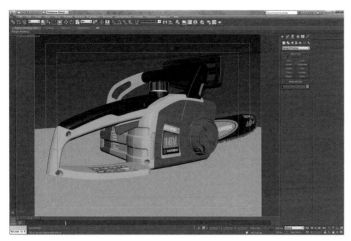

produce global illumination. If your renderer doesn't support IBL, it is worth experimenting with GI to bounce indirect light onto a model's surfaces from the inside surface of a spherical surface surrounding your model.

Shadows

Shadows cast by models onto the ground surface and surfaces of nearby objects are required to achieve a realistic render, but too many shadows can create an unrealistic and distracting effect. Lighting settings on most renderers enable shadows to be switched off for some of the lights in the scene, if required. Shadows vary in their realism from renderer to renderer, with the more capable programs using a process called 'ray tracing' to accurately calculate how surrounding and bounced light interacts with shadows to soften their appearance with greater distance from the model. Shadow density and colour can also be adjusted for more realistic shadows.

Caustics

Caustics are the bright, focused light effects created on surrounding surfaces when light shines through glass, transparent plastics and liquids, or bounces off such highly reflective materials as polished stainless steel. Good-quality renderers will be able to simulate these effects, which are necessary for rendering highly reflective, transparent and semi-transparent materials realistically.

Materials

A good-quality rendering program will include a vast library of different materials and, for each material, a large number of variations. Materials will range from plastics, ceramics, glass and metals to accurate representations of more visually complex materials, such as fabrics and woods. Materials help to create a realistic rendered image, and are either procedural or image based.

Procedural materials

A procedural material is one where the appearance has been determined in the software using a series of combinations of colours and layered pattern effects. Procedural materials take up little memory and are quick to render, but often do not produce high levels of realism, especially when used to replicate such visually complex materials as wood.

Image-based materials

These make use of image maps (or texture maps) to add realism to a material. Image maps are images used to recreate the appearance of the colours, patterns, roughness, transparency, highlights and internal illumination (glow) of specific materials. Some materials may utilize one image map; others may use several.

Fig. 61 (left)
CAD model of a Gardena chainsaw designed for Husqvarna Group by i4 Product Design ready for rendering in 3ds Max.
Fig. 62 (right)
High-quality render created by i4 Product Design demonstrating ray-traced reflections, shadows and realistic material finishes.

Fig. 63
Classic Material Editor showing a range of
shaders, and the related Material/Map Browser,
in 3ds Max software. Materials can either be
selected from a library of predetermined
materials, or created to match specific
requirements using one or more shaders.
Image maps can be assigned to shaders to
control the appearance of materials.

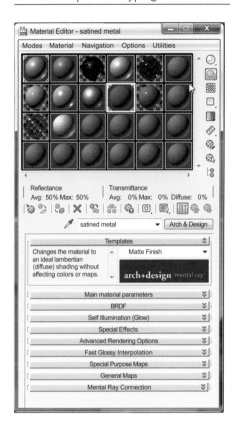

Fig. 64
3ds Max Material/Map Browser in Slate Material
Editor mode being used to assign materials to a
model. The Slate Material Editor is a node-based
editor, showing each component of a material as
a separate module that is connected to slots.

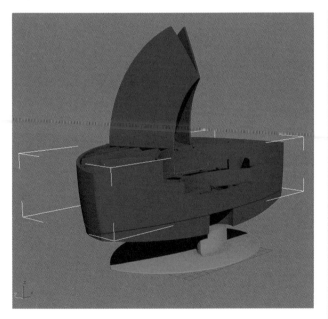

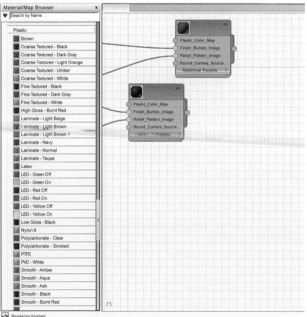

Shaders

The surface appearances of different materials are controlled by shaders – adjustable settings that determine how a material will reflect light. A diffuse setting for reflections, for example, will produce soft reflections of light and surfaces that appear matt. A glossy setting will produce defined light reflections and somewhat shiny surfaces. A specular setting for reflections will produce well-defined light reflections and very shiny surfaces. Whichever setting is specified, the size of highlight can be adjusted in either the material settings or the lighting settings. Shader settings affect the appearance of all materials whether they utilize texture maps or not.

Ground surface material

In scenes set up to create a studio shot, the material specified for the ground surface should be given careful consideration as it will significantly affect the rendered image. One consideration is whether or not you want the surface to be reflective and, if you do, how reflective. While it is always a good idea to be creative and experiment with different options for ground surface materials, a good starting point is to study the variety of materials that other designers have used in their renders. The websites of rendering software providers include galleries of renders created using their software and are a good place to start.

Creating materials

If a material you need to use in a render doesn't exist in the material library of your renderer, you will need to either edit a library material or create your own. To do either of these requires an understanding of commonly used types of image map and how they will affect your material. Common examples of image maps are:

- **A colour map** (or diffuse map) is simply an image of the material you wish to replicate in the rendering, which replaces the main material surface colour (usually grey by default). If the colour map needs to be repeated (a process known as 'tiling') to create the correct material scale in the render, the image needs to be edited first in image editing software to make it seamless so that it can be repeated without it becoming obvious where one image stops and the next begins. Most maps included with rendering programs are seamless, and many seamless maps are available to download from the internet
- **A bump map** is a texture map that creates the appearance of surface roughness
- **A displacement map** is similar to a bump map but actually distorts the surface of the model to achieve the surface roughness
- **A specular map** is a texture map that controls where specular highlights will show on a glossy material
- **A transparency** map is a texture map that controls which parts of a material will be transparent and which parts opaque
- **A luminosity map** (or incandescence or ambience map) is a texture map that enables part or all of the material to appear as if it is glowing, illuminated from within.

All these maps (apart from colour maps) use tonal values of black and white pixels to create the opposite extremes of the effects in images.

Fig. 65
Example of a render created by Pixela Render from a CAD model, recreating the appearance of different materials.

Fig. 66
Example of the use of bump maps within a render of in-ear monitors designed by Robrady for Sleek Audio. The bump maps recreate subtle variations in material finish.

Anti-aliasing

Rendered images are made up of lots of tiny mosaic-like pixels. In order that the edges of objects or shadows in renders don't appear jagged or stair-stepped, a smoothing process known as 'anti-aliasing' is used. As a render is created, this process adjusts the colour and tonal value of pixels in between the steps of colour representing the edge of the object or shadow, giving the appearance of a smoother edge. Higher-quality anti-aliasing settings result in smoother edges but slower render speeds.

Image resolution

Image resolution refers to the number of horizontal and vertical pixels in a rendered image. The number of pixels specified for a render determines the size the rendered image can be viewed at on a computer monitor and also the physical size it can be printed at. For images to display crisply at full size on a computer screen, they must have either the same or more pixels as the computer

Fig. 67
Anti-aliasing settings can affect the quality of a product rendering; note the changes to the shadow and the top surface of the product as a result of improved anti-aliasing quality settings.

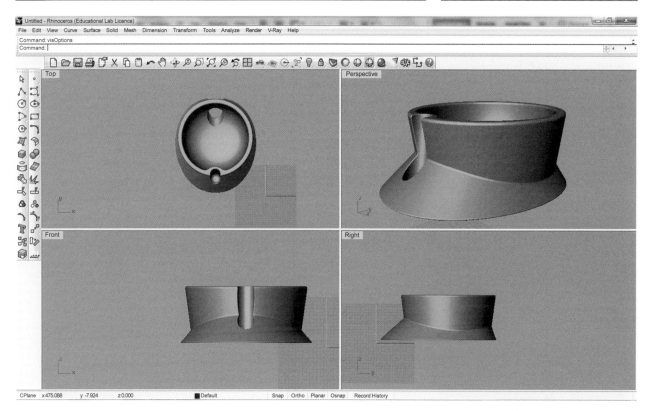

monitor display (this varies from monitor to monitor). To print a render at high quality the rendered image requires a resolution of between 150ppi (pixels per inch) and 300ppi. (N.B. 300ppi actually means 300 x 300 – or 90,000 – pixels in every square inch of image space.)

As a general rule, smaller images require the higher resolution of 300ppi because they are observed more closely than large images. For printed poster images between A2 size (594 x 420mm, 23.39 x 16.54in) and A0 size (1188 x 840mm, 46.77 x 33.07in), a resolution of 150ppi is perfectly sufficient, and for larger banners at twice A0 size or larger, 100ppi is enough. As an example, a render destined to be printed at A3 size (420 x 297mm, 16.54 x 11.69in) at 300ppi requires pixel dimensions of 4961 x 3508 pixels to be specified. Some rendering programs make the process of specifying pixel dimensions for print easier by enabling the user to input both the physical size and the desired resolution for the render, thus helpfully removing the need to use a calculator or image editing software such as Photoshop to calculate the required pixel dimensions.

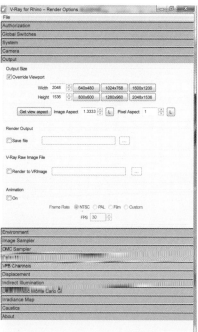

Fig. 68
CAD model of the bowl of a motor-driven pestle and mortar ready for rendering in V-Ray software. The associated Render Options dialogue box shows a range of typical settings, including Output, where the Output Size (pixel dimensions for the render) is specified.

Case Study
Stefano Giovannoni

Products: AlessiPhone and AlessiTab
Clients: Telecom Italia (AlessiPhone),
Promelit (AlessiTab)
Material: polycarbonate
Dimensions: AlessiPhone: 45 x 195 x
55mm (1.77 x 7.68 x 2.17in); AlessiTab:
258 x 183 x 108mm (10.16 x 7.20 x
4.25in)
Designer: Stefano Giovannoni
Design to production: AlessiPhone:
14 weeks; AlessiTab: 16 weeks
Modelling software: Autodesk Alias
Design, Maxon Cinema 4D Studio,
Robert McNeel & Associates
Rhinoceros 3D
**Visualization and rendering
software:** Maxon Cinema 4D Studio
Website: www.stefanogiovannoni.it

Introduction
Stefano Giovannoni was born in Italy in
1954 and has taught and conducted
research at a number of universities in
his home country. Now based in Milan,
Giovannoni works as an industrial
designer, interior designer and
architect, and his designs form part
of the permanent collections of the
Pompidou Centre in Paris and the
Museum of Modern Art in New York.
The AlessiPhone and AlessiTab are just
two of a number of designs he has
created for Alessi, including a previous
telephone in 2003.

Approach
The receiver and docking components
of most telephones are usually clearly
differentiated from each other. The aim
with the AlessiPhone was to design an
object that provided a fluid
combination of these two elements,
creating a unique product form. The
most challenging aspect was the
extremely tight project timescale of
just three to four months.

Designing the AlessiTab also
presented a significant challenge,
requiring Giovannoni to deliver an
entirely new kind of product. The
concept was for a multimedia,
interactive touch-screen tablet,

and, while a common product today,
AlessiTab had already been designed
when rumours first appeared that
Apple might be developing what is
now the iPad.

Process
For both projects, five or six initial
concepts were explored. The second
step of the design process involved
moving quickly into 3D to better
visualize the objects and to be able to
work on them dynamically. To gain a
better sense of size, drawings were
created from the CAD models and
printed at 1:1 scale. For key designs,
mock-up models were created from
the drawings and rapid prototypes
were produced from the 3D CAD files.
For each product, only two prototypes
were produced during their
development: one basic and one final.

Cinema 4D software was used for
the initial concept exploration, then
Alias and Rhinoceros were used to
generate the IGES or STEP files
needed to produce the prototypes.
Internal components for both products
were provided by Telecom Italia and
Promelit at the beginning of the
process for Giovannoni to design
around, and ensuring that these
components would fit inside the phone

Fig. 69
CAD modelling was an integral part of
developing the fluid form of the AlessiPhone's
handset and base.

Fig. 70
Realistic visualizations of the AlessiTab. CAD files were used to create both product renders and rapid prototypes.
Fig. 71
By turning the AlessiTab over, the screen can be viewed at two angles: 30 degrees for the touch screen, and 70 degrees for the TV feature.

was especially important during the CAD surface modelling process for that product.

Two colour variations were developed for both products and presented to Alessi. Cinema 4D was also used to create realistic product renderings. For both projects, once a final concept had been developed, an internal focus group was used to gain quick feedback.

Result

The AlessiPhone presents a desirable alternative to existing cordless telephone designs, with their typical vertical handset and horizontal recharging dock. When the handset is paired with the base, the face-down orientation of the AlessiPhone discreetly hides the OLED screen and keypad; the deliberate gap between the base and the handset, which glows when the phone rings, enables the handset to be lifted easily; and the ergonomically shaped and almost featureless smooth, glossy polycarbonate exterior provides a natural fit with the hand.

The L-shape of the AlessiTab keeps together the two parts, the screen and its front foot. This shape, with a gravitational sensor that rotates the screen image through 180 degrees, makes it possible to use the tablet at two different angles: at 30 degrees, to use the touch screen, and at 70 degrees (obtained by turning over the AlessiTab), to use the TV feature. This product is designed to be used primarily in the kitchen, and is the first all-Italian Android tablet computer.

Case Study
Philips Design

Product: DesignLine television and home cinema system
Materials: glass, PC, ABS, aluminium
Dimensions: 645 x 1007 x 39.4mm (25.39 x 39.65 x 1.55in)
Designers: Rod White (creative director), Anthony Smith (product design), Yang Tah Ching (product design implementation), Ang Chin Boon (product graphics)
Design to production: 9 months
Modelling software: Autodesk Alias Design and Robert McNeel & Associates Rhinoceros 3D
Visualization and rendering software: Chaos Group V-Ray
Website: www.designphilips.com
Awards: Goed Industrieel Ontwerp 2011, iF 2012, Janus de l'Industrie 2011, Red Dot Award 2012

Introduction
Philips Design is one of the largest design organizations in the world. They undertake in-depth research into social and environmental contexts and employ a collaboration of designers, psychologists, ergonomists, sociologists, philosophers and anthropologists to help create commercially successful products that work in intuitive ways.

Approach
The goal for the DesignLine television and home cinema system was a design that offered uncompromised picture-quality performance and 'interior fit' through application of materials, innovative design solutions and engineering finesse. Following a design briefing, a design workshop started with product, interaction and communication designers working together on sketches, followed by CAD visuals, models and design testing to refine the final product.

Process
The design team began by exploring modern living spaces, with the aim of creating a product that would reflect both lifestyle and aesthetic needs. They then created concepts for a 40in LED television, a 2.1 home cinema system, a small-screen range of 20 and 26in LED televisions and accompanying remote controls that were to be fully aligned in appearance and behaviour across the range.

Sketching and then modelling was done in Rhinoceros 3D and Alias Design, with visualization undertaken in Chaos Group's V-Ray renderer. The designers worked on location with their mechanical engineering counterparts, who worked in PTC Pro/Engineer software (now Creo), with transfer back and forth between designers and engineers via IGES and STEP files.

During development, many models of the corner of the bezel were created to investigate the behaviour of light on glass and to find the optimum surfacing to give the tightest perceived volume. 'Sketch level' CAD was quickly created in-house and sent to external model makers. (Market testing throughout the process required full-scale aesthetic models with all detailing included.) 'Screen captured' images were used frequently to communicate 3D surface status between designers, mechanical engineers and marketing teams, allowing instant translation into solid visuals and keeping the project time

Fig. 72
DesignLine television and home cinema system.

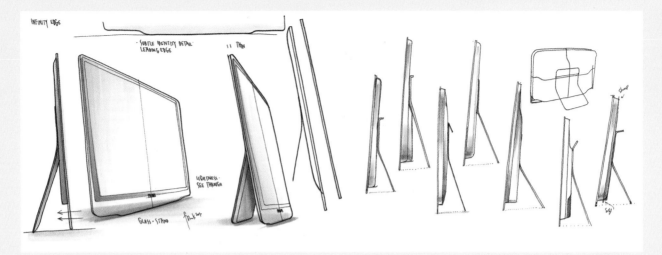

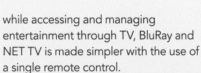

down. Models with working TV panels were made from Pro/Engineer surfaces.

At a certain project milestone, ownership of the reference CAD file passed from the designer to the mechanical engineer, after which the design had to be as close to final as possible. When fully prepared by the mechanical engineer in Pro/Engineer, the CAD files were then passed to the suppliers and tool makers to prepare for production. The final Pro/Engineer CAD data was used in parallel to render the communication material in V-Ray, which was used on packaging and promotional material.

while accessing and managing entertainment through TV, BluRay and NET TV is made simpler with the use of a single remote control.

CAD modelling and rendering tools played a vital role in the creation of this product range, both as design and visualization tools and as a means of communication with project engineers.

Result

The DesignLine television and home cinema system expresses high quality and performance through its materials, aesthetic qualities and engineering. The innovative use of angled glass plate for the LCD TV results in a modern, elegant design, while Air Touch Controls appear to 'float' on the transparent glass, making them unobtrusive when not in use, yet highly ergonomic when required. This level of usability is carried through into the icon-based onscreen user interface,

Clockwise from top:
Fig. 73
Concept sketches of the television screen. Hand sketches were used to explore initial ideas before CAD modelling.
Fig. 74
V-Ray was used to create high-realism product renders, which were used on packaging and promotional material.
Fig. 75
Rhinoceros 3D and Alias Design were used for CAD modelling. Transfer of models between designers and engineers, who worked in Pro/Engineer, was made via IGES and STEP files.
Fig. 76
Render of the remote control, created in V-Ray from the final Pro/Engineer CAD data.

Case Study
Priestmangoode

Product: Moving Platforms
Designers: Paul Priestman, Son Tran, Dan Window
Design to production: 7 weeks
Modelling software: Autodesk Alias Studio Tools (now Alias Design)
Visualization and rendering software: Autodesk 3ds Max and Chaos Group V-Ray
Website: www.priestmangoode.com
Awards: International Design Excellence Awards (Bronze award in Transportation) 2012

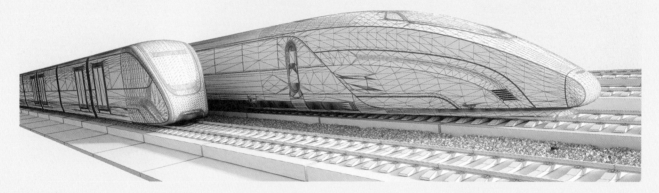

Fig. 77 (top)
Render showing a tram drawing alongside a high-speed train. V-Ray was used to create concept renders.
Fig. 78 (above)
3ds Max was used to create polygonal CAD models of the tram and high-speed train.
Opposite, clockwise from top left:
Fig. 79
CAD model of a local tram docking with a high-speed train.
Fig. 80
Tram and train interiors were modelled in detail prior to rendering and animation.
Fig. 81
Render of an internal transfer zone between tram and train.
Fig. 82
Render of a frame of an animation showing a local tram docking with a high-speed train. Transfer of passengers between train and tram would take place at lower speeds.

Introduction

Priestmangoode is a multidisciplinary design consultancy specializing in transport, aviation, environment, branding, product and packaging design, with user- and passenger-focused designs ranging from the first lie-flat airline seat for Virgin Atlantic to designing the fastest trains and the smallest hotel rooms in the world. Continuing Priestmangoode's drive to improve rail travel, Moving Platforms is a concept design for a completely interconnected rail infrastructure where local trams connect to a network of non-stop high-speed trains, enabling passengers to travel from their local stop to a local address at their destination (even in another country) without getting off a train.

Approach

Observing that billions were being spent on high-speed rail across the world, but that trains were often running on networks invented in the nineteenth century, Priestmangoode concentrated on improving the connectivity of the rail network as the best solution to getting people off roads and short-haul flights. Their aim was to create an infrastructure that would work with, and not against, high-speed train technology, and to create a seamless passenger experience from start to destination.

A new network of major stations would necessarily be costly, in terms of space, finance and environmental impact. Another problem is that high-speed trains are not very fast. Slowing down and speeding up as they

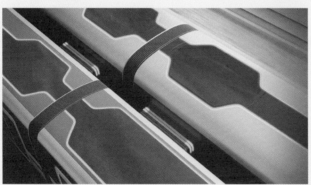

move between stations means they are able to travel at their full speed only for limited periods of time (wasting vast amounts of energy in the process). A huge amount of people's time was being lost in transit, waiting at stations to change trains.

Priestmangoode's approach was to mimic the way the internet works, connecting isolated computers via a series of networks. The concept is based on a joined up local and international rail network that allows passengers to transfer directly from one moving tram or high-speed train to another.

Process

The process of modelling the concept took around one week using Alias Studio Tools, which Priestmangoode found to be the best software for surface modelling. The associated animation (which can be seen online) then took a month to create. Both the animation and renders for the project were created using 3ds Max and V-Ray.

The main challenge for this small consultancy was finding sufficient time outside their client work to develop this self-generated project; their visualizers spent evenings and weekends on the project. Budget was also a challenge; the cost to Priestmangoode, financial and in man hours, was significant.

Result

On long journeys, the non-stop high-speed train could save a vast proportion of any journey time. Many rail passengers also use cars to get to their main-line embarkation station, so being able to link up to the high-speed train directly from a local tram or train service would also reduce car usage.

Track infrastructure is already in place in many areas. On each train line, there are two tracks, one high speed and one local, next to each other, so Moving Platforms would potentially not take up any more land. Existing local stations would serve the feeder trams, enabling passengers from rural areas to access the high-speed line easily.

Moving Platforms could also be used for local deliveries and freight, helping to get lorries off the road and ease congestion on motorways and in towns. A journey planner app would tell you which local tram or train to get on in Manchester to go to a local address in Liverpool, for instance, making travel simpler and easier.

CAD proved an invaluable tool for Priestmangoode to communicate their speculative concept in an engaging manner, facilitating the production of high-quality visuals and an animation that not only provides information about Moving Platform's appearance, but also effectively communicates how the concept works.

Animation

Animations are used for a range of different purposes. Animation software, often integrated within CAD programs, enables designers to communicate more fully the story of a design concept and how a product might be used. It is able to explain the workings of products with moving parts and can also be used to explain the product assembly process. Sophisticated rendered animations are often used in marketing and advertising to present concepts in ways that would not be possible using real products. In film production, 3D modelling programs are now used extensively to create virtual environments, buildings, rooms and products, and it is often impossible to tell reality from virtual reality. In summary, animations are primarily used to:

- Help designers explain products to clients or marketing departments
- Enable inventors to communicate their new product concepts to potential investors
- Market products to consumers through online and television advertising
- Manipulate objects, characters and environments in films.

Animation principles

In order to create the appearance of smooth-flowing movement, film displays a certain number of frames (images) – usually 24 – every second. In computer animation, each frame is a render of the 3D scene. Multiple renders are created and can then be played back as a film. Animations of 3D models are created through a process called 'key framing', whereby positions of models and parts of models are determined at different key points in time (key frames). The animation software then cleverly calculates the positions of the models at all the frames in between the key frames. The greater the complexity of movement required, the more frequently key frames need to be placed. For film production, polygon mesh CAD programs (see page 13) are most frequently used to create 3D models, including realistic virtual models of actors.

Using NURBS or solid models in animations

If models for films are created in either NURBS or solid modellers, they must be converted into polygon meshes to be imported into the animation software. To animate such complex polygon meshes as character models, the 3D model is given

Fig. 83
Animating a 3D character using avars.

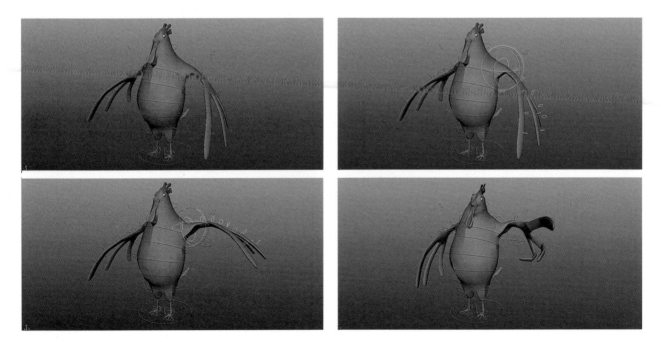

hinges, or 'avars', inside the polygon mesh, which an animator will use to make a model move. A complex 3D character model requiring sophisticated movement might require hundreds of these hinges. As the hinges are moved, the polygon mesh deforms at the joints. Rather than laboriously moving the character joint by joint, frame by frame, a process called inverse kinematics (IK) enables the animator to move the joints to the desired locations at key frames, and the movement of all the joints associated with that joint is then calculated by the software for the in-between frames, with the polygon mesh deforming smoothly as the joints move.

Animating a product model

To create an animation of a product model, you first decide how long you would like your animation to last and then determine the number of frames required – usually based on 24 frames per second, although for simple animations this number can be lower. The process of creating the animation is as follows:

– Create a timeline of frames
– Place your model(s) where you want it to be located at the beginning of the animation
– Record a key frame
– Move your model(s) and/or camera to a position at which you require it to be located at a second point in time
– Record another key frame.

This process of moving models or parts of models and recording key frames is then repeated until the models and parts are located where required at the end of the animation. The animation can then be played and the software will

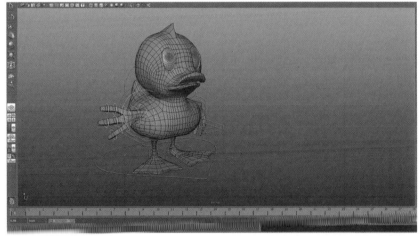

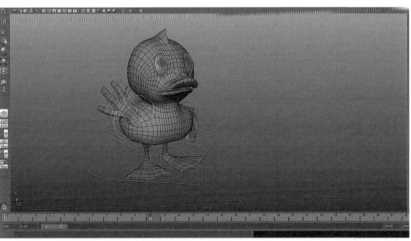

Fig. 84
Start and end phases of an animation showing key framing on an animation timeline.

Fig. 85
Ease-in/ease-out curves for controlling movement.

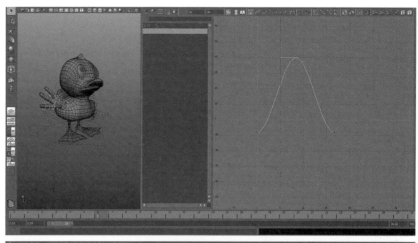

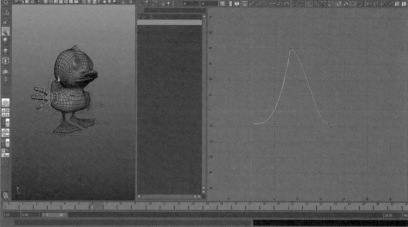

automatically calculate the transitional movements of the objects for every frame between the key frames. Popular programs for creating animations include Autodesk Maya, Autodesk 3ds Max Design, Autodesk Softimage, Bunkspeed Pro, Dassault Systèmes 3DVIA Studio Pro, Luxion KeyShot, Maxon Cinema 4D Broadcast, Maxon Cinema 4D Visualize, PMG Messiah Studio Pro and Side Effects Software Houdini Escape.

Creating natural movement in animations

The key to creating realistic speed of movement in an animation is to think about how far an object or part of an object would move within a given period of time. To better control the movement of objects, a type of graph called a 'function curve' is used. As a simple example, let's say you want to animate the lid of a box closing: you want the lid to start slowly, speed up, then slow down for the closure. Recording a key frame at the beginning and end positions for the lid would result in a constant speed from start to finish. By assigning a function curve to the lid, it can be made to travel more slowly at both the beginning and the end. This type of movement is known as an 'ease-in/ease-out'.

Using key framing and function curves to determine the movement of objects over time, it is possible to create animations of the movement of a model and the movement of several parts on that model all at the same time. Animations of different models in a virtual scene, moving at different speeds and on different trajectories, is possible, as is animating the movement, brightness and colour of lights and the movement of the camera.

CAD software for product design

A bewildering number of software programs are available to the product designer, covering a range of the processes involved in designing and communicating a product, including sketching, 2D drafting, 3D modelling, product assembly, simulation and analysis of components and assemblies, documentation, rendering and animation. Some CAD programs have capability across all these areas, while others are highly capable in just one category; most have capability across two or more. Many CAD vendors sell themselves as product lifecycle management (PLM) software suppliers, and support programs with capability across these areas. Some programs are designed to suit the entry-level occasional user, while others are aimed at the specialist professional, and the range of prices reflects this broad market.

The price of software is usually a reasonable guide to capability, although it is not always an accurate reflection of performance or ease of use. Lower-priced software and freeware can be very capable, so keep an open mind and try out free demos to discover what best meets your requirements and budget. Your knowledge of CAD software will likely come down to a combination of the software you have been taught while in education and the software you have been required to learn while working professionally. While compatibility between different programs is improving, learning and becoming familiar with several different programs is always a good idea – you will avoid becoming entrenched in one particular way of working, and it will come in useful if you need to liaise with manufacturers or other designers using different software to you. As a general

Fig. 86
Popular CAD software interfaces. Clockwise from top left: PTC Creo Parametric; Dassault Systèmes SolidWorks; Autodesk AutoCAD; Robert McNeel & Associates Rhinoceros 3D.

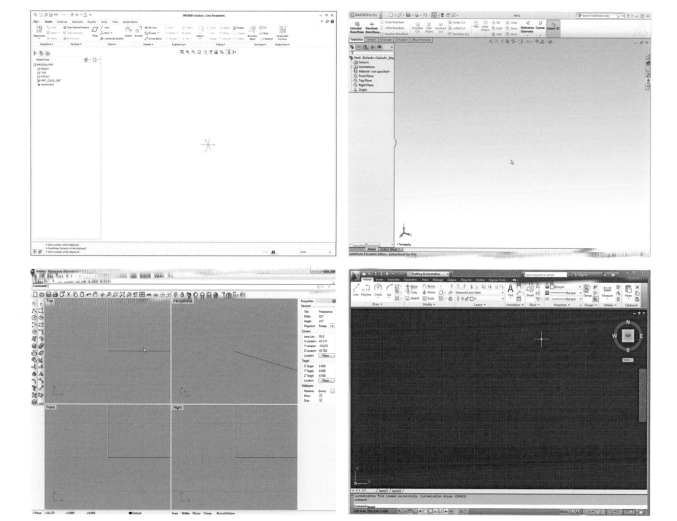

rule, the more CAD software you learn, the easier it becomes to pick up others, as there are many similiarities between different programs. (An extensive list of available software can be found on pages 167–169.)

2D CAD software

The generation of 2D drawings is done using 2D CAD programs, such as Autodesk AutoCAD and Ashlar-Vellum Graphite. A complete set of 2D drawings showing different orthographic (plan, elevation, section) views of components used in a product and different views of the assembled product can be used to communicate with manufacturers responsible for producing the components and assembling the product. The 2D CAD files can also be output directly to subtractive manufacturing processes, such as laser cutting and water-jet cutting (see page 70), and they can be used as the basis from which to create 3D computer models in 3D CAD software, most of which have built-in 2D drafting and dimensioning functionality. Most 3D CAD programs are able to automatically

Fig. 87
Interface of Autodesk AutoCAD, showing a 2D drawing and typical drawing and editing tools.

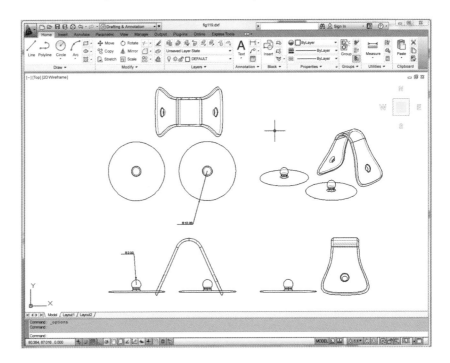

Fig. 88
Drawing sheet showing an engineering drawing of the base plate for a cash-handling machine.

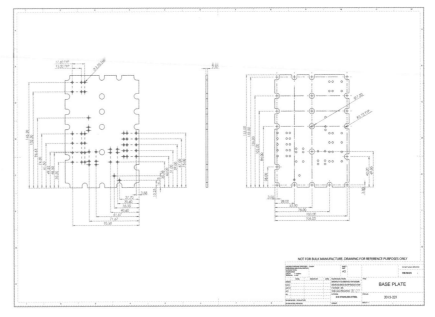

generate 2D drawings from 3D models, and some programs are able to automatically dimension 2D drawings created from 3D models.

These processes are useful time savers – the designer no longer needs to create 2D drawings separately from the 3D model. However, while accurate, these processes are not yet fully automatic; the designer must still usually position drawing views, reposition dimensions and add further dimensions and any other required information to these 2D drawings before they are ready to be discussed with a manufacturer. In order to make these changes, you must be familiar with the standard conventions and industry requirements for layout, dimensioning and tolerance information required on orthographic 2D drawings, which are a primary form of communication between designer and manufacturer.

3D CAD software

A wide variety of industries use 3D CAD programs for the creation of 3D models:

- The medical industry uses them to create detailed models of organs
- The film industry uses them to create and manipulate objects, characters and environments in the production of animations and films
- The video game industry uses them to create objects, characters and environments for video games
- The science sector uses them to create models of chemical and biological compounds
- Architects and landscape architects use them to create models of proposed buildings and landscapes
- Civil engineers use them to design new structures
- Electrical engineers use them to design electrical circuits and printed circuit boards (PCBs)
- Mechanical engineers use them to design machines and engines
- Product and automotive designers use them in combination with mechanical and electrical engineers in the design of cars and devices.

Some 3D CAD programs excel in their ability to enable quick and direct modelling, and these programs are often used to complement sketching and physical model making in the early, exploratory stages of developing a new product. With these programs the designer can concentrate on exploring the appropriate form and proportions of a product concept at a stage when exact

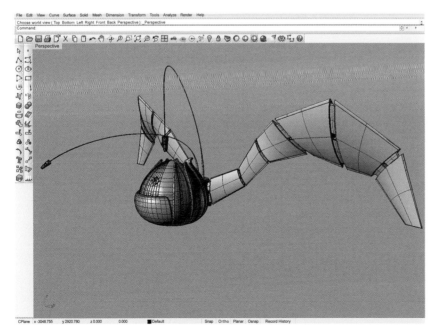

Fig. 89
Model of a character from a comic by Kenichi Kusano, created in Rhinoceros 3D software.

Fig. 90
CAD model of the pestle component of a motor-driven pestle and mortar, created in SolidWorks (see also page 49).

dimensions are less important or have not yet been finalized. Other programs are more suited to detailed design work later in the design process, when accuracy, precision and creating specifications for manufacture are required. These programs often include libraries of industry-standard components that can be used in product assembly models and avoid the need to repeatedly model frequently used components. Models of components created in the software can be added to these libraries for future use.

Every design consultancy and manufacturer has their own preference for a particular program or combination of programs. Popular programs are Autodesk Alias Design, Autodesk Inventor, Ashlar-Vellum Xenon, Dassault Systèmes CATIA, Dassault Systèmes SolidWorks, PTC Creo Parametric (formerly Pro/Engineer), Robert McNeel & Associates Rhinoceros 3D, Siemens Solid Edge and Siemens NX 8. Whichever software is used, one drawback to modelling in a virtual environment is that scale can be difficult to determine, so to evaluate scale effectively, mock-up models and rapid prototyped parts produced from computer models are required in addition to CAD modelling.

Learning 3D CAD software

Learning a new 3D CAD application can seem a daunting prospect, with the initially unfamiliar 3D modelling interface and what can seem like endless tools and options to learn. Depending on the software, a program can take anything from a few days to several months to master. Some programs are designed for ease of use; others are more complex, both to learn and to use, but are designed to facilitate the production of highly accurate models of components and product assemblies, which can be worked on collaboratively by designers and engineers and used for the production of mould tools for manufacturing processes.

Sadly, few CAD software developers prioritize the user, and place the number of tools, features and capabilities provided by their products ahead of intuitive interfaces, ease of comprehension and ease of use. However, with most programs it does not take long to master navigation within the interface and grasp the fundamental modelling techniques. Before long, modelling a virtual 3D product will become second nature. It is only when product designers become truly proficient with the use of 3D software that they are able to visualize in the virtual 3D environment in an unrestricted manner, just as they are less able to sketch fluently and explore a product concept on paper if their sketching skills aren't fully developed. When new to CAD modelling, it is important to use CAD in conjunction with sketching by hand and model making, or you risk your designs being limited by your CAD skills. Training manuals, online video tutorials and user

Fig. 91

CAD development model of the Franke Pebel PBG651 kitchen sink designed by Crumauie Ltd and modelled in Creo.

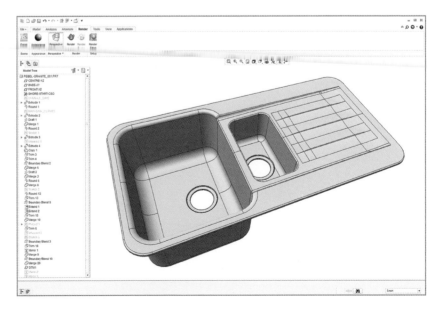

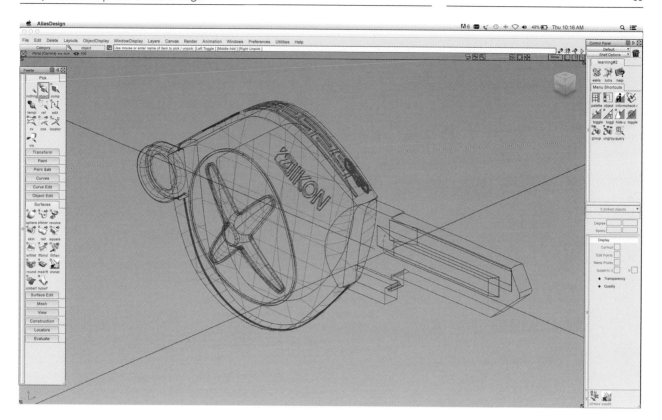

forums all help to support the learning process, and researching which of these resources are provided before committing to learning a particular CAD program is time well spent.

Fig. 92
CAD model of a key fob in Autodesk Alias Design software.

Rendering software

Computer rendering software is now able to give highly realistic impressions, enabling designers to create life-like representations of their products without the need to commit to the creation of realistic physical appearance models before an evaluation can be made. This has helped to speed up the design process significantly. Commonly used rendering software includes Autodesk 3ds Max, Autodesk Showcase, Bunkspeed Shot, Chaos Group V-Ray, Luxion KeyShot, Next Limit Technologies Maxwell Render, Maxon Cinema 4D Visualize, Nvidia Mental Ray and SplutterFish Brazil. Some of these rendering programs are stand-alone, while others are available as plug-ins for a range of 3D modelling software.

The capability to create photorealistic images has been the main driver of rendering software developers in recent years, so this type of image is becoming ever easier and less time consuming to create. However, photorealism may no longer be sufficient or even desirable, especially for product design graduates hoping to differentiate themselves from other graduates in the hunt for employment. It may now be the ability to use rendering software to create a sense of individuality – much as in the past designers created their own hand rendering signature style – that is becoming more important. In addition, one of the drawbacks to producing a highly realistic product visual in the early stages of the design process is that it suggests to a client that a quick idea is more developed and considered than it is, which may dissuade the client from inputting in the way they might if presented with 'looser' design sketches. Highly realistic renders also give the designer the responsibility of ensuring that the manufactured product will appear exactly as the computer renderings have suggested.

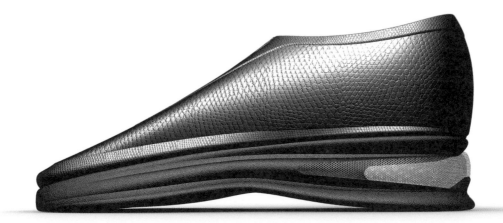

Fig. 93
Render of a casual athletic shoe concept.

Computer-aided engineering software

Computer-aided engineering (CAE) software refers to programs, either stand-alone or included within CAD programs, that enable the automation of several difficult engineering calculations. These calculations are often required as part of the virtual prototyping of a product, prior to physical prototyping. CAE programs enable the designer or engineer to specify particular materials for parts models and simulate stresses in parts receiving specified forces at particular locations. CAE software is used to test parts for tensile strength, yield strength, stress, strain and reaction to temperature. Product components and assemblies can be virtually loaded and impact tested to ensure the product will meet required standards of strength, safety and durability. These forms of testing are known as finite element analysis (FEA); they help to minimize the risk of product failure, optimize designs to lower production costs, prevent over-engineering, reduce the use of materials and validate product behaviour.

CAE software can also enable one or more moving components to be animated using motors, to check for correct movement, clearances and connections with other components. Computational fluid dynamics (CFD) is

Fig. 94
Development render of the sink shown in Fig. 91, rendered in KeyShot.

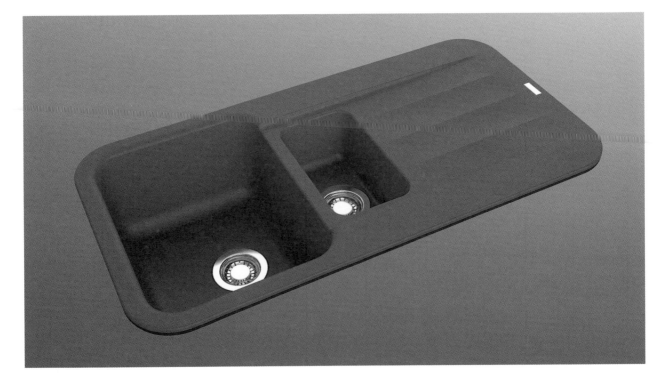

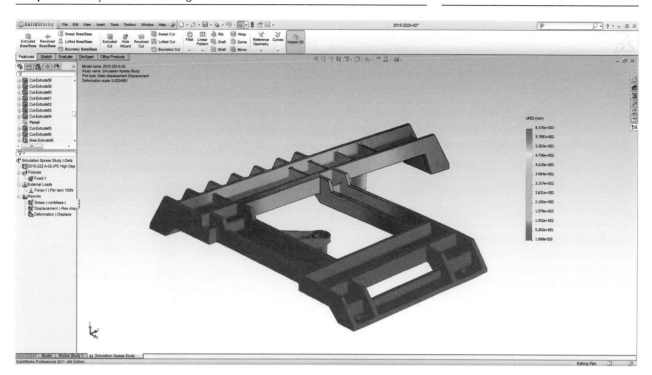

Fig. 95
CAE Simulation Xpress Study within SolidWorks
CAD software. The analysis results provide a
visual indication of the expected displacement
caused by applying an external load, equivalent
to a force of 100 newtons, to the area of the part
shown in red. Blue areas of the part show no
displacement, with red representing maximum
displacement.

related software used to test the movement of air and liquid through the internal
or over the external surfaces of a product. CFD software can also be used to test
the flow of plastic into a virtual injection mould cavity (the negative of the plastic
component to be manufactured).

CAE software therefore allows the refinement of a design as a virtual
prototype to ensure optimum performance and manufacturability, and helps
to reduce the number of working prototypes that need to be created and tested.
Engineers and tool makers are also able to simulate the manufacturing process
in advance of the tooling process, determining the amount of material and time
required for both the tooling process and for a production run so that costs
can be calculated. CAE software also reduces the likelihood of failure in the
moulding or casting process (which can be an expensive problem to solve),
and the failure of a product during its lifetime, which for certain products
would have serious safety consequences.

RAPID PROTOTYPING

What is rapid prototyping?

Rapid prototyping (RP) is a term encompassing a variety of processes used to fabricate models and prototype parts for products using CAD data from computer models. RP most commonly refers to a set of processes that utilize 3D CAD data to create three-dimensional prototype parts, but the term can also refer to automated processes that utilize 2D CAD data to create prototype parts from sheet materials. CAD software programs facilitate the RP process. Some RP processes are subtractive, whereby a design is cut from a sheet or block of material to create the desired part, and others are additive, whereby the part is built up through layer-by-layer addition of material.

The term 'rapid' is used to describe these processes for several reasons. They are able to fabricate prototype parts in hours, rather than the days or weeks required using traditional processes. They facilitate the rapid production of prototyping tooling for use with more traditional prototype-making processes. For certain applications, they can also be used for the manufacture of parts, bypassing the tooling processes required for some conventional manufacturing processes. The benefits of RP include potential cost and time savings during product development, the physical evaluation of parts, improved quality control, earlier discovery of errors during product development, reduced requirement for changes to production tooling and, for certain materials and applications, even the potential to remove the need for tooling altogether.

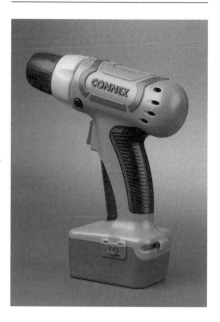

Fig. 1
A rapid prototype of a battery-powered drill. This prototype was output using the PolyJet process developed by Objet, which allows concurrent printing in materials of differing properties.

What is rapid prototyping used for?

RP enables designers to quickly create accurate physical representations of their design concepts so that they can see and feel them as objects in the real world. They can then check that they look, fit together and function as intended, prior to a client or manufacturer committing to the expensive process of tooling (creating moulds) for mass production. These checks can also avoid endangering the planned launch of a product. During the development of new products, rapid prototypes have a number of uses:

- In-house design evaluations
- Physical testing of the fit/assembly, function and ergonomics of a design
- Clarification of design changes
- Presentations to clients
- Gauging market reaction to new products through focus groups
- Evaluating customer demand at trade exhibitions prior to tooling for production
- Obtaining quotes from manufacturers
- Creating master patterns to facilitate the production of silicone moulds
- Creating master patterns for investment (lost wax) casting and sand casting
  Tooling for injection moulding (one of several processes used to create plastic parts)
- As a visual aid for tool makers
- As temporary placeholder parts used in product assemblies until real parts become available.

Rapid prototyping processes

Subtractive RP processes use CAD data inputted and converted in computer-aided manufacture (CAM) software to control a machine cutting head that removes material from a sheet or block of material inserted into the machine. Examples of subtractive RP processes are:

Fig. 2
Tuta coat hanger designed by Nendo for
Cappellini, an example of a laser-cut product.

Fig. 3
A rapid prototype of an inhaler. The cross-
sectional layers are clearly visible on the surface.

– Laser cutting
– Water-jet cutting
– Plasma cutting
– Milling
– Routing
– Hot-wire cutting
– Wire electrical discharge machining (wire EDM).

Additive RP processes, which the term 'rapid prototyping' more commonly describes, refers to a set of processes in which 3D parts are built from 3D CAD data using either liquid or powdered materials. In additive RP, CAD models are sliced by RP system control software into many two-dimensional cross-sectional layers or slices. These slices are then reconstructed layer by layer in the RP machine until the part is built. Examples of additive RP processes are:

– Stereolithography apparatus (SLA)
– Jetting systems
– Direct light processing
– Selective laser sintering (SLS)
– Selective mask sintering (SMS)
– Direct metal laser sintering (DMLS)
– Fused metal deposition
– Three-dimensional printing (3DP)
– Fused deposition modelling (FDM).

Rapid manufacturing and additive manufacturing

An exciting recent and ongoing development is the uptake of additive RP processes for manufacturing in addition to prototyping. Rapid manufacturing (RM) refers to the use of any RP process for the production of end-use product components. As no tooling is required, this can be economically viable for lower production volumes compared with traditional tool-based manufacturing processes. Additive manufacturing (AM) refers to the production of product components using additive RP processes. As the use of additive RP processes for manufacturing is a relatively recent development, several alternative terms are used to describe it, including additive layer manufacturing (ALM), solid freeform fabrication and 3D printing. In this book, 'AM' will be used when referring to the use of RP processes for manufacturing.

AM frees designers from traditional manufacturing constraints, enabling them to design products of any conceivable form. AM technologies create the possibility for on-demand manufacture of goods and enable the design and production of unique, customer-specific, customized or one-off products. Hearing aids are a typical example of a customer-specific product. For a hearing aid to fit perfectly, it must match the shape of the inner ear, but this shape is different in each of us. Each hearing-aid shell is therefore created in CAD from the 3D scan of a wax impression taken from the inner ear of a specific customer, and then output to additive manufacturing, providing a perfectly fitted product. Other current customer-specific applications for AM include dental and medical implants, and anatomical models used for practice by surgeons prior to real operations. The ability of RM to produce customized parts relatively quickly enables designers and manufacturers to offer customized variations of a given design and, depending on the size and functionality of the product, with no extra production cost.

Advantages of additive manufacturing

In addition to enabling economic low-volume production, AM also enables what would traditionally be separate product parts to be combined as one. This creates the added advantage of the removal of split lines (where separate components fit together) on products consisting of more than one part. Hinged components and geared mechanisms traditionally assembled from separate pieces can also be created together in one process.

One of the main advantages of AM over traditional manufacturing processes is that there are very few design restrictions. Since part complexity does not affect the production cost, and as the process does not involve moulding or casting, there are few constraints other than ensuring that the amount of material used to create a part is optimized for that part's given function, and that the design is optimized for the AM process used. There is no need to consider the location of parting lines, found on the surfaces of moulded and cast parts where separate components of the tool or mould used to create the part have met. The freedom to design according to clients' requirements and not around manufacturing constraints also means that the design of purely functional structural components can be optimized to avoid unnecessary material use and thus reduce product weight. This is key within the aerospace industry, for example, where weight savings of just a few kilograms can mean significant reductions in fuel consumption.

Fig. 4
Direct metal laser sintered engine block prototype designed by Within Technologies and produced on an EOS M270. Standard versions have two pipes meeting each other at a right angle, creating a point of resistance in the flow of liquid. Additive manufacturing in stainless steel allows curved pipe to run through the block. The lattice design can bear heavy loads, while being lighter than traditional cylinder blocks.

Fig. 5
Hearing-aid shells built using a high print resolution EnvisionTEC Perfactory 3 Digital Shell Printer, which uses the direct light processing RP process. The high print resolution produces a high-quality surface finish. The machine builds up to 40 shells in 2–3 hours. More than ten different resins can be used, ranging from transparent for ear moulds to skin tones for shells.

Subtractive RP

Subtractive RP processes are older than additive processes and have been in popular use for both prototyping and manufacturing for many years. They are used for a wide range of prototyping and manufacturing applications across the manufacturing, engineering and construction industries. Their particular advantages are:

- Good accuracy
- Good surface finish
- Efficient volume fabrication
- Structural integrity of materials
- Suitability for large workpieces.

Several commonly used subtractive RP processes are described below, and the case studies that follow provide examples of their use by designers.

Laser cutting

Laser cutting uses a laser beam to precision-cut materials from 0.2 to 40mm (0.0079 to 1.57in) thick, with thin sheet materials enabling faster cutting speed. The cut is created by the material melting, burning or vaporizing on contact with the laser beam. Many materials can be laser cut, including paper, card, plastics, composites, textiles, metals, glass, ceramics, man-made boards and timber. Laser cutting machines vary in size and power and not all machines are suitable for processing all these materials. Laser cutting leaves a relatively clean edge to cuts, particularly on thermoplastics, minimizing material finishing time and cost. Man-made board materials and timbers are left with a burnt edge to cuts. Laser cutters can be set up to score rather than cut right through material, enabling the creation of engraved surface patterns. Two-axis laser cutters are suitable for use with flat sheet material, while five-axis robotic laser cutters enable cuts on the surface of formed sheet materials.

Water-jet cutting

Water-jet cutting forces water, sometimes mixed with a selected size of abrasive powder (e.g. fine silicate), at high pressure and high velocity through a fine nozzle, producing a cutting beam with a diameter of 0.5 to 1mm (0.02 to 0.039in). The nozzle on most water-jet cutters is located on a CNC controlled gantry, able to travel and cut along the X and Y axes over the surface of the workpiece. Robotic CNC water-jet cutters are able to cut in five axes, enabling them to make more complex cuts in formed materials. The water is collected in a chamber beneath the workpiece, sieved and reused. Water-jet cutting can cut a range of materials, including plastics, composites, textiles, glass, ceramics, stone, wood and metals. It can also cut through stainless steel up to 60mm (2.36in) thick, mild steel up to 100mm (3.94in) thick, glass up to 100mm (3.94in) thick and granite up to 160mm (6.3in) thick. As a result of the water/water-abrasive mix flaring out as it passes through the workpiece, thicker materials result in a tapered cut, whereby the entry cut is narrower than the exit cut. Water-jet cutting is a cold process, so will not burn materials, but it can only be used to cut materials not adversely affected by water.

Plasma cutting

Plasma cutting is a means of cutting metals – usually steel or aluminium – using an inert gas blown through a small, water-cooled nozzle onto the surface of the workpiece. Some of the gas is converted to very high-temperature plasma when it comes into contact with an electrical arc created between a negatively charged electrode located in the gas nozzle and the positively charged surface of the workpiece. At around 25,000°C (45,000°F) the plasma easily melts the metal,

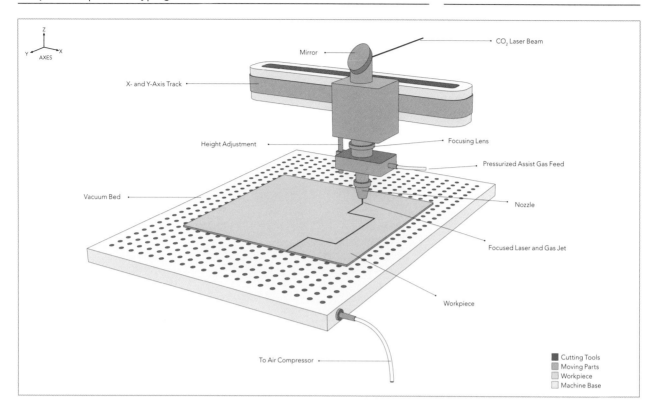

Fig. 6
Laser cutting.

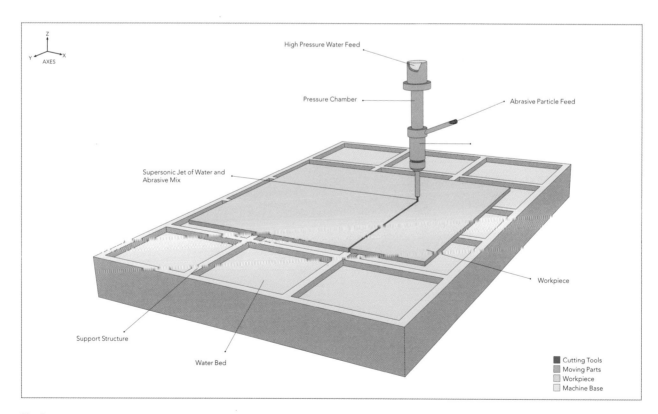

Fig. 7
Water-jet cutting.

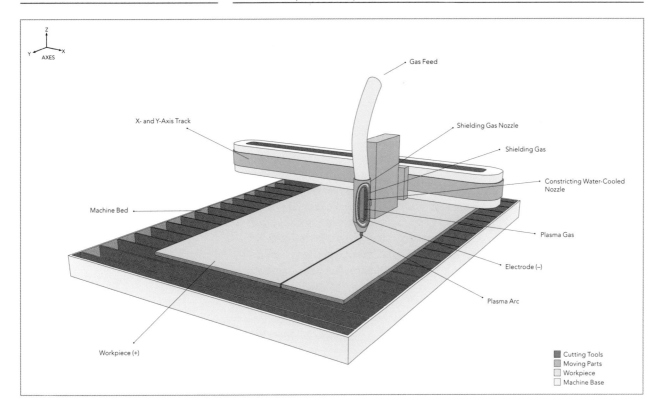

Fig. 8
CNC plasma cutting.

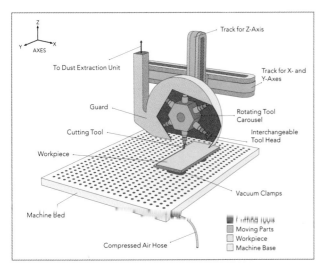

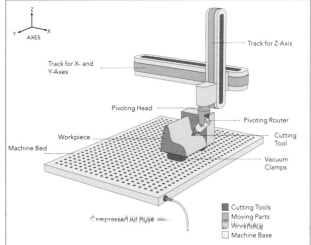

Fig. 9
Left, 3-axis CNC milling/routing; right, 5-axis.

which is subsequently blown away from the workpiece by the pressure of the gas. The process can be used to cut metals from 2 to 150mm (0.079 to 5.9in) thick, although due to the high heat it may distort sheet metal thinner than 8mm (0.31in). The level of finish on the cut edge is good but depends on the cutting speed; slower speeds create a better finish. Not as precise as laser cutting, plasma cutting is typically accurate to within tolerances of plus or minus 1.5mm (0.059in). Two-axis CNC plasma cutters, which enable cutting in the X and Y directions, are suitable for use with sheet metals, while five-axis robotic plasma cutters enable cuts on the surface of formed metal materials.

Milling and routing

Used for both prototyping and manufacturing, milling and routing refer to the process of removal of material by either a CNC or manually operated machine. For historical reasons, 'milling' is more commonly used when referring to the machine cutting of metal substrates, and 'routing' for the machine cutting of man-made board and wood substrates; however, the terms are interchangeable. A range of other materials can be used with these processes too, including plastics, composites and stone. In this process material is removed from the workpiece with the use of a high-speed rotating cutting tool, which follows a predetermined path over and around the substrate. Cutting is typically achieved along three, four or five axes, with the first three axes referring to movement of the workpiece on the two horizontal planes and one vertical plane. The fourth axis enables the workpiece to be rotated and the fifth axis enables the cutting tool to be rotated. Fully robotic machines allow up to nine axes of movement of the workpiece and cutting tool. Many different types and sizes of cut can be achieved using different shapes of cutting tool. On some machines, tools can be changed automatically. Milling and routing can be used to prototype and manufacture a wide range of object sizes, and allow for the creation of complex forms. In the automotive industry, for example, appearance models of full-size cars are prototyped from large blocks of modelling clay.

Hot-wire cutting

Hot-wire cutting is used to cut foams with relatively low melt temperatures. This includes expanded polystyrene (EPS), extruded polystyrene (XPS) and expanded polypropylene (EPP) foams. In this process, a thin, taut nickel chromium or stainless steel wire, 0.2 to 0.5mm (0.0079 to 0.02in) thick, is heated to around 200°C (390°F). When the wire is introduced to the foam, it vaporizes the foam just before making contact. Depending on the set-up of the machine used, cuts can be vertical, horizontal or angular. The movement of one end of the wire can be controlled independently from the other end, enabling tapered cuts and transitioning cuts that can produce different shapes at the top and bottom of the workpiece. Using lathe, turntable and bowl cutter attachments, which use a thicker wire preformed into a desired profile, curved surfaces can also be created. Larger machines are able to cut material volumes as large as 4800 x 4800 x 2400mm (189 x 189 x 94.5in) and are accurate to plus or minus 0.025mm (0.00098in).

Wire electrical discharge machining (wire EDM)

Similar to hot-wire cutting, yet much more accurate, wire EDM (or wire erosion) is a process used to cut through metals using rapid electrical discharges (sparks) created between a high-voltage, negatively charged, thin copper or brass wire and a positively charged metal workpiece. The wire, ranging from 0.02 to 0.25mm (0.0008 to 0.0098in) in diameter, is tensioned to enable straight-sided vertical or angled cuts. Cutting takes place in a bath of continuously running water, used to clear debris from the cutting area. To prevent the wire from eroding during the process, it is constantly fed into the workpiece, continuously wound between two spools. The X–Y movement of the top of the wire can be controlled independently

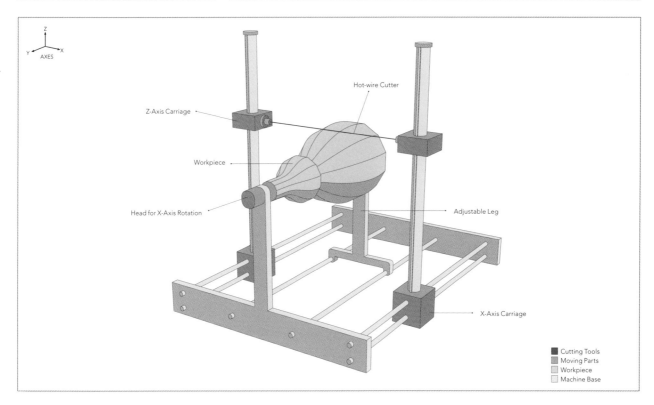

Fig. 10
CNC hot-wire cutting.

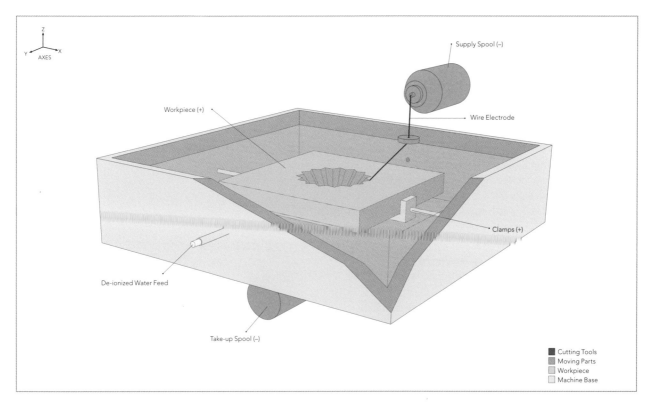

Fig. 11
Wire electrical discharge machining.

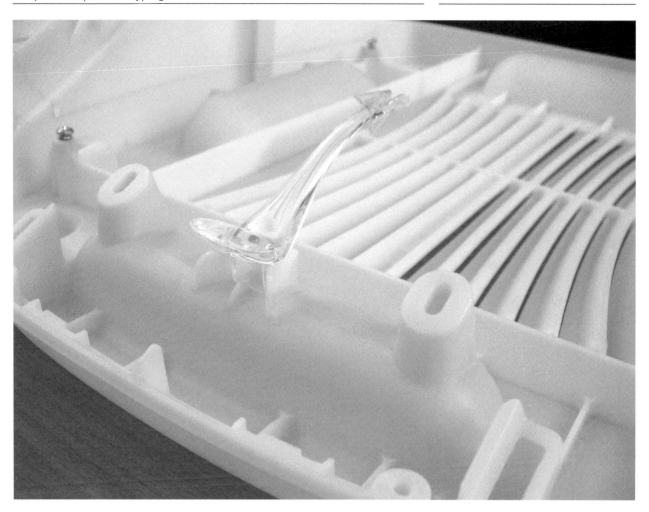

from the bottom, enabling tapered cuts with side wall angles of up to 45 degrees, and transitioning cuts that can produce different shapes at the top and bottom of the workpiece. Accurate to plus or minus 0.001mm (0.0004in), and able to cut metals up to 600mm (23.62in) thick, wire EDM is used to cut metals when other methods would not be possible due to the required depth of cut, when greater accuracy is required, or when very intricate cut shapes are required on parts too small for CNC milling, plasma cutting or water-jet cutting.

Fig. 12
Although similar in appearance to an additively rapid prototyped part, this prototype of a plastic casing was created using a computer numerical control (CNC) milling machine.

Case Study
2Form

Product: Memento Rug
Material: wool felt
RP process: laser cutting
Dimensions: 1700 x 2400mm
(66.93 x 94.49in)
Designer: Ksenia Stanishevski
Design to production: 12 months
Modelling software: Adobe Illustrator
Website: www.2form.no
Awards: Forum AID Award nomination
2007

Introduction

Ksenia Stanishevski moved from her native Estonia to Norway to study industrial design, and established 2Form there in 2005. She combines materials, handcraft techniques and the latest technology to create rugs that seek to combine art and design. By evoking experiences of natural and man-made environments with colours, patterns and surface textures, the designs aim to create a product that will push beyond interior decoration and transport its owner to other places. The company creates rugs for both private and corporate clients and exports niche volumes internationally.

Approach

Stanishevski is not aligned to any particular manufacturing technique. For every new rug, the concept for the rug drives the selection of materials and manufacturing processes. The objective for the Memento Rug was to play with different notions of contrast: black/white, positive/negative, old/new, handcraft/technology.

Process

The design was first drawn in Illustrator. To create the rug, traditional hand-tufting techniques were initially explored but the results didn't produce the desired aesthetic or sit well with the concept. Digital manufacturing techniques were then explored. The design was exported from Illustrator as a DWG file, a type of CAD drawing file able to be processed by laser-cutting machine control software. The most time-consuming part of the development process was sourcing industrial wool felt from India and finding suitable manufacturing facilities in Norway.

Five layers of felt were loaded into the laser cutter and took eight hours to be cut, which for the complex pattern and multiple layers was substantially faster than cutting by hand. The cut-out pieces of material were then removed by hand. Although this is an automated process, the time taken to cut the patterns was a challenge, limiting production volume and increasing production costs, and making high-volume production uneconomical.

Fig. 13 (opposite)
The reversible design of the Memento Rug allows a change in colour from white to black.

Fig. 14 (above)
The cut pattern allows the floor surface to show through and become an integral part of the design.

Fig. 15 (left)
The Memento Rug updates a classic damask textile pattern.

Result

Made from two layers of felt – one black and one white – the pattern is cut through both, enabling the floor surface to be seen through the cut-outs and become an integral part of the design. The geometric visual qualities of Memento, contrasting between solid and void, light and dark, update a classic woven damask textile pattern.

The manufacture of the rug also plays on contrasts, with the use of wool felt – the world's oldest textile – and laser cutting, a high-tech subtractive process. Although the laser cutting process reduced labour costs, the other costs associated with limited-volume production of rugs make the product suited only to limited-batch production. However, there is vast potential to further explore the combination of laser cutting and textiles.

Case Study
Lauren Moriarty

Products: Noodle Block Cube, Stitch Studies, Geometric Structure Cushion
Materials: Noodle Block Cube and Geometric Structure Cushion: EVA foam; Stitch Studies: PVC
RP process: laser cutting
Dimensions: Noodle Block Cube: 600 x 600 x 600mm (23.62 x 23.62 x 23.62in); Stitch Studies: 1000 x 500mm (39.37 x 19.69in); Geometric Structure Cushion: 350 x 350 x 70mm (13.78 x 13.78 x 2.76in)
Designer: Lauren Moriarty
Design to production: Noodle Block Cube: 6 months; Stitch Studies: 3 months; Geometric Structure Cushion: 2 months
Modelling software: Adobe Illustrator
Website: www.laurenmoriarty.co.uk
Awards: Noodle Block Cube: iF Product Design Award (Materials) 2005, Jerwood Applied Arts Prize (Textiles shortlist) 2002

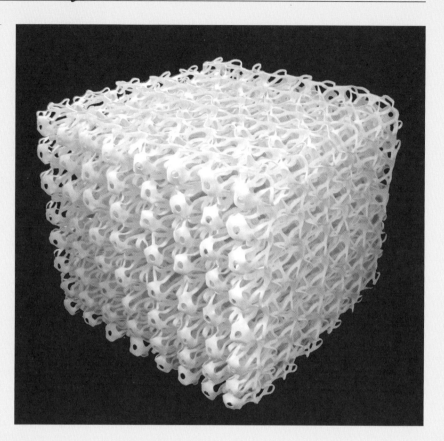

Fig. 16
Noodle Block Cube.
Fig. 17 (opposite above)
Stitch Studies.
Fig. 18 (opposite below)
Geometric Structure Cushion.

Introduction

With a background in both textiles and industrial design, British designer Lauren Moriarty mixes these disciplines to create new concepts for products and interiors that explore the potential of pattern, materials and three-dimensional textiles. She works with a variety of materials – predominantly plastics, rubber and fabrics – and uses a range of processes, including screen printing, laser cutting, die cutting and 3D modelling, to produce one-off experiments, limited-batch collections and commissions for a range of international clients.

Approach

Moriarty's textile collections form a study of fabric structures, referencing both hand making and mechanized techniques. Her approach is to explore textile structures, examining woven structures, lace and open-weave constructions, threads and embroidered surfaces. Her aim with the design of Noodle Block Cube, Geometric Structure Cushion and Stitch Studies was to explore the use of repeat geometric patterns using CAD in combination with laser cutting to achieve new forms of layered structural and woven textiles.

Process

The design process began with research for visual inspiration and intensive concept sketching, alongside research into weave patterns and lace structures. Moriarty then took her designs into Illustrator to investigate ways of reconstructing the patterns to form unique designs. Once a section of pattern had been created, this was then scaled and repeated to fit the size of the material being used. As each piece was made from a series of separate layers, the layers were designed individually in Illustrator. Moriarty then used either a plotter cutter (a CNC knife-cutting process) or a laser cutter to cut out each intricate layer before exploring ways of assembling the layers by hand. Depending on the design and scale of the piece, upwards of eight separate layers of material were used.

Result

By taking an experimental approach to working with materials, Moriarty pushes the boundaries of the discipline to discover what textiles are capable of. Using CAD cutting techniques in conjunction with heat forming and hand finishing provides an insight into how hand-making and machine-making processes can be combined to create an end result. The Noodle Block Cube demonstrates how an imaginative approach to using CAD, a sheet material and an RP/RM process can achieve an intricate and intriguing three-dimensional form. By bonding individual layers of EVA foam to create a three-dimensional structure, Geometric Structure Cushion challenges both existing preconceptions about the appearance of cushions and the methods used to create them. The use of layered CAD/CAM cut pieces of PVC material within Stitch Studies reinterprets and explores new fabric structures. The use of laser cutting enables each piece to be created using a different repeat pattern and gives an intricacy to the cutwork that could not otherwise be achieved.

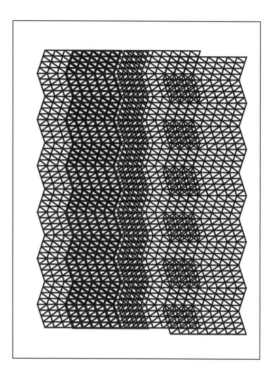

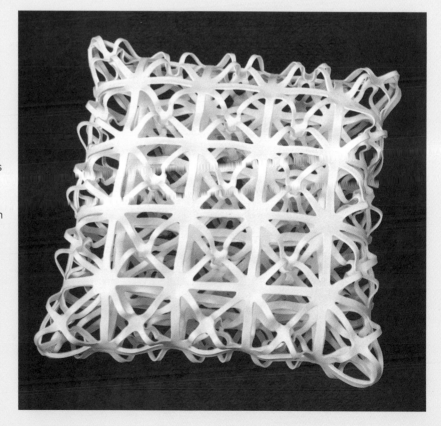

Case Study
David Trubridge

Products: Kina, Dream Space
Materials: Kina: bamboo plywood with nylon clips; Dream Space: cedar and aluminium
RP process: CNC routing
Dimensions: Kina: 440 x 200mm (17.3 x 7.9in), 800 x 370mm (31.5 x 14.6in), 1000 x 420mm (39.4 x 16.5in), 1400 x 650mm (55.1 x 25.6in), Dream Space, 4200 x 2400mm (165 x 94in)
Designer: David Trubridge
Design to production: Kina: 6 months (in combination with other projects); Dream Space: 3 months at the time of writing (still in development)
Modelling software: Robert McNeel & Associates Rhinoceros 3D and Grasshopper
Website: www.davidtrubridge.com
Awards: Kina: Good Design Award 2011, Design for Asia Award (Merit) 2011, IFDA Award (Silver Leaf) 2005, DINZ Best Design Award (category winner) 2005

Introduction
Originally from the UK, David Trubridge moved to New Zealand in the early 1980s. For much of his working life he was a self-employed designer/maker of crafted furniture. After the initial success of his Body Raft designs in Europe, one of which was licensed for manufacture by Cappellini in 2002, he established a larger company. With the development of lighting designs and the purchase of a CNC router, the company grew, and it now comprises two parts: manufacturing and design. Environmental concerns lie at the heart of the company, informing all aspects of their operation.

Approach
While developing a design for an ottoman, it was discovered that plywood thin enough to bend into the intended form wouldn't be strong enough to carry the required load. This inspired the idea to use the thin plywood to create lighting instead. The aim then became to produce an attractive, decorative lightshade that cast beguiling shadows, while using the minimum of material. Exploring the larger-scale use of the same techniques to create architectural spaces then led to the creation of Dream Space.

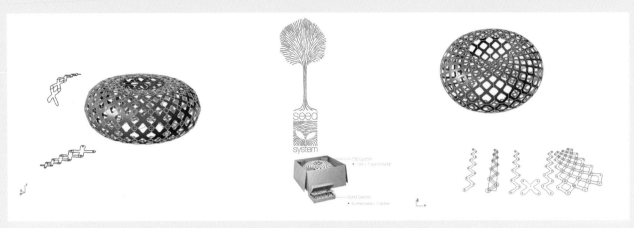

Fig. 19 (opposite)
Dream Space, a garden gazebo prototype
developed from the design of Kina, an
award-winning light.
Fig. 20 (top)
Design revisions to Kina to enable flat packing for
self-assembly.
Fig. 21 (above)
The original design for Kina.

Case Study
David Trubridge

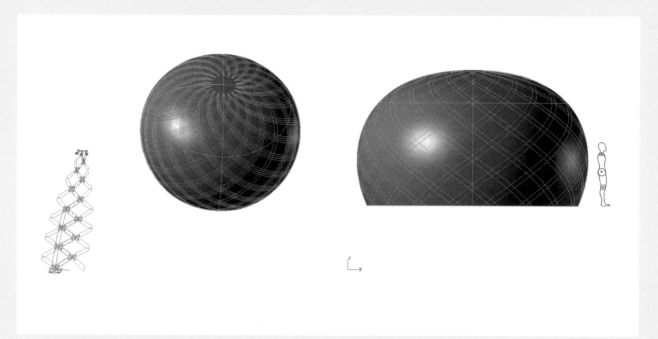

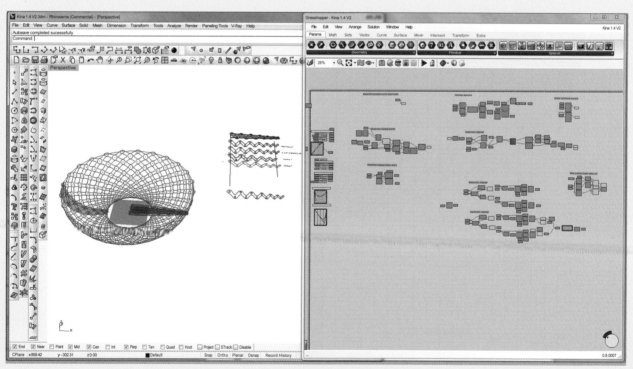

Fig. 22 (top)
Early CAD model of Dream Space.
Fig. 23 (above)
Modelling using Rhinoceros 3D plug-in
Grasshopper.

Process

The design for the Kina light was initially modelled in Rhino, by breaking down the surface of the form into vertical strips, then fitting X-shaped pieces onto the unrolled strips. Later, in similar designs the designers used Paneling Tools (a plug-in for Rhino) to array the X-shape module onto a grid on the built surface. The pieces of initial prototypes were cut out using a band saw; later, a CNC router was used. Each X-shaped piece in the strip was different, so the assembly of the original design was too complex to make it a flat-pack kitset. Instead, the pieces were riveted together on jigs.

It transpired that freight (and thus environmental) costs for the light, which when packaged consisted of approximately 99 per cent air, often exceeded the cost of producing it. Kina was therefore redesigned with different, zigzag-shaped components – all identical – to be sold flat-packed for self-assembly, while still retaining a similar appearance to the original design. The virtual model of the redesigned light was built in Grasshopper, so that a series of Kina lights could be created by scaling the model up or down, while at the same time adding or reducing the number of components or zigzags to suit the scale. The CAD model was converted to CNC machine control G-code in Visual Mill, and the pieces were then cut out on a CNC router, with all the fastening holes predrilled prior to cutting.

As with Kina, Dream Space was modelled in Rhino, converted to CNC Machine control G-code in Visual Mill, and cut out on a CNC router. All the rivet holes were predrilled prior to cutting. The strips of cedar are connected together using pairs of aluminium connectors 1.5mm (0.06in) thick. The dome was built from the bottom up in rings, each pair of connectors riveted together through the wood sandwiched in between. Developments are underway to release the product as a kitset; currently it is only available ready-assembled.

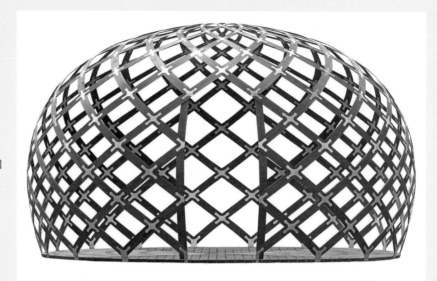

Result

'Kina' is the Maori name for a sea urchin local to New Zealand, whose shell the light resembles. CAD and CNC routing make economical use of thin sheet plywood to produce beautiful three-dimensional forms – the natural material creates a warming glow, while the intricate latticework casts attractive shadow patterns. The flat-packed components, at approximately one-fortieth of the volume of the assembled light, enable efficient transportation.

Dream Space is an elegant and contemporary alternative to existing gazebos. It obtains its strength from the accumulated compound curvature of all its thin pieces held in tension. The wood strips and aluminium connectors in each horizontal ring are identical, but different from those in the ring above and below. Although the wood is only 5mm (0.19in) thick, the structure is rigid and little affected by the inclusion of an entrance. Built from the ground up on a wooden deck or, for indoor use, a circular aluminium ring, the design creates a contemporary space with a minimum of materials.

Fig. 24 (top)
Dream Space, fabricated from thin pieces of cedar held together with aluminium connectors, makes efficient use of materials and is an elegant alternative to existing gazebos.
Fig. 25 (above)
Early scale prototype of Dream Space.

Case Study
Daniel Rohr

Product: Colander Table
Materials: aluminium, glass or acrylic tabletop
RP process: CNC milling
Dimensions: 1600 x 950 x 720mm (63 x 37.5 x 28.5in)
Designer: Daniel Rohr
Design to production: 12 months
Modelling software: Dassault Systèmes CATIA, PTC Pro/Engineer (now Creo Parametric), Robert McNeel & Associates Rhinoceros 3D
Rendering software: Autodesk Showcase
Website: www.danielrohr.com
Awards: Country Life/LAPADA Object of the Year 2011

Introduction

Born in Germany in 1968, Daniel Rohr studied industrial design and fashion accessories design in Milan before working for ten years as a product designer for the automotive and shoe industries. He began working on his own furniture designs in 2005, and has exhibited his work around the world.

Approach

Having designed aluminium products for the automotive industry, Rohr had a strong desire to use aluminium for furniture. The idea was to design a table suitable for batch production. Removing many of the constraints so often required for mass production would provide greater design freedom.

Process

Rohr first explored the concept with multiple paper sketches. Then, to evaluate the proportions and details more accurately, dimensions were determined and the design was modelled at 1:1 scale using Rhinoceros 3D. To visualize the product as it would appear in aluminium, the model was then imported into Showcase and rendered from various viewpoints. For evaluation as a physical object, the design was remodelled using Pro/Engineer and a 1:1 wooden prototype was produced using a robotic seven-axis CNC router. Constant changes to the shape, proportions and product details during the design process were time consuming but essential to creating the desired optical qualities.

To prototype the table in aluminium, Rohr collaborated with a manufacturing company producing large steel and aluminium moulds for the automotive industry. Prior to machining, the design was modelled again using parametric software (CATIA), which enabled changes to be made to such details as the size and positioning of holes without recreating the model from scratch.

Fabrication began with a 408kg (899lb) block of aluminium being clamped to the table of a four-axis CNC milling machine. A high-speed rotating cutting tool then followed a tool path calculated by machine control software from the CAD model, removing material in several passes in different directions over the workpiece; for a smooth finish, a succession of ever smaller, finer cutting tools was used with each pass. The CNC machine also engraved the name and number of each table, and the designer's signature. To create curved forms on both upper and lower surfaces, the workpiece was rotated by 180 degrees. The component was then polished, first with a hand-held powered rotational buffer, then with cloths.

The table legs were produced from a large-diameter, round-section aluminium bar. The bar was cut into pieces and each piece secured in a CNC lathe. A cutting tool then followed the predetermined tool path to remove material and reproduce the tapered outer form. Each leg was then transferred to a three-axis CNC machine to create the channel features. The legs were then polished using a powered buffing wheel, sandpaper and polishing cloths.

The complete production process for each table took around four weeks: three weeks for machining and one week for polishing.

Result

This time-consuming and expensive-to-make table was produced as a limited edition of eight pieces, two prototypes and two artist's proofs. Its striking design achieves several optical effects. The bowl-like curved upper surface of the aluminium creates space underneath the glass top, which, when

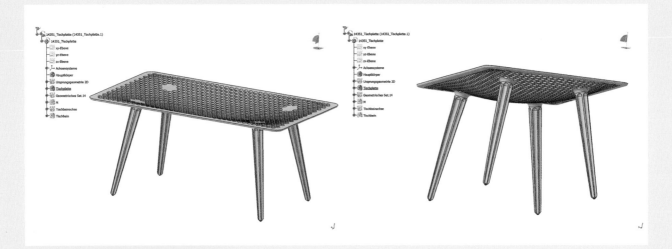

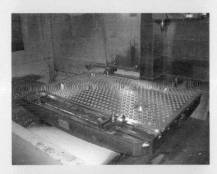

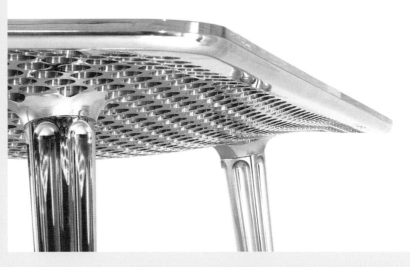

viewed from certain angles, seems to disappear – objects placed on it appear to float. The 909 holes enable light to pass through the table, making it appear lighter and creating an interesting pattern of light and shadow on the floor. The alternating light and dark reflections that result from the cross-sectional shape of the legs create the illusion that they have been fabricated from a transparent material.

Although the CNC process used for this design might seem inefficient in material and energy use, the table was produced in such limited numbers and designed to be so long lasting that such environmental concerns become insignificant when compared with the CNC production of such mass-produced goods as computer casings, which have a lifespan of only a few years.

While this product caters to a very small, exclusive market, its impactful design promotes fresh thinking about ways of employing CNC machining and aluminium, which is rarely used for large pieces of furniture.

Fig. 26 (opposite)
Colander Table.
Fig. 27 (top)
CAD model of the Colander Table.
Fig. 28 (above)
Detail of the curved aluminium surface.
Left, top to bottom:
Fig. 29
CNC machining the top.
Fig. 30
CNC machining the underside.
Fig. 31
Completed underside.
Fig. 32
Polishing the Colander Table.

Case Study
Paul Loebach

Product: Shelf Space
Material: basswood
RP process: CNC routing
Dimensions: 1140 x 380 x 530mm
(45 x 15 x 21in)
Designer: Paul Loebach
Website: http://paulloebach.com

Introduction
Born in 1974, Paul Loebach is a New York City-based furniture and product designer. His work incorporates digital modelling and manufacturing technology, combined with a deep analysis of furniture history and traditional crafting techniques. Loebach works as a manufacturing consultant for major furniture companies and is an adjunct professor at the Rhode Island School of Design. His projects have been exhibited internationally and published broadly in books, blogs and periodicals.

Approach
Loebach's approach to the design of Shelf Space was to 'explore referential form through the parameters of advanced wood machining technology, for the purpose of pushing the limits of recognizable aesthetic form, to push the limits of what a given material can do, and to challenge what we are conditioned to recognize as "normal".'

Process
The design was first explored on paper using pencil sketches. From there, forms were explored using 3D computer modelling in order to develop a range of 'paths' that a given moulding profile could follow. Once a design had been determined, a dialogue began with an engineer at a manufacturer of aerospace machinery, who programmed and operated the

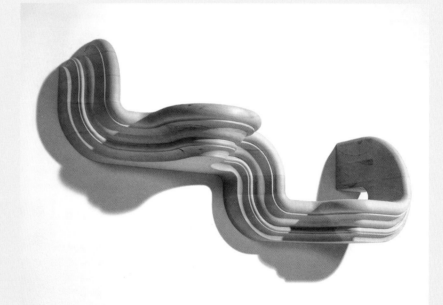

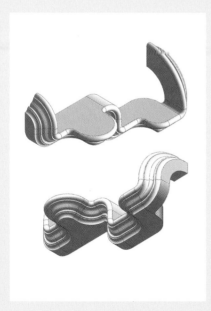

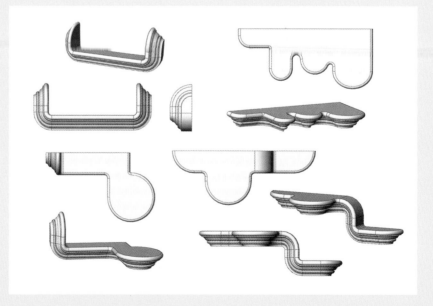

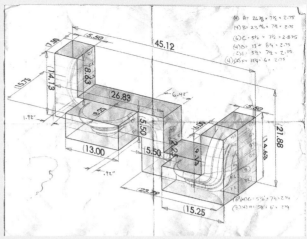

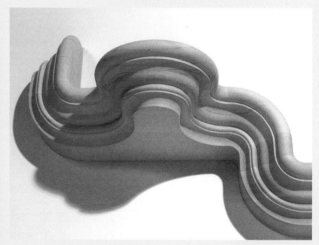

five-axis CNC routing machine. At this stage there were many exchanges and revisions back and forth to figure out how the required blank would be built up from pieces of basswood, and to determine ways to hold the blank down on the machine's table. The cutting tool then followed a predetermined tool path to cut the final object from the large wood blank, which consisted of several pieces of basswood glued together.

Result

Referencing historical American moulding profiles from the early 1900s, Loebach makes use of technology to re-contextualize these profiles within a fluid and dynamic undulating shelf. Emerging from the wall and twisting and turning through space before seeming to re-enter the wall, the design pushes the limits of wood machining to create a form only possible with multi-axis CNC routing machinery. Shelf Space successfully

combines the warmth of traditional wood craft with contemporary methods of production. Revisiting forms from the past, the product feels familiar yet at the same time unexpected, creating a link between tradition and technology and successfully challenging our understanding of how existing materials and processes can be used

Fig. 33 (opposite above)
Shelf Space.
Fig. 34 (opposite below)
Exploratory CAD models of Shelf Space.
Clockwise from top left:
Fig. 35
Sketch of basswood assembly prior to CNC machining.
Fig. 36
Dimensioned CAD drawing of basswood assembly prior to CNC machining.
Fig. 37
Detail of the finished shelf.
Fig. 38
Assembled pieces of basswood ready for CNC machining.

Additive RP

Additive RP refers to a set of automated fabrication processes that utilize 3D CAD data to build three-dimensional parts layer by layer without any requirement for tooling. In additive RP processes CAD models are converted to a special type of file format, which can then be sliced by RP machine control software into many horizontal cross-sectional slices or layers. Depending on the RP process and software settings used, the thickness of these layers ranges from 0.1 to 0.015mm (0.0039 to 0.00059in). These processes are used for part prototyping, for the creation of patterns and tooling for traditional manufacturing processes, and more recently also for low-volume and one-off, high-value part manufacturing. Some of these processes create parts from photosensitive liquid polymers and others from powdered polymers, metals or ceramics. The term 'additive manufacturing' (AM) is used when these processes are used for the manufacture of parts. At the time of writing, around 20 different RP processes exist. A range of commonly used additive RP/AM processes are described below, with case studies presenting examples of the use of some of these by designers.

Although additive RP processes can be used to prototype large parts, such as car dashboards, they are not yet suited to the high-volume production of large parts. However, with growing uptake of the technology, reduction in material costs and further technological advances, in the future both higher volume and the production of both small- and larger-scale parts are likely to be possible. Indeed, the manufacture of entire aircraft wings using AM is already being explored by the aerospace industry, and it is possible that entire aircraft may one day be manufactured in the same way.

Stereolithography apparatus (SLA)

Background
Developed, named and subsequently patented by Chuck Hull in 1986, with the first machine produced by 3D Systems in 1987, the company he founded with Raymond Freed to commercialize the process. Stereolithography was the first commercially available RP process.

Process
The SLA process uses slice data from the CAD file to control a UV (ultraviolet) laser to cure thin layers of photo-curable resin. The layer thickness ranges from 0.05 to 0.15mm (0.002 to 0.006in), depending on the SLA machine used and the machine settings for the build. In the SLA process, the part is built on a horizontal perforated platform located in a vat of the liquid resin. The bed initially sits at the top of the vat, lowering into the liquid resin by the layer thickness set for the build. After one layer of resin has been cured (solidified) by the UV laser, the bed again lowers by the layer thickness, enabling a sweeping arm to pass a layer of uncured resin over the first cured layer. When cured by the UV laser, this next layer bonds to the first cured layer.

Before small, delicate parts are built, the same build process is used to create a supporting structure between the platform and the part. This structure prevents the part being damaged when being removed from the build platform. Any parts with overhangs that fan outwards also require a supporting structure to be built between the build platform and their lower surfaces in order to stop the overhangs bending down during the build process. These supporting structures are generated automatically by the software controlling the machine but can be adjusted by the machine operator. After the part has been built, it is removed from the machine and placed in a chemical bath to remove excess resin.

Once supporting structures have been manually removed, parts are then fully cured using a UV oven. (During the build, the UV laser first cures the outline of the cross-sectional shape of the part layer and then cures the resin inside the

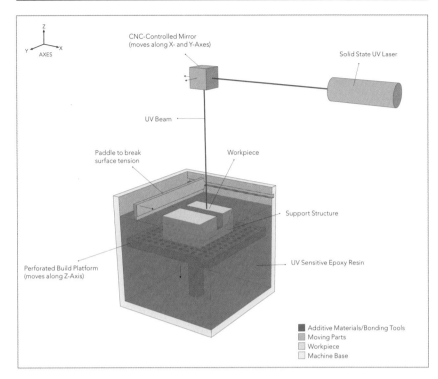

Fig. 39
Stereolithography.

Fig. 40
An SLA prototype produced by Ogle Models and Prototypes using an IPro 8000 SLA machine with their SLA Clear (Sl 7870) resin.

cross-sectional outline in a grid pattern, which results in small areas on the inside of the part remaining uncured.)

Advantages

SLA produces accurate parts with tolerances down to 0.05mm (0.002in) with very good surface finish, similar in appearance to (although not as strong as) injection-moulded components. The largest machines are able to build parts up to a maximum size of 2100 x 700 x 800mm (82.68 x 27.56 x 31.50in). A wide range of photosensitive epoxy and acrylate-epoxy composite resins can be used with the SLA process to achieve a variety of desired material properties. Because of this variety, and the accuracy of the process, SLA is frequently used to produce functioning product prototypes. Flexible and clear parts can be produced using SLA materials.

Drawbacks

The need to support overhanging sections places some limitations on part design and can make highly complex part geometries difficult to realize. The strength, impact resistance and long-term stability of the resins used in SLA are poor compared with some other AM processes. Although build time is relatively quick, the additional time required for the UV oven-curing stage can make SLA slower than some other RP processes. Enclosed volumes will trap uncured liquid resin inside unless a small drain hole is integrated in the CAD model to allow the resin to drain out after part creation.

Jetting systems

Background

First introduced by 3D Systems in 1996 and subsequently also by Objet in 2000, these inkjet-based technologies use photo-curable liquid resins as in SLA, but here the resin for the part is deposited by print heads and cured by a UV lamp.

Fig. 41
3D illustration of a jetting system. Several variations of this process (above) exist.

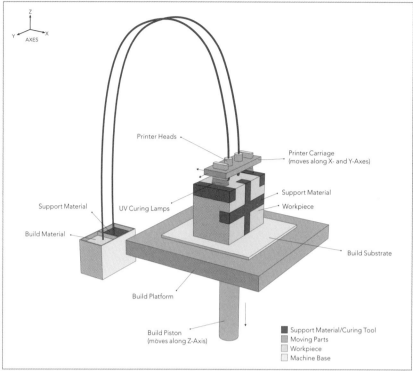

Process

Jetting processes use multiple print heads to print both the part and the support material. In Objet's PolyJet process, the support material is cured to a gel, which can be removed post-build using a water jet or by hand. In 3D Systems' InVision 3D printer multi-jet modelling (MJM) process, the part material is an acrylic photo polymer and the support material is built from an easily removed wax. These jetting processes build parts layer by layer from the bottom up. The print heads, or jets, deposit material only where required.

Advantages

Jetting systems are accurate to within 0.02 to 0.08mm (0.00079 to 0.0031in). They are fast compared with other RP processes, with very fine layer thickness as low as 0.016mm (0.00063in), resulting in parts with little or no visible stair-stepping (see page 118). This enables accurate replication of very small, intricate details and minimizes part finishing time. Wall thickness can be as thin as 0.6mm (0.024in) or even less, depending on the material used. Objet's PolyJet machines work with over 100 different materials and can print a single part consisting of 14 different materials. This enables the creation of parts with a wide range of physical and mechanical properties, for example, soft, hard, transparent and opaque materials, of varying grades and colours. Materials that are resistant to temperatures up to 80°C (176°F) can be used. The water-soluble support structure can be washed off, enabling complex geometries. For most applications, no post-curing of parts is required.

Drawbacks

As with SLA, the strength of parts created using jetting systems is not as high as with selective laser sintering (SLS) (see page 92). Maximum build size is relatively small at 500 x 400 x 200mm (19.69 x 15.75 x 7.87in) for the PolyJet system and 298 x 185 x 203mm (11.73 x 7.28 x 7.99in) for InVision.

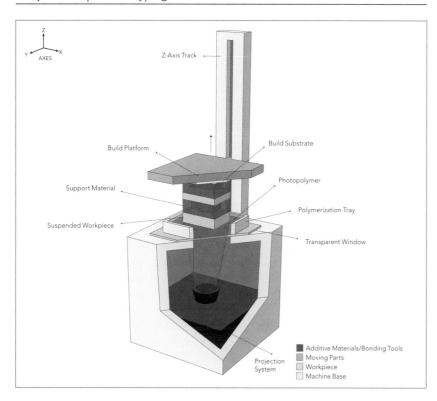

Fig. 42
Direct light processing.

Direct light processing

Background
Developed by EnvisionTEC and commercialized in 2003, their Perfactory machines use digital light processing (DLP) technology developed by Texas Instruments to selectively cure fine layers of an acrylic photo-curable polymer. The process is widely used by the hearing aid, jewellery and dental industries.

Process
Like jetting processes, DLP cures parts as they are being built from a photo-curable resin. The difference is that this process cures volumetric pixels (voxels) using multiple mirrors that reflect UV light from a source onto the appropriate locations of a very thin layer of resin, making the process approximately three times faster than SLA. DLP builds parts upside down, with the build platform located at the top and the model suspended below. Support material is created to support overhanging sections from above and to enable the part to be removed from the build platform without damage.

Advantages
In comparison with other RP processes DLP is relatively fast. A choice of ten different resins is available to create parts with different material properties, from transparent to coloured opaque materials to soft materials. Medical-grade polymers are available for use with this process and some wax-like build materials are suitable for subsequent direct casting in metals. Depending on the material used, the height of the voxels (akin to layer thickness) can be down to an industry-leading 0.015mm (0.00059in), resulting in parts with no visible stair-stepping. This enables accurate replication of very small, intricate details and minimizes part finishing.

Drawbacks
The highest precision machine is currently limited to building small parts with a maximum size of 160 x 100 x 160mm (6.3 x 3.94 x 6.3in). Lower-precision machines enable slightly larger parts of up to 267 x 165 x 203mm (10.51 x 6.50 x 7.99in).

Fig. 43
Selective laser sintering. Above, a lampshade by Freedom Of Creation under construction in an SLS machine.

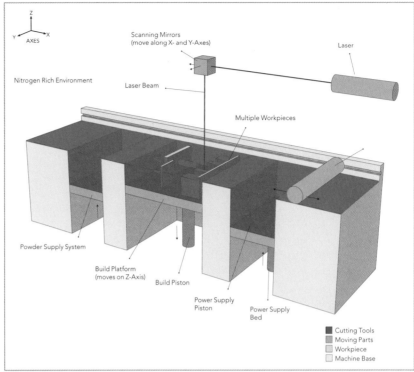

Some materials require parts to be further cured using a photo flash process, which hardens the photo-curable material. Enclosed volumes will trap uncured liquid resin inside unless a small drain hole is included in the CAD model to allow the resin to drain out after part creation.

Selective laser sintering (SLS)

Background
First proposed and patented by Ross Householder in 1979, the SLS process, as it is currently known, was developed and patented by Carl Deckard at the University of Texas in the late 1980s and first commercialized by the DTM Corporation in 1992, and subsequently in 1994 by EOS. In 2001 DTM was acquired by 3D Systems.

Process
The SLS process uses a laser to sinter (fuse) a fine thermoplastic powder. The process is similar to SLA, with the part built on a lowering platform inside a build chamber, but instead of a liquid resin being swept across the part with each lowering of the platform, a resin in powdered form is used. As the laser fuses a layer of powdered polymer, it bonds to the already fused layer below. Once a layer of a part has been fused by the laser, the platform drops, another fine layer of polymer powder is swept across the part and the process repeats until the part is built. Layer thickness ranges from 0.05 to 0.2mm (0.002 to 0.008in). Prior to the build, the polymer powder is heated to just below its melting point, making it easier for the laser to fuse the powder.

Advantages
The materials used in SLS lead to the creation of parts with relatively good mechanical properties that can be used to create functioning parts. Polyamide (nylon) is most common, and can be filled with glass fibres, carbon fibres, aluminium and other fillers to give it a range of properties, including flexibility for the creation of living hinges and snap fits and resistance to high temperatures of up to 184°C (363°F). Polystyrene is used for the creation of investment casting patterns, and elastomeric materials for the creation of gaskets, seals and other

parts requiring rubber-like qualities. Small details can be as thin as 0.5mm (0.02in), and part wall thickness down to 0.7mm (0.03in). Larger SLS machines can build large parts with maximum dimensions of 700 x 380 x 600mm (27.56 x 14.96 x 23.62in). Complete functional mechanical assemblies can be built in one process (rather than built separately and assembled later).

Another advantage of SLS is that no supporting structure needs to be built to support overhanging sections; the powdered material next to the sintered part performs this task. This enables the creation of highly complex forms. Parts can also be built in 3D space without contacting the build platform, which allows parts to be nested together in the build chamber, increasing production efficiency.

Drawbacks

The surface finish on SLS parts is not as good as on SLA parts and, depending on the layer thickness specified for the build by the machine operator, the process can leave visible stair-stepping on curved surfaces of parts and on flat surfaces oriented at low angles relative to the horizontal in the build chamber. Because of how SLS parts are created, their surface remains porous, so, depending on the intended end use, it may be necessary to seal the surface using lacquer, water-based urethane, two-part urethane or epoxy. Enclosed volumes will trap powder inside unless a small drain hole is included in the CAD model to allow the powder to drain out after part creation.

Selective mask sintering (SMS)

Background

SMS was developed by Ralf Larson, who founded Speedpart in 2000 to commercialize the technology. In the same year, the intellectual property rights were transferred to Sintermask, another of Ralf Larson's Swedish companies. In 2007 a machine was successfully produced to prove the technology, and in 2009 the company moved to Germany. Sintermask now market a machine that utilizes this process for additive manufacturing in low to medium batch sizes.

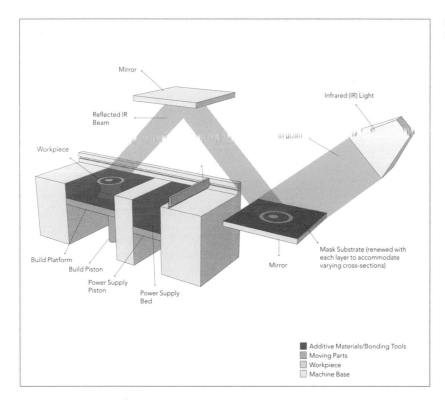

Fig. 44
Selective mask sintering.

Mirror

Infrared (IR) Light

Reflected IR
Beam

Workpiece

Build Platform

Build Piston

Power Supply
Piston

Power Supply
Bed

Mirror

Mask Substrate (renewed with
each layer to accommodate
varying cross-sections)

■ Additive Materials/Bonding Tools
■ Moving Parts
□ Workpiece
□ Machine Base

Process

The process is initially similar to SLS insofar as a thin layer of powdered material is swept across a build platform. However, instead of a single laser beam travelling over the polymer powder to fuse the section shape of the corresponding slice layer of the CAD model, an infrared lamp is used to cure the entire slice layer in one flash. Parts of the layer not to be fused are masked off on a reflective mirror using an electrostatic coating of reusable ceramic powder. The infrared lamp then projects infrared radiation onto the mirror, which reflects the radiation from the areas that haven't been masked onto a second mirror. This in turn reflects the radiation onto the layer of powdered polymer, fusing the entire layer. The build platform then lowers, the next layer of polymer is swept across and the process repeats. The process creates parts with a layer thickness of between 0.025 and 0.25mm (0.001 and 0.01in). Depending on the material used and layer thickness specified, the SMS process has a build speed of 5 to 10 seconds per layer, equivalent to a part height per hour of 9 to 180mm (0.354 to 7.09in).

Advantages

SMS eliminates the need for a laser and, unlike SLA, SLS, FDM, 3DP and, to an extent, jetting systems, the speed of build is independent of the build area. Build time is easier to predict than with laser-based processes. Various types of material can be used to create end-use parts, functional prototypes and air-permeable master patterns for casting for thermoforming processes. Materials include polyamide, polyethylene, polypropylene, polystyrene, polycarbonate, wax and coated sands, metal and ceramic powders. Similar to SLS, the creation of a supporting structure is not necessary as the powder surrounding the fused part supports overhanging sections. This also makes it possible to fabricate a part of any shape (part wall thickness dependent) and nest parts during the build process. The relative low cost and speed of this process, and the fact it has been designed for the continuous production of parts with minimal operator involvement, makes it well suited to AM.

Drawbacks

SMS is not yet as widely used or as available in RP/AM bureaus as SLA and SLS. The layer thickness results in visible stair-stepping on curved surfaces of parts and on flat surfaces oriented at low angles relative to the horizontal in the build chamber. Because of the way SMS parts are created, their surface remains porous and, depending on the intended end use for the part, it may be necessary to seal the surface using lacquer, water-based urethane, two-part urethane or epoxy. Enclosed volumes will trap powder inside unless a small drain hole is included in the CAD model to allow the powder to drain out after part creation. Maximum build size is currently 200 x 310 x 500mm (7.87 x 12.20 x 19.69in), which is smaller than SLA and SLS, although the technology is scalable, so larger machines are likely.

Direct metal laser sintering (DMLS)

Background

DMLS was developed in the 1990s by EOS as a method of creating metal parts from metal powders. The process is very similar to selective laser melting (SLM), first commercialized by MCM-HEK (now SLM Solutions) in the early 2000s, and LaserCusing, introduced by Concept Laser in 2004. A number of other similar processes exist, including 3D Systems' indirect metal laser sintering and Trumpf's direct laser forming. DMLS is well suited to additive manufacturing and is similar to SLS, although instead of using polymer powders it uses a range of metal powders. It is currently most commonly used for prototyping metal parts, for the direct manufacture of high-value parts for the aerospace, motorsport, dental and medical sectors and for the production of small tools and tool inserts for injection

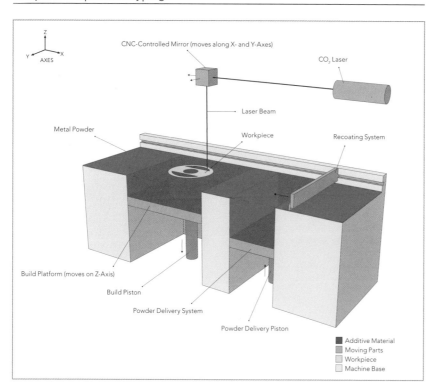

Fig. 45
Direct metal laser sintering.

moulding. Arcam's electron beam melting (EBM) is a very similar process, using an electron beam instead of a laser to melt steel and titanium metal powders.

Process

A fine layer of powder is swept from a powder chamber onto a build platform in the build chamber. A high-powered CO_2 laser melts an area of the metal powder corresponding to the slice of the STL CAD file and the process repeats until the part is built. A supporting structure for overhanging sections is built from the same powder and is removed once the part has been built. The build chamber of most DMLS machines is 250 x 250 x 250mm (9.84 x 9.84 x 9.84in), although some have capacities up to 500 x 500 x 500mm (19.69 x 19.69 x 19.69in).

Advantages

Layer thickness is fine, from 0.02 to 0.1mm (0.00079 to 0.0039in) according to the machine setting specified for the build. Fine layer thickness results in accurate parts with good replication of details and relatively good surface finish. No tooling is required to produce the metal parts. In comparison with parts produced using traditional metal manufacturing processes, it is possible to create parts with more complex geometries with internal features and passages that could not be cast. Part design can be optimized for function and performance rather than for manufacture. By building parts with integral geometric lattices, parts with very high strength-to-weight ratios can be produced. Solid areas of parts are very dense, with properties similar to wrought alloys, and comparable to parts produced using die casting. Unlike casting, no tooling is required for the production of metal parts, making it an efficient process for one-off and low-volume production. A range of metals can be used, including bronze, cobalt chromium, nickel bronze, nickel chromium, maraging steel, stainless steel, titanium and zinc. Part wall thickness can be as low as 0.25mm (0.01in).

Drawbacks

DMLS parts require a support structure for overhanging features, so this process produces less-complex part geometries than are possible with SMS and SLS. The support structure is created from the same metal powder as used to create the

Fig. 46
Fused metal deposition.

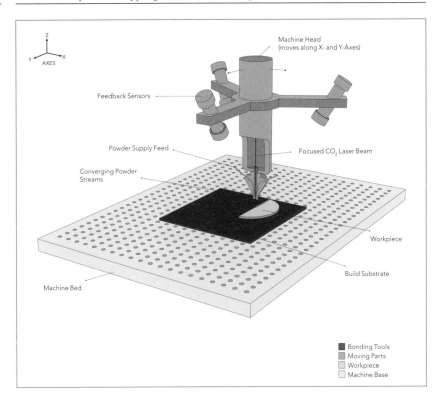

part and is joined to the build platform. Wire EDM (see page 73) is used to remove the metal support structure from the platform and part. Accurate grinding, lathes and mills are used to remove any remaining support structure from the part and to finish surfaces. These additional processes are time consuming and add cost. In order to achieve very smooth and polished surface finishes, part surfaces have to be post-processed. Part cost is high.

Fused metal deposition

Background
Fused metal deposition processes include laser engineered net shaping (LENS), developed by Sandia National Laboratories in the US and commercialized by Optomec, and direct metal deposition (DMD), commercialized by POM. Fused metal deposition is most commonly used for prototyping fully dense metal parts, for the direct manufacture of high-value parts for the aerospace, defence and medical sectors, and for making small tools and tool inserts for injection moulding.

Process
These processes use metal powders that are fed through a nozzle into the path of a laser beam, which melts the metal powder, depositing it onto the build platform/previous part layer. As the molten metal is deposited, the laser also melts the previous layer, facilitating a high-quality bond between deposited layers. Metals used include a range of stainless steel alloys, aluminium, titanium, maraging steel, nickel chromium, cobalt and copper. Maximum part size is 305 x 305 x 305mm (12 x 12 x 12in). Minimum part wall thickness is 1.5mm (0.06in).

Advantages
No tooling is required to produce metal parts. The mechanical properties of fused metal deposition parts are equivalent to, or better than, those produced using traditional manufacturing processes. The hardness of some metal materials can be controlled during the deposition process. The process is able to create parts using multiple metals, combining metals with such materials as ceramics and varying the material composition within a single part. These are known as

functionally graded materials. Deposition of the metal can be tailored according to desired accuracy and speed of build. Fused metal deposition can also be used to repair or add features to existing metal parts, whether built using this process or traditionally fabricated.

Drawbacks

The typical layer thickness of 0.1 to 1.6mm (0.0039 to 0.063in) is not as fine as DMLS. The method used by these systems to deposit material using a five-axis robotic head limits part complexity. Metal is deposited slowly, making larger parts less cost effective for manufacture. As with DMLS, parts need to be separated from the build platform using wire EDM, and smooth finishes require extensive post-processing by grinding, lathing and milling. No support material is built, making overhanging sections problematic. Part cost is high.

Three-dimensional printing (3DP)

Background

Three-dimensional printing was developed by researchers at MIT in the early to mid-1990s and commercialized by Z-Corp (later acquired by 3D Systems) in 1997.

Process

This process uses inkjet printing technology to build parts layer by layer by depositing a liquid binder onto thin layers of plaster, corn starch or polymer powder. Once one cross-sectional part layer has been bonded, the build platform drops by the layer thickness, a roller sweeps a fresh layer of powder over the previous layer and the process repeats. At the end of the build, after the binder has set, excess powder is removed from the build chamber and cleaned from the part using compressed air. Maximum part size is 508 x 381 x 229mm (20 x 15 x 9in). Minimum wall thickness is 0.5 to 1mm (0.02 to 0.039in) for details, and 2 to 3mm (0.079 to 0.12in) for weight-bearing parts of the model. Three-dimensional printing processes that utilize other powdered materials, such as ceramics and metals, have also been developed; these require additional sintering, infiltration

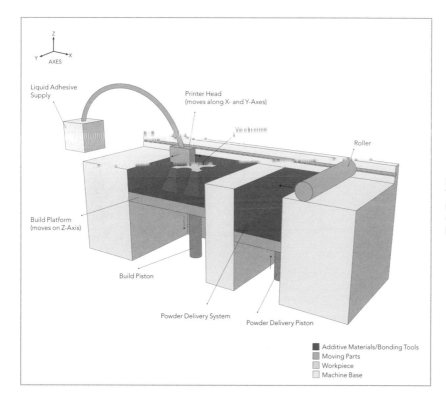

Fig. 47
Three-dimensional printing. Above, a rapid prototype of an underwater propulsion device created in multiple colours using the 3DP process on 3D Systems' Z-Printer.

and heat treatment steps to fuse the powders together, burn off the binder and ensure adequate material density and surface finish.

Advantages
The build process is fast compared with other RP processes, with a typical build speed of around 20 to 30mm (0.79 to 1.2in) per hour, depending on part size and complexity of internal geometry. No supporting structure is required, enabling complex part geometries. High-end machines with five print heads can print parts comprising multiple colours and are able to print 390,000 different colours, many more than other RP systems. The cost of parts is low.

Drawbacks
With a layer thickness of 0.1mm (0.0039in), 3DP is not as accurate as other RP methods. Parts are not as strong as those produced using other RP processes and can only be used for visual aids and concept appearance models. The surface finish of parts straight off the machine is not as good as with other processes. The surface of parts remains porous; achieving a smooth finish requires sealing the surface using wax, cyanoacrylate or epoxy infiltrants. Enclosed volumes will trap powder inside unless a small drain hole is included in the CAD model to allow the powder to drain out after part creation.

Fused deposition modelling (FDM)

Background
FDM was developed by Scott Crump in 1988 and commercialized by his company, Stratasys, in 1991. A number of different machines are available. One of the most popular RP systems, FDM is used to produce prototypes, patterns, jigs and end-use parts across a wide range of industries, including automotive, aerospace, industrial, consumer and medical products.

Process
A thin filament of solid thermoplastic polymer is heated above its melting point

Fig. 48
Fused deposition modelling. Above, a Stratasys Dimension FDM machine.

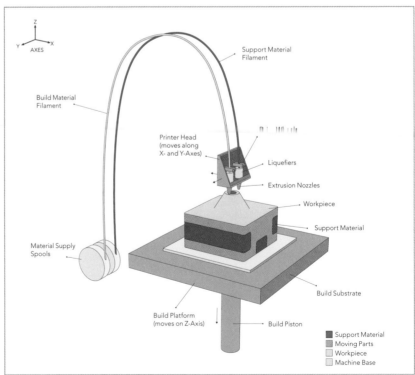

and extruded through a small nozzle, which deposits the semi-liquid melted plastic onto the build platform. The plastic is deposited in the appropriate places according to the cross-sectional shape of a part slice. The build platform then lowers by the layer thickness, and another layer of plastic is deposited, fusing to the previous layer. The process repeats until the part has been built. Support material is built under overhanging sections and is deposited as the part is being built. The support material is then broken off or, if water-soluble support material is used, removed in a water-filled tank. Maximum part size on the largest machine is 600 x 500 x 600mm (23.6 x 19.7 x 23.6in). Minimum wall thickness for parts is 0.5mm (0.02in).

Advantages

FDM is a clean process with no excess liquid or powder materials to deal with, making it suitable for use in offices. FDM can build large, strong, durable parts, and can be used for both concept models and prototypes that require functional testing. Materials used are some of the same production-grade engineering polymers used in traditional plastics manufacturing processes and have good impact strength, relatively high tensile strength and good resistance to scratching and to chemicals. Parts can also be used as patterns for tooling and master patterns for casting. The process works with several polymers, including ABS, ABSi, polycarbonate and polyphenylsulfone. A range of coloured plastics can be used. When water-soluble support structure material is used, the process allows for complex geometries.

Drawbacks

The size of the nozzle used to deposit the polymer limits the resolution of the build and the quality of finish of parts straight off the machine. Layer thickness is 0.13 to 0.33mm (0.005 to 0.013in), depending on the machine used and the specified settings. The process is relatively slow.

Fig. 49
Rapid prototyped tap in white ABS polymer created using fused deposition modelling (FDM).

Case Study
Fuseproject

Product: SAYL Office Chair
Client: Herman Miller
Materials: polyurethane, stainless steel, cast aluminium, glass-reinforced plastics, self-skinning polyurethane foam, nylon
RP processes: stereolithography apparatus (SLA) and fused deposition modelling (FDM)
Dimensions: 870–984 x 622 x 622mm (34.25–38.75 x 24.5 x 24.5in)
Designer: Yves Béhar
Design to production: 3 years
Modelling software: Autodesk Alias Studio
Website: www.fuseproject.com
Awards: IDEA Award (Bronze 2012, Silver 2011), Good Design Award 2011, FX Award (Best Workplace Seating) 2011, Mix Interior Award (Product Design of the Year) 2011, Core77 Design Award (Furniture and Lighting) 2011, D&AD (Notable in Product Design) 2011, Australia International Design Award (Best of Architectural and Furniture Design) 2011, Treehugger Best of Green 2010, International Design Award (Product Design of the Year) 2010

Introduction

The work of Fuseproject, founded in 1999 by industrial designer Yves Béhar, spans brand and market strategy, identity and naming, packaging design, product development and communications design. Béhar's innovative designs have garnered more than 150 awards, his work forms part of the permanent collections of several prominent museums, and in 2009 he was one of two industrial designers invited to speak at the World Economic Forum in Davos, Switzerland.

Approach

Designing a work chair can be an intimidating design challenge, with so many functional and tactile parts needing to work together. The aim was to create a comfortable, beautiful and visually cohesive task chair, yet at a fundamentally lower price than anything the client had previously accomplished. Initial ideas took inspiration from the structural towers and cable suspension system of the Golden Gate Bridge, near Béhar's home in San Francisco, exploring the use of a tower to provide support and cables for back tension and comfort.

Process

Early sketch ideas were explored as mock-up models and prototypes in 3D using such materials as wood and rope to establish the engineering principles of the chair. Further iterations of prototypes enabled refinement to the back of the chair to mirror spine curvature. Over 70 prototypes were produced during the development of the product, in a process of continual designing, building, testing, breaking and starting over. Even small details, such as movement control knobs, were continually revised and refined through multiple prototypes, each successively removing material while refining the functional and visual characteristics.

CAD software was used to create 3D computer models almost from the beginning. Alias Studio was used

weight. Every part was detailed so as to remove as much material as possible and to create shapes that were expressive and tactile. To avoid the assembled-kit appearance of many task chairs, parts were designed to run fluidly into one another: the arms were made to 'grow' out of their height adjustment posts; the frameless back was designed to be visually integrated with the Y-tower, its pattern expressing the tension distribution from the top attachment points while visually following the tower's form.

While 3D modelling and RP formed part of the development process, the majority of it took place in the workshop and on the drawing board, with real prototypes leading to failures and successes, highlighting that even for visually and technically complex products, traditional techniques still play a crucial role.

Result

Many office chairs are large and visually dominant, but SAYL's visual lightness, created by reducing material usage wherever possible, enables it to appear smaller in scale and to become more transparent and discreet within its environment. The design of the back and the material used allow it to both conform to and move with the body, encouraging a full range of movement and providing natural dynamic support without the need for back adjustment control knobs. Produced using 10 per cent recycled materials, SAYL is also 93 per cent recyclable, contains no PVC and uses less material and fewer parts than typically required for a task chair.

almost exclusively because of its flexibility and power in creating both rational, geometric forms and fluid, organic surfaces. Fuseproject also found the program well suited to ideation in 3D, enabling them to generate 3D forms quickly and produce multiple variations of these. Scale rapid prototyped models and full-scale rapid prototyped samples for nearly every detail were produced from CAD models. SLA was primarily used for prototyping every part of the chair; FDM was used for those full-scale, functional parts that required a better material approximation of plastic, such as the adjustment knobs and levers. In addition, many handmade mock-ups were created using paper, urethane foam, fabric and wire.

One hundred different variations of the mesh pattern for the back were prototyped, exploring pattern density, thickness and level of tension. The final design settled on an injection-moulded polyurethane sheet suspended between a Y-shaped tower and a lower arc at the level of the seat. The result of this iterative prototyping was a breakthrough; hard material used to create the frame around most chair backs could be eliminated, allowing greater movement and the first frameless suspension back.

The arm structure and tilt mechanism undercarriage were fused into a single triangulated part, creating a multifunctional part that enabled significant reduction in material use while also reducing the chair's visual

Fig. 50 (opposite above)
SAYL Office Chairs.
Fig. 51 (opposite below)
Drawing the mesh pattern of the chair back.
Fig. 52 (top)
Making an early mock-up of the chair back.
Fig. 53 (above)
Detail of the mesh back.

Case Study
Freedom Of Creation

Products: Dahlia Wall Light, Palm Pendant Light, Macedonia Tray, Trabecula Tray, Punch Bag, V Bag
Material: polyamide
RP process: selective laser sintering (SLS)
Dimensions: Dahlia: 160 x 150mm (6.3 x 5.9in), 320 x 150mm (12.6 x 5.9in), 500 x 170mm (19.7 x 6.7in); Palm: 160 x 110mm (6.3 x 4.3in), 230 x 140mm (9.1 x 5.5in), 320 x 190mm (12.6 x 7.5in), 500 x 290mm (19.7 x 11.4in); Macedonia: 320 x 320 x 40mm (12.5 x 12.5 x 1.2in); Trabecula: 700 x 365 x 32mm (27.7 x 14.4 x 1.2in); Punch Bag: medium 300 x 280mm (11.8 x 11in), large 340 x 300mm (13.4 x 11.8in); V Bag: 510 x 200mm (20 x 7.9in)
Designers: Janne Kyttanen (Dahlia, Palm, Macedonia, Trabecula), Janne Kyttanen, Janne Kyttanen and Jiri Evenhuis (Punch Bag and V Bag)
Website: www.freedomofcreation.com

Introduction
Freedom Of Creation was founded by Janne Kyttanen in Helsinki, Finland, in 2000. The company, which relocated to Amsterdam in 2006, specializes in exploring the use of additive processes to manufacture desirable consumer products, and their work is included in the collections of museums around the world. In 2011 Freedom Of Creation was acquired by 3D Systems, for whom Kyttanen is now creative director.

Approach
Inspiration for Kyttanen's designs comes from 'the mathematics of nature and its astonishing shapes'. Preferring not to sketch but to transfer his ideas directly onto computer, Kyttanen uses a variety of 3D modelling software to experiment and to model his designs but often uses polygon modelling software for the freedom it provides to create organic forms. With each design, he attempts to push the boundaries of form generation.

Process
Due to the complexity of their forms, each design presented challenges for the computer modelling process, although Kyttanen saw these as a fundamental part of the process of creating innovative designs. SLS was chosen for the manufacturing process as it facilitates economic batch production by enabling several products to be built in a machine together and requires no support structure. The SLS process, which took up to a day, resulted in products with the required strength and enabled light to pass through the polyamide material used. The optional metallic appearance on the trays and bags was achieved with electroforming.

Result
The visually complex, symmetrical forms and patterns of light and shadow of the Dahlia Wall Light and Palm Pendant Light reflect similar forms generated in nature, drawing parallels

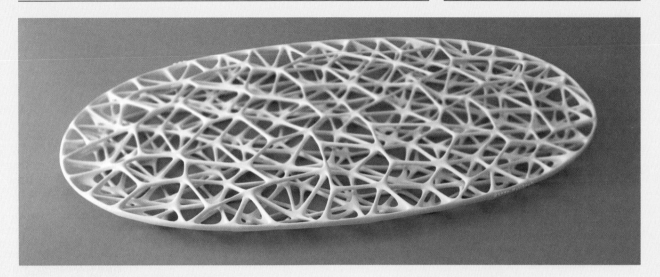

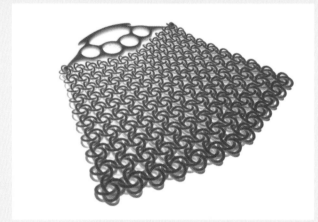

between mathematically driven computer-modelling processes and the unseen mathematical models driving natural growth. The structures of the Macedonia Tray and Trabecula Tray draw on natural materials that are both strong and light, such as bone. Punch Bag and V Bag pioneer the creation of flexible interwoven materials.

Recognizing that product lifespan is decreasing while the number of new mass-produced products is increasing, Freedom Of Creation believe that their approach to product development will change the world; they draw parallels between additive manufacturing and the ways in which MP3s changed the music industry. Their vision is to enable consumers to become more involved in the creation of products, meaning that value for consumers will increase and waste will decrease. Whether or not this vision will become reality, the company's success is evidence of growing consumer demand for additively manufactured products.

Fig. 54 (opposite above)
The Dahlia Wall Light, inspired by the flower, is an arrangement of petals in a compact semi-sphere.
Fig. 55 (opposite below left)
The Palm Pendant Light comprises uncountable delicate petals with light flooding through them.
Fig. 56 (opposite below right)
The Macedonia Tray, inspired by soap bubbles and the structures they create. In Spanish *macedonia* means 'fruit salad', and the tray, filled with fruit, creates a kind of fruit salad with each piece of fruit in its own space.

Clockwise from top:
Fig. 57
Trabecula Tray, inspired by low-density bird bone. The structure is very lightweight, but extremely strong.
Fig. 58
Punch Bag, based on the concept of 3D printed textiles. The pattern uses flexible, Möbius strip-like links. The handle design was inspired by knuckle dusters, hence the bag's name.
Fig. 59
V Bag. The chainmail pattern was inspired by medieval armour.
Fig. 60
Macedonia Tray with a metal coating.

Case Study
Ryuji Nakamura & Associates

Product: Insect Cage
Material: TSR-821 resin
RP process: stereolithography apparatus (SLA)
Dimensions: 121.3 x 121.3 x 105.6mm (4.78 x 4.78 x 4.16in)
Designers: Ryuji Nakamura, Makiko Wakaki, Toru Uranaka
Design to production: 3 months
Modelling software: AutoDesSys Form Z
Website: www.ryujinakamura.com

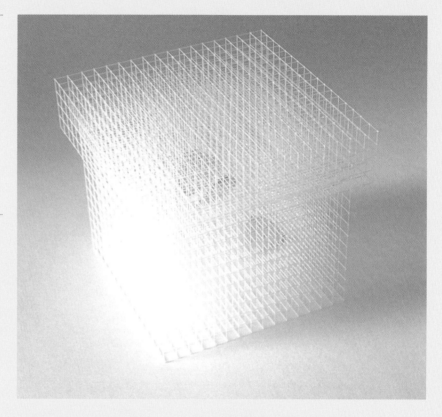

Introduction

Born in 1972 in Japan, Ryuji Nakamura completed an MA in architecture at the National University of Fine Arts and Music, Tokyo, in 1999. From 2000 to 2003 he worked at Jun Aoki & Associates before establishing Ryuji Nakamura & Associates in Tokyo in 2004. His company has exhibited globally and been the recipient of numerous international awards.

Approach

In 2007 curator and director Eizo Okada invited five young architects to each create a unique one-off piece of work, based on the theme 'box', for an exhibition in Tokyo entitled 'DEROLL Commissions Series 1: Box'. Inspired by furniture and lighting designed by young Japanese architects, Okada was keen to commission architects rather than product designers. Ryuji Nakamura & Associates decided to design a box in which to put a butterfly.

Process

Sketching first by hand on paper and then using Form Z CAD software, the designers conceived a box that would have no front or back and would comprise a lattice-like structure with a void in the centre for the butterfly.

Instead of capturing the insect inside an enclosed volume, as with a standard clear acrylic box, the open latticework was designed to enable the viewer not only to see but also to 'feel' the butterfly. Exploring the limits of accuracy, latticework thickness and resulting visual phenomena, four early study models were prototyped using SLA. Each prototype presented an alternative lattice density and a different relationship between the lid and the bottom of the box. The prototype and final design were produced by Japanese prototyping bureau CAD2Solid.

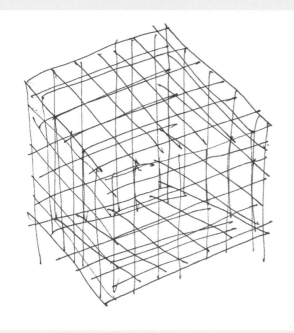

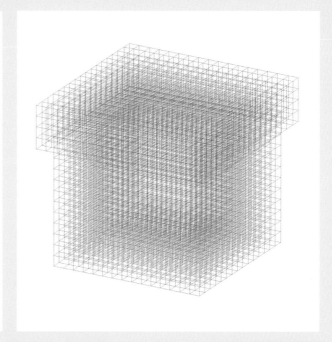

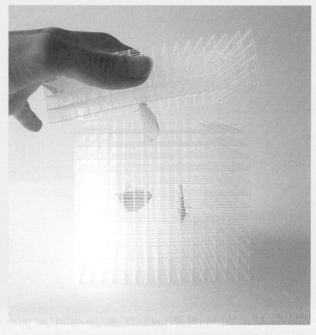

Result

The final design for the Insect Cage consists of fine, 0.3mm (0.012in)-diameter intersecting rods spaced 7mm (0.276in) apart. The box comprises 2902 cells and is 99 per cent air. The lattice-like box not only makes economical use of material, but also results in an immediately engaging visual experience that varies as the viewer moves around it. From some angles the box almost disappears, providing an uninterrupted view of the enclosed butterfly, and from others, the box appears less transparent and

the view of the butterfly within is partially obscured. The delicate design enables closeness and interaction with the enclosed insect, while the structural approach dematerializes the box and questions notions of division between internal and external space.

Fig. 61 (opposite)
When the Insect Cage is viewed from an angle, the butterflies within become partially obscured.
Clockwise from top left:
Fig. 62
Initial sketch of the concept for Insect Cage.
Fig. 63
Wireframe concept drawing.
Fig. 64
The holes within the design mean the structure becomes less apparent when seen from the side, providing a clearer view of the butterflies within.
Fig. 65
Close-up showing how the designers pushed the limits of the SLA process in creating an extremely fine structure.

Case Study
Michaella Janse van Vuuren

Products: Chrysanthemum, Krizant .MGX

Clients: Nomili, Materialise

Material: PA2200 polyamide

RP process: selective laser sintering (SLS)

Dimensions: 250 x 82mm (9.84 x 3.23in)

Designer: Michaella Janse van Vuuren

Design to production: 10 weeks

Modelling software: Materialise Magics, MeshLab, Netfabb, Robert McNeel & Associates Rhinoceros 3D

Website: http://nomili.co.za

Awards: Design Indaba Most Beautiful Object in South Africa 2009

Introduction
After training in performing arts and then electrical engineering, Van Vuuren went on to work in custom implant design using CAD and additive manufacturing at the Central University of Technology in Bloemfontein, South Africa. During this time she recognized the unique potential of 3D printing processes to merge her artistic and technical interests, and in 2008 she founded Nomili to further this pursuit. Her work includes lighting, sculptures, functional objects and jewellery.

Approach
Van Vuuren states, 'my work is about experimentation and evolution, about art and science, and new materials and processes. I look at technology as a creative tool, and have turned to new methods of manufacturing and design that have pushed the boundaries beyond what could ever be achieved by conventional processes.' The Chrysanthemum centrepiece was conceived as a personal project to promote Nomili. To capture the attention, the design had to be intricate and unique.

Process
Several variations of the design were explored using paper sketches, then technical drawings followed. Once a final design had been determined, a basic bowl shape was created in Rhinocerous 3D; this was converted to a wireframe that formed the layout pattern for the leaves. The computer model of the final design was carefully planned to ensure a 'watertight' (see page 126) solid model that could be laser sintered. The leaves were then added and kept thick enough to be printed so as not to disintegrate in the build process.

Once the final diameter of 250mm (9.843in) had been determined, Magics was used to hollow out the inside of the piece to give it a 2mm (0.0787in) wall thickness. The thickness required careful consideration as this determined not only the strength of the product but also how much light would be able to penetrate it. A disc was then cut out from the dome and a recessed structure added to house an LED tea light. To ensure enough light would pass through the centrepiece and create the desired glowing effect,

Fig. 66
Close-up of Krizant, a wall light included in the .MGX by Materialise principal collection and developed from the Chrysanthemum design.
Fig. 67 (opposite above)
Chrysanthemum bowl and LED tea-light holder.
Fig. 68 (opposite below)
CAD model of Chrysanthemum and, on the far right, the adaptation of the CAD model into Krizant.MGX.

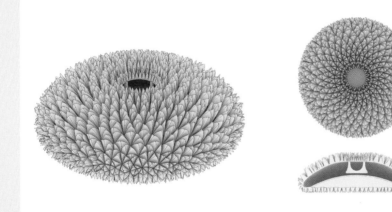

small wedge-shaped areas were then removed between the leaves.

Most of the design development work was carried out in Rhinoceros 3D, but other software was also used to add detail and to check the integrity of the 3D mesh. To avoid the possibility of having to repair the 3D model after it had been created, it was converted into a mesh and checked numerous times using these other software programs. SLS was chosen as the manufacturing process for the light; however, this required sponsorship due to the expense of the process for an object of this size.

Result

Chrysanthemum can be used as a bowl or an LED tea-light holder, depending on which side faces upwards. The SLS process provided the freedom to design intricate textures and details

that would have been near impossible to create by hand, yet the centrepiece still retains the beauty and tactility of a natural object. The polyamide (nylon) material enables light to be diffused to varying degrees through the thick, thin and open sections of the repeating surface pattern, bringing the form of the product to life.

Chrysanthemum captured the attention of Belgian rapid prototyping company Materialise, who requested that the design be converted into a wall sconce to form part of their .MGX by Materialise collection. The adaptation, which took around five days, made it possible to stack the shades like shells within the SLS machine for more economical manufacturing. Krizant.MGX remains part of the Materialise collection.

Case Study
WertelOberfell Platform

Product: Fractal.MGX Table
Client: Materialise
Material: epoxy resin
RP process: stereolithography apparatus (SLA)
Dimensions: 980 x 610 x 420mm (35.58 x 24.02 x 16.54in)
Designers: Matthias Bär, Gernot Oberfell, Jan Wertel
Design to production: 12 months
Website: www.platform-net.com

Introduction

WertelOberfell Platform was founded in 2007 by Jan Wertel and Gernot Oberfell, both of whom studied industrial design. The duo share a strong interest in new technologies and manufacturing processes, and the possibilities of computer-aided design. Their work combines experiments using 3D software with the logic and beauty of organic forms and the appropriate use of materials, production processes and ergonomics, and ranges from furniture and lighting to industrial products.

Approach

The organic fractal growth patterns found in nature were the inspiration for the Fractal.MGX Table. These patterns, which display a property known as 'self-similarity', can be split into parts, each of which is approximately a reduced-size copy of the whole. The designers were inspired by a range of sources displaying such patterns: the interior structure of Stuttgart airport, the subtropical dragon tree, patterns generated by the Sierpinsky fractal plug-in for Rhinoceros 3D, and images of mathematically generated fractal line drawings.

Process

Working directly on computer from the start, polygon-based 3D modelling software was used to experiment with different ideas and methods of

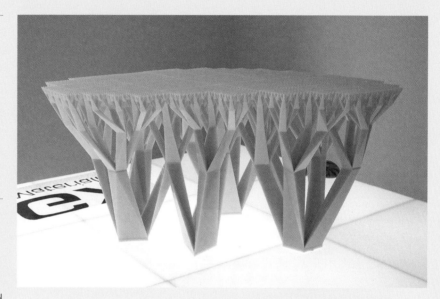

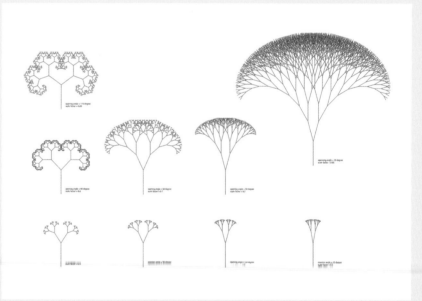

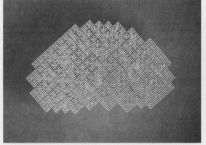

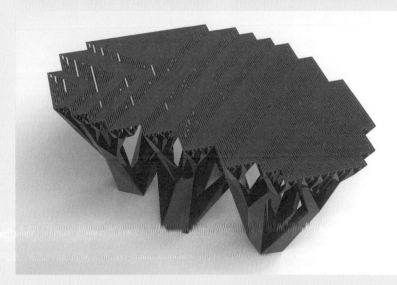

modelled and prototyped to find the right balance between the desired fractal geometry aesthetic and the structural requirements of the product. The final improved prototype, produced in a brown-coloured resin, was modelled and produced hollow, saving material and reducing the printing time, and then filled with polyurethane resin to add strength.

Result

The tree-like stems of the Fractal.MGX table, which was launched in 2009, grow into smaller branches that become progressively dense towards the top to form a quasi-surface. The design is organic in nature yet also has a structured, mathematical quality. It begins in a relatively unorganized manner at the bottom, becoming progressively more organized until ending in a regular grid, representing a progression from an approximate fractal to a fractal with exact self-similarity.

Produced to order by Materialise as a limited edition of 25 pieces, each table is created as a single piece in their Mammoth SLA machine; it is grown upside down, starting with the more complex, intricate top and finishing with the thicker base elements. Both in terms of size and complexity, Fractal.MGX pushes the manufacturing process to its limits and promotes speculation about the possibility of economical furniture production using AM processes.

modelling 3D fractal-like forms. One of the problems with the complex geometries was that in order to evaluate the design, the entire model had to be created, which was time consuming. If a design element required modification, the modelling process often had to be started again. Adjustments to the CAD model were then made according to the technical requirements of the material and the SLA machine. A NURBS-based

modelling program was used for analysis of the model and for better control when converting it into the required STL file format ready for output on the SLA machine.

In 2008 an initial white prototype of Fractal.MGX was shown at the Salone Internazionale del Mobile in Milan. This was then developed through design refinements, and several small-scale test studies of alternative 3D fractal patterns were

Case Study
Erich Ginder

Product: Materialized Vase
Materials: epoxy resin, plaster, porcelain
RP process: stereolithography apparatus (SLA)
Dimensions: 178 x 127 x 229mm (7 x 5 x 9in)
Designer: Erich Ginder
Design to production: 8 weeks
Modelling software: Dassault Systèmes SolidWorks
Website: www.erichginder.com

Introduction
Seattle-based designer Erich Ginder founded his eponymous studio in 2004, shortly after studying at Chicago's School of the Art Institute. Much of his work draws upon imagery from his youth growing up in the rural Pacific Northwest. Through irreverent application of technology and the handmade, he aims to imbue products with emotion and meaning. In addition to designing and manufacturing his own range of products, Ginder has been commissioned to create public artworks, design commercial lighting and provide art direction and interior design for a range of clients.

Approach
The initial concept for this product was to use laser scanning technology in conjunction with CAD software in order to create a series of angular, baroque forms that were free of the designer's hand.

Process
Ginder sourced an old, classically shaped vase from a flea market, which was then digitally scanned at a local bureau. This resulted in a virtual model, consisting of around 70,000 triangular-shaped polygons that accurately recreated the form of the original vase. The model was imported into SolidWorks and, inspired by the process of natural erosion, the number

of polygons was reduced, turning the smooth exterior form into a faceted version of the original vase.

To make the vase, a rapid prototyped master pattern was first created in epoxy resin using SLA. The CAD model and prototype were oversized by 14 per cent to account for the predicted shrinkage during the firing process when producing the vase in porcelain. A manufacturer in Thailand was sourced to slip cast, glaze

and fire the vase, but actual shrinkage after firing was discovered to be 17 per cent, requiring another, larger master pattern to be created. In an exemplary display of traditional making skills, instead of scaling up the CAD model and producing another SLA epoxy pattern, the Thai company handcrafted another master pattern from plaster, identical to the original SLA pattern but exactly 3 per cent larger.

Result

Completed in 2008, the Materialized Vase highlights the potential for the creative use of reverse engineering. This process, in which existing product components are 3D scanned in order to recreate CAD data that either is missing or was non-existent in the original product, provided the opportunity to bring contemporary aesthetics to a traditional product and material. Integrating the unique capabilities of 3D scanning and CAD software within the design process, Ginder was able to realize his vision of creating forms free of the designer's hand and, in so doing, transported the visual language of low-resolution polygonal computer models from the virtual to the real.

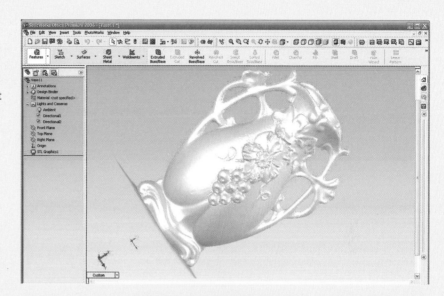

Fig. 75 (opposite)
Materialized Vase, an experiment in the use of 3D scanning and CAD modelling.
Fig. 76 (above)
A laser scan of the original vase imported into Solidworks CAD software prior to reducing its polygon count to create the faceted appearance. This method of creating an object from an existing product is known as reverse engineering.
Fig. 77 (right)
The finished vase, a faceted transformation of the classically shaped vase.

Case Study
Michael Eden

Products: Wedgwoodn't Tureen, Vortex (both 2010), Maelstrom IV, Bloom (both 2011)

Materials: Wedgwoodn't Tureen: plaster and gypsum with a unique non-fired ceramic coating; Vortex, Maelstrom, Bloom: polyamide with mineral soft coating

RP processes: 3D printing (3DP), selective laser sintering (SLS)

Dimensions: Wedgwoodn't Tureen: 400 x 255mm (15.8 x 10in); Vortex: 240 x 220 x 165mm (9.5 x 8.7 x 6.5in); Maelstrom: 400 x 290 x 180mm (15.8 x 11.4 x 7.1in); Bloom: 340 x 285 x 180mm (13.4 x 11.2 x 7.1in)

Designer: Michael Eden

Design to production: Wedgwoodn't Tureen: 100 hours; Vortex and Maelstrom: 60 hours; Bloom: 40 hours

Modelling software: Materialise Magics, Robert McNeel & Associates Rhinoceros 3D, Sensable FreeForm

Website: www.edenceramics.co.uk

Awards: Wedgwoodn't Tureen: RSA Design Directions Award 2008

Introduction

Michael Eden formed his studio in 1987 and, until 2006, designed, made and sold contemporary slip-decorated earthenware. From 2006 to 2008 Eden undertook a Master of Philosophy at the Royal College of Art, London, to explore how his interest in digital technology could be combined with his traditional pottery skills. Since then he has concentrated on the design and creation of additively manufactured artworks, attempting to push CAD software beyond its limits and extend the range of materials available for additive manufacturing.

Approach

For the Wedgwoodn't Tureen, Eden decided to redesign an iconic object from the Industrial Revolution (the Wedgwood tureen) and 'turn it into a child of the new industrial revolution'. In addition to fully exploiting CAD, he also wanted to experiment with using non-fired ceramic materials in additive fabrication processes in a way that would be impossible using conventional industrial ceramic techniques. The form of the Wedgwoodn't Tureen was inspired by bone texture, thus also referencing the natural objects that inspired many of Wedgwood's own designs.

The aim with Vortex and Maelstrom was to emulate digitally the technique of coiled pottery construction, where coils of clay are used to build the walls of vessels. Bloom was intended as a test, to push technology and to seduce the viewer by revealing something unexpected or seemingly impossible.

Process

For the Wedgwoodn't Tureen, Eden developed numerous iterations and played with geometry and proportion using Rhinoceros 3D and FreeForm. The CAD models of the base and lid were then exported as STL files for transformation into the artificial bone

Fig. 78
Wedgwoodn't Tureen (2010), an archetypal ceramic object given a contemporary twist with an imaginative approach to the use of CAD software and 3D printing.

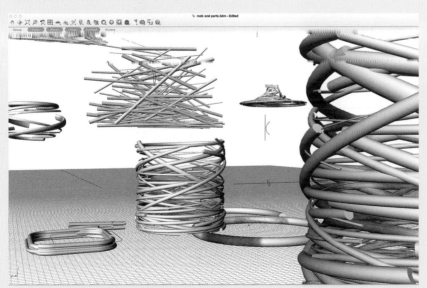

Fig. 79 (top left)
CAD model of Wedgwoodn't Tureen modelled in Rhinoceros 3D modelling software prior to export to Magics software.

Fig. 80 (top right)
CAD model of Wedgwoodn't Tureen after trimming in Magics software to create the artificial bone-like structure.

Fig. 81 (above)
Maelstrom IV (2011), an experimental rethink of traditional coiled pottery construction.

Fig. 82 (left)
Screen grab capturing initial experiments in modelling the Maelstrom and Vortex series using Rhinoceros 3D. Rhinoscript was used to generate rods, which were manipulated to form basic shapes that were tapered, stretched and scaled.

Case Study
Michael Eden

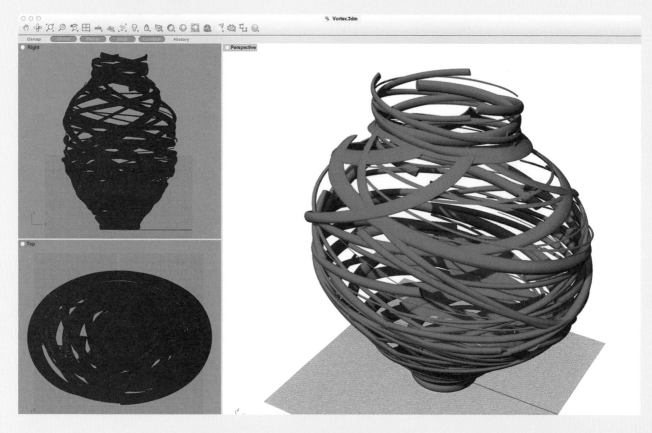

Fig. 83
CAD model of Vortex (2010), created with the aid of Rhinoscript, a programming language used in Rhinoceros 3D modelling software to automate form generation.

structure in Magics. A 2D pattern similar to a cross-sectional slice through bone was created using black and white slip (liquid ceramic), which was then photographed and 'tiled' in Photoshop to enable it to be repeated over a larger area. Finally, it was positioned over the 3D models in Magics and used to trim the STL model files, creating the holes.

The design was then tested on a Z Corp 510 3D printing machine, which revealed the difference between exploring the virtual form on screen and engaging with the real object. The body of the tureen was initially too fragile and parts broke off during the first production test, so the design was amended to strengthen the weak areas and make it strong enough to infiltrate, a process required to further strengthen the plaster material ready for the application of the final surface coating material. The powder material

used for printing was also changed to produce stronger parts.

After infiltration, the piece was cured with a UV lamp, oven dried, then coated in a non-fired ceramic material – a non-toxic, food-safe, acid- and alkali-resistant waterproof material, developed by a French company to allow 3D printed parts produced on Z Corp machines to become fully functional products. Eden formulated the first coating to closely resemble Wedgwood Black Basalt, and subsequently developed a wider range of colours.

For the 'coil construction' of the Vortex and Maelstrom pieces, Eden used Rhinoscript – a programming language used to automate form generation – to produce a series of cylinders of varying length and diameter. He then selected a group of the cylinders and manipulated them to form a vessel, which was stretched

and shaped until the desired form was created.

Bloom was conceived to test 3D modelling and 3D printing technology. Drawing its inspiration from the familiar image of a profusion of flowers, Bloom was designed to seduce the viewer. The main challenge in modelling Bloom on a computer was creating a 'valid' object that could be arrayed, arranged and trimmed. The process of joining components often resulted in an 'invalid' object that could not be 3D printed. Close collaboration with the expert responsible for printing the pieces was required to overcome these issues.

Result

These pieces represent an extraordinary step forward in ceramic design, presenting forms never possible before in this material. By referencing iconic pieces of the past,

the silhouettes gain a familiarity that draws the viewer in, while also emphasizing the uniqueness of their design. In combining his knowledge of ceramics with an experimental approach to the use of CAD and AM processes, Eden has explored the opportunities that these materials, tools and processes present to designers to break free from the constraints of 'design for manufacture' and the limited forms able to be produced using traditional ceramic materials and production processes. In 2010 Wedgwood'n't Tureen was named by *Apollo* magazine as one of the 24 most important international museum acquisitions of the year.

Fig. 84
Bloom (2011), inspired by the culturally familiar image of an arrangement of flowers in a decorative container.

Case Study
Bathsheba Grossman

Product: Klein Bottle Opener
Materials: stainless steel and bronze
RP process: 3D printing (3DP)
Dimensions: 45 x 40 x 79mm
(1.8 x 1.6 x 3.1in)
Designer: Bathsheba Grossman
Design to production: 2 months
Modelling software: Materialise
Magics, MeshLab, Robert McNeel &
Associates Rhinoceros 3D, Autodesk
T-Splines plug-in for Rhino, Surface
Evolver
Website: www.bathsheba.com

Introduction

In 1998, having previously made bronze sculptures using traditional techniques, US designer Bathsheba Grossman began to use CAD and RP techniques in her work. Grossman now creates sculptures, jewellery and mathematical models, and has been influential in popularizing the use of direct-metal printing as an art medium. Several of her lighting designs form part of the .MGX by Materialise collection by Belgian company Materialise. Grossman is also founder of Protoshape, an RP/AM bureau.

Approach

The form of the Klein Bottle Opener originates from Grossman's interest in physical forms that represent mathematical oddities – in this case, an external surface that becomes an internal surface. As the inner and outer surfaces are the same, the inner and outer spaces become one, meaning that from a mathematical viewpoint, no volume is enclosed.

Process

A 3D model of a bottle cap was initially created in Rhinoceros 3D, with a network of curves used to create the surface. This was then converted to a mesh before being exported to Surface Evolver to 'relax' the linear mesh and control the size and aspect ratio of the mesh triangles. Grossman then wrote scripting code within Rhinoceros, which was used to adjust the edges and vertices of the mesh, to add planar (flat) surfaces, and to offset the mesh surface to give it the thickness required to output as a 3D object. The model was then again imported into Surface Evolver to create a more complex mesh using a smoothing algorithm. To generate the triangular holes in the model and give it thickness, Grossman wrote scripting code in Perl. Finally, a shape was designed both to act as the mechanism for prising the cap from the bottle and for the infiltration metal to flow into. However, Grossman was unhappy with the look of this design and decided to start again.

The second model was made in three parts – left and right sides with a strip in between. In addition to improving the look of the design, this approach also enabled the software to make a clear distinction between inner and outer surfaces, and provided a more solid area near the feature designed to prise off the cap.

A hexagonal pattern was drawn in Rhinoceros, then stretched and squashed to vary the size and shape of the hexagons. The pattern was cut into two halves and applied onto the two halves of the model using the Sporph command, then adjusted on the model to fit onto the complex curving surface. The pattern was then used to trim the surface of the model, and the surfaces were converted to meshes and given thickness using the Offset Mesh tool. The model was exported as a mesh to Surface Evolver, the number of triangles was increased and a smoothing operation was used to smooth the edges of the hexagonal holes. The three solid parts were joined together in Magics, and, finally, the feature used to prise off the cap was modelled and added.

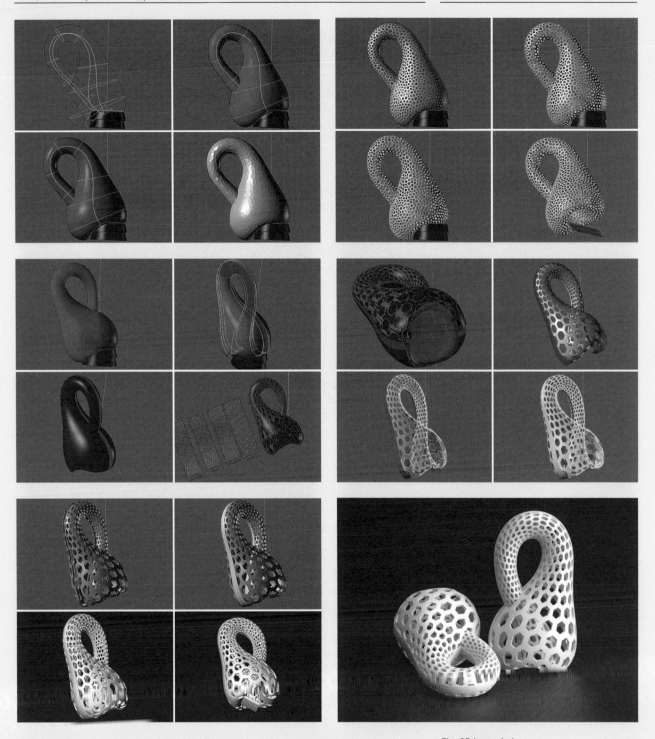

The piece was created using 3DP with a mixture of stainless steel and bronze metal powders. For a smooth surface finish, it was repeatedly tumbled using ceramic beads, steel shot and then either walnut shell or corn cob pieces.

Result

The Klein Bottle Opener demonstrates how taking advantage of the modelling and model editing capabilities of a range of compatible CAD software, and the latest additive manufacturing processes, can create forms otherwise impossible to realize as physical objects. Grossman's mathematical knowledge and highly developed skills in CAD software enable her to generate extremely complex, intricate and often beautiful forms.

Fig. 85 (opposite)
Klein Bottle Opener.
Fig. 86 (top row)
An early model, rejected by the designer.
Fig. 87 (centre row)
A further iteration of the design.
Fig. 88 (bottom row)
CAD render of the final design.

Finishing additive RP models

Parts created using additive RP processes are not always created with the required level of surface finish for the intended application for the part, which may be for an appearance model, a functional prototype, a master for creating a casting mould or an end-use product. This means that RP parts may need to be post-processed or finished manually, which, depending on the RP process used, can involve removing excess build material or support material, cleaning or curing the part, sanding, polishing or painting.

Removing excess build material

In some additive RP processes, such as SLA, SLS and DMLS, parts are created surrounded by material that has not been solidified by the laser. Once the part has been created it must be separated from this unused build material. Any excess liquid resin (SLA) or powder (SLS, DMLS) located in difficult-to-access areas must be removed. In SLS, to ensure consistency of material properties, typically only one-half to two-thirds of the unused build material is reused for subsequent builds.

Removing support material

In some additive RP processes, such as SLA and FDM, as a part is being built, a support structure is created underneath thin, overhanging sections to prevent them from bending or breaking off. The orientation of the part in the machine determines the amount of support structure required and where on the part it will be attached. Orientation is determined by the machine operator, who will aim to minimize the amount of support structure required. The operator will also consider how to best orient the part to avoid a stair-stepped surface appearance. Stair-stepping can occur on surfaces positioned at shallow angles to the horizontal, and on curved surfaces as a result of the way in which parts are built from multiple horizontal layers. Once the part has been created, the support structure material, attached to the underside of overhanging areas of the part, must be broken away. Depending on the RP process used, this is first partly removed by hand and/or jetted off using water, and then either soaked in a 2 per cent sodium hydroxide (NaOH) solution in water, or bead blasted.

Fig. 89
Removing excess build material from an SLS part.

Post curing

Post curing using UV light is required to fully solidify SLA parts. The process is undertaken in a separate machine and the time taken depends on the size of the part. (The time required for post curing is a drawback of the SLA process.)

Creating a smooth surface

Once any support material has been removed from the part, the next step is to create the desired surface smoothness. The amount of work required will depend on the material used, and the thickness of each layer used to create the part, which varies according to the process used and the specified machine settings for the build. Thinner layers create smoother surfaces but increase build time. The quality of surfaces produced using RP processes, which print dots of photo-curable liquid polymer, is also affected by the size of the printed dots, which vary from 0.1 to 0.05mm (0.0039 to 0.002in) in diameter.

Sanding

Dry sanding, using 200, 220 and 320 grit sandpaper, is used to remove roughness, imperfections and any visible stair-stepping. Wet sanding, using 400, 600 and 1000 grit sandpaper, is used to remove any light scratches caused by earlier sanding. Water is used during sanding to clean away waste debris. For removing any larger undesired indentations, or if stair-stepping is particularly prominent, two-part car-body filler paste is applied with a spatula and sanded smooth.

For transparent or semi-transparent and glossy surfaces, on which any scratches would be noticeable, micro-mesh finishing cloths and pads of grades 1500, 1800, 2400, 3200, 3600, 4000, 6000, 8000 and 12000 are used to achieve a perfect surface finish. Either soapy water or vegetable oil is used during this stage to help lubricate the surface of the part. Parts are then carefully polished using a buffing wheel and polishing compound before all traces of the compound are removed with a clean buffing wheel and a polishing cloth.

Creating the desired final surface appearance

A range of surface finishing techniques are used to replicate the finish of manufactured parts on rapid prototyped appearance models.

Dyes

To achieve a coloured transparent surface appearance, transparent prototype parts can be dipped in a warm bath of water with added coloured clothing dye. The darker the desired colour, the more dye is added to the water. Alternatively, for translucent coloured finishes, alcohol-based aniline dyes used for leather or wood can be applied to transparent prototype parts. The dye is added to the part using a brush or by dipping the part in the dye. Dyes are available in a range of colours but can be mixed to achieve new colours. Colours can be lightened by diluting with alcohol before application. Part surfaces must be thoroughly cleaned prior to dyeing, first using water and then, after drying, with a lint-free cloth and isopropyl alcohol.

Sand blasting

To create a frosted appearance on transparent or semi-transparent materials, parts can be masked off and the unmasked areas sand blasted.

Paint

Water-based, solvent-based or hard-wearing two-pack paints can be either brushed or, more usually, sprayed onto a part to add colour and to achieve a variety of different paint finishes, including matt, semi-gloss, gloss, pearlescent, iridescent, metallic and colour shifting. Colours can be matched to requirements and are often specified from a colour reference system, such as RAL or Pantone. Soft-to-touch two-pack paint finishes that mimic the surface feel of rubber, velvet

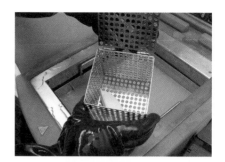
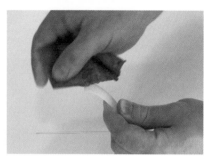

Fig. 90 (top)
FDM prototype being washed in a mild acid bath to dissolve support material.
Fig. 91 (above)
RP part being sanded to give a smooth finish for painting.

Fig. 92 (left)
RP taken from an FDM machine prior to finishing.
Fig. 93 (right)
RP parts after the removal of build material,
sanding and painting.

and leather are also used. To provide better paint adhesion to a part, two or three light coats of primer paint are applied. The primer is lightly wet-sanded between each coat, before applying three or four light top coats of the desired colour. The application of primer also helps to show up any remaining surface imperfections that require further sanding before priming the part again. Final colour coats can also be lightly wet-sanded with 1000 grit between coats to remove any unwanted surface roughness caused by spray paint partially drying before reaching the part. A paint gun is used to apply lacquer paint. Single-colour aerosol spraycan paints can also be used. As with dyeing, part surfaces must be thoroughly cleaned prior to painting, first using water and then, after drying, with a lint-free cloth and isopropyl alcohol.

Varnish and lacquer
Clear varnish or lacquer, available in matt, semi-gloss and gloss finishes, can be brushed or sprayed onto painted parts to seal them and to provide added protection.

Vacuum metallization
This process is used to create a range of different finishes on RP parts, including chrome, gold, bronze, coloured chrome and such matt metallic finishes as satin nickel and matt silver. It involves melting and evaporating metals inside a vacuum chamber, and then condensing them onto the rapid prototyped part. Parts are first cleaned and spray coated with a primer to help adhesion of the metal and to help ensure a reflective finish. Once the metallization of the part has taken place, a clear or tinted top coat of lacquer is applied to help protect the metal finish. Vacuum metallizing is an alternative to the more expensive electroforming process.

Electroforming
The process of electroforming, also known as metal encapsulation and metal coating, coats an RP substrate with metal. To enable the metal to adhere to a non-metal RP substrate, the part is first covered in a thin layer of silver powder applied by brush. The RP substrate is then lowered into a tank of electrolytic solution and given a negative charge. The metal for coating is placed into the same solution and given a positive charge, dissolving metal ions in the solution, which are then deposited on the silver, building the metal coating. Metals used for coating include copper, nickel, silver and gold, each with a variety of finish appearances. The thickness of the coating can be controlled accurately, and ranges from 0.005mm (0.0002in) upwards to any desired thickness, but is typically around 0.15mm (0.0059in). When tolerances are critical, an intended 0.15mm (0.0059in) coating would require the CAD model being undersized by 0.15mm (0.0059in) and any holes on the model increased in diameter by 0.3mm (0.012in).

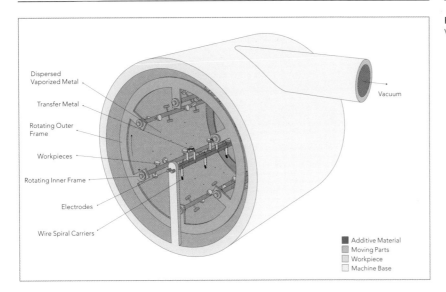

Fig. 94
Vacuum metallization.

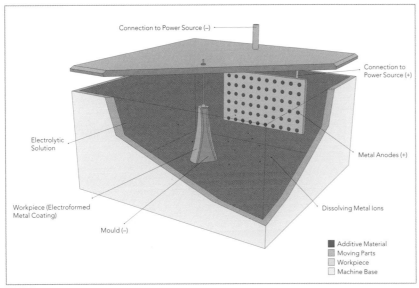

The electroforming process can be used either to fully encapsulate RP parts in metal or to create hollow metal parts. To create a hollow metal part, either the RP part is used as a mould to be removed once coated or, for more complex forms with undercuts, a wax RP part is used and the wax later melted out, leaving the hollow metal part.

Considerations for CAD models destined for RP

In order to build physical parts from CAD models, all software supporting RP systems reads STL files. This file type was originally developed to support SLA, the first commercially available RP process, and has subsequently become the standard file type read by all RP systems in order to generate parts from CAD models. Virtually all CAD programs are able to save or export STL files. Depending on the CAD software used, saving/exporting as an STL file converts either a NURBS or a polygon mesh model into a mesh of triangles that approximately represents the model. The way in which a CAD model has been built affects whether it will be translated successfully into an STL file and outputted correctly on an RP machine. If too little care is taken during the modelling process, errors will be created in the translation to an STL file. This is not normally an issue in parametric CAD modellers but can be in non-parametric CAD software. Although specialist software is available for the task of repairing

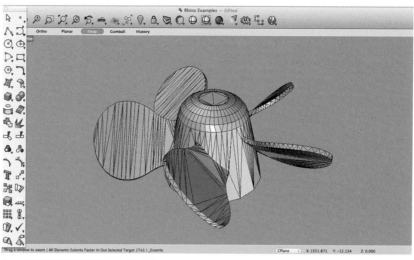

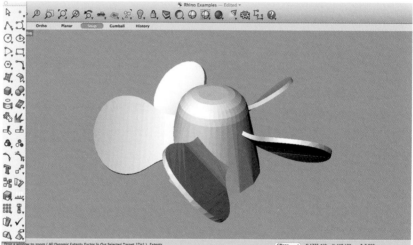

poor-quality STL files, it is better practice to model and save/export correctly in
the first instance. A number of factors require consideration by product designers
during the modelling and saving/exporting processes to ensure an RP part will
appear as designed and modelled in CAD.

Faceting

When saving/exporting an STL file, triangles are created. A simple way to think
about the process of representing curved surfaces with triangles is to think of a
circle that, instead of consisting of a continuous curved line, is made up from a
series of small, connected straight lines. The shorter the straight lines, the greater
their number and the smoother the circle appears. If a sufficient number of
straight lines are used to create the circle, the circle will appear smooth.
Depending on the radius of the circle and the number of straight lines used, using
fewer straight lines may result in a faceted appearance. Now picture a sphere
made up from many triangles joined together along their edges. If an insufficient
number of triangles is used, facets (flat spots on the surfaces of the sphere) will be
created. The greater the number of triangles used, the smoother the appearance
of the sphere. To represent a CAD model with complex and tightly curved
surfaces correctly as an RP part, therefore, a large number of triangles must be
generated to represent those surfaces correctly in the STL file.

　　　　Facets on curved surfaces of an RP part can be avoided by adjusting
settings in the STL save/export options. Different CAD programs utilize a number
of different mesh adjustment settings to achieve this.

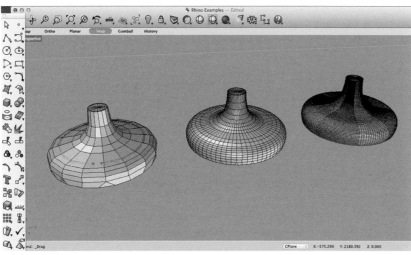

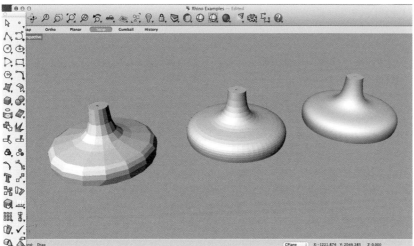

Fig. 97
Three copies of the same CAD model with different polygon counts and surface smoothness.

Number of polygons

One potential solution to a lack of surface triangles causing faceting on curved surfaces is to maximize the polygon number, creating as dense a mesh of triangles as possible. Although this solves the issue of faceting, it can make the file size unnecessarily large, which results in a longer build time. When exporting CAD models as STL files it is possible to determine whether or not you have generated a sufficient density of mesh by opening and viewing the STL file after saving/exporting. Some CAD programs offer particular shading modes or a preview of the tessellation that displays the faceting more visibly, which can help determine whether or not an increased mesh resolution is required. Determining the correct mesh density often involves a trial-and-error approach; to ease this process, NURBS-based CAD programs with integrated mesh tools enable NURBS models to be translated into separate mesh models within the CAD model space.

As a rule of thumb, if the triangles forming the mesh on the curved areas of a CAD model are the same size as the layers creating the RP part – between 0.015 and 0.1mm (0.00059 and 0.0039in), depending on the RP process, particular machine and machine setting used – the result will be as good a surface finish as possible. If the triangles are larger than the layer thickness, faceting on curved surfaces will be visible. If the triangles are smaller than the layer thickness, the STL file size will be unnecessarily large and the part will take longer to be created.

Chord height

Chord height – also known as maximum distance, triangulation tolerance or facet deviation, according to the CAD software used – specifies the maximum distance

Fig. 98
Chord height and corresponding chord length.
Chord height is the maximum distance the
mesh is created from the original NURBS surface.
For curved surfaces, decreasing chord height
increases the mesh density and accuracy.

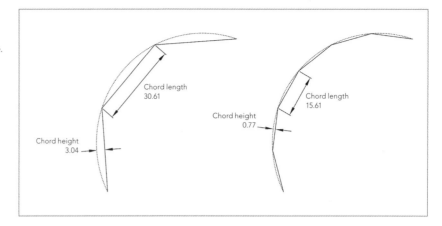

Fig. 99
White arrows indicate surface normals.
Reducing the angle between surface normals
increases the number of triangles used to
represent curved surfaces, resulting in a denser
and more accurate mesh.

the mesh will be created from the original NURBS surface. Settings are usually between 0.1 and 0.001mm (0.0039 and 0.00039in), depending on the size of the object being modelled and the acceptable deviation from the NURBS surface. Smaller objects require smaller chord height settings. Decreasing the chord height increases the number of triangles used to represent curved surfaces and surface edges, resulting in a denser, more accurate mesh but with a larger file size that will take longer to prototype.

Angle
Angle refers to the angle between the surface normals of the mesh triangles. Surface normals can be thought of as invisible lines perpendicular to the surfaces of the triangles. Using lower values for angle reduces the angle between the normals of adjacent triangles, therefore increasing the number of triangles used to represent curved surfaces.

Edge length
Edge length refers to the length of the edges of the triangular facets that make up the mesh. Decreasing the maximum edge length setting for mesh triangles will correspondingly increase the number of triangles used to represent a surface on a CAD model. This setting is applied uniformly to every surface on the model and thus flat surfaces will have an equally high mesh density as curved surfaces. This can result in unnecessarily dense meshes on flat surfaces. Increasing the minimum edge length setting prevents triangles from becoming too small.

Initial grid quads
When creating a mesh from a NURBS model, CAD programs divide the surfaces of the model into a series of quadrangles (four-sided polygons), which are later subdivided into triangles. Setting the initial grid quads to a predetermined minimum value ensures that small complex surfaces on the model will be meshed using a greater number of polygons than this minimum number. This ensures that detail on those surfaces of the model is retained.

Aspect ratio
Aspect ratio controls the proportions of the initial quadrangles and, subsequently, the triangles that form the mesh. Higher values for aspect ratio result in long, thin triangles, while smaller values result in more equilateral polygons and a denser mesh. The effects of adjusting aspect ratio are most noticeable on flat surfaces and surfaces that curve in only one direction.

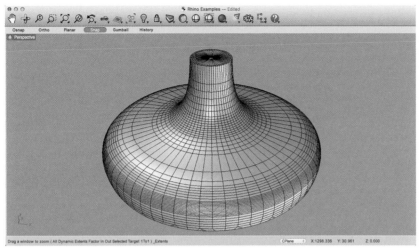

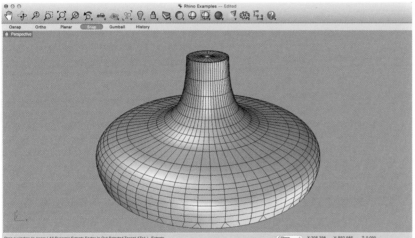

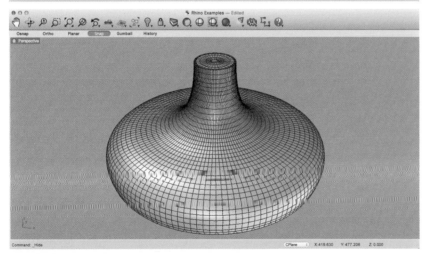

Fig. 100
Adjusting maximum angle, maximum distance and maximum edge length settings affects the polygon count and distribution on the surface of a CAD model.

Surface overlaps

If two adjacent surfaces on a CAD model are intended to meet each other but instead overlap due to modelling error, this will cause the formation of open edges, also known as indeterminate or 'naked' edges, which are not joined to other surface edges. These surface overlaps may be very small and not immediately noticeable during the modelling process. Open edges cause errors in the translation to an STL file and subsequent build errors in the RP process. Surface edges can be analysed in some CAD programs to check for any open edges.

Fig. 101
Examples of surface overlap and gaps between surfaces of a CAD model that would cause problems when saving or exporting the model as an STL file.

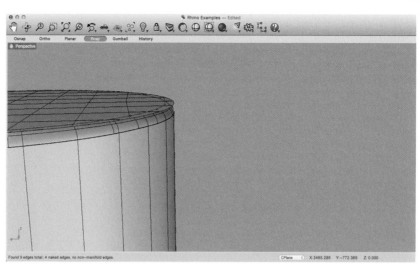

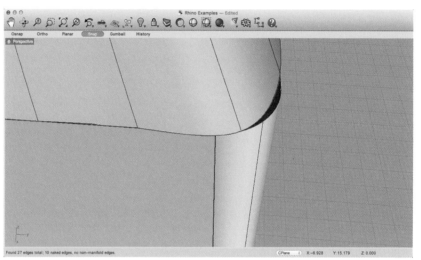

Gaps

If two adjacent surfaces on a CAD model are intended to meet and be joined to each other but a gap remains between them, the CAD model is not 'watertight' – it does not completely enclose a volume and is therefore not a solid model. When converted to an STL mesh, the resulting mesh will be an open mesh, and RP machines cannot create parts from open meshes. These gaps can be very small and therefore difficult to spot during the modelling process. To remedy this problem, any discovered gaps need to be closed either by creating a surface to fill the hole or by recreating the original surfaces, ensuring the surface edges meet as intended. One method used in some CAD programs to check for gaps is to analyse the volume of the model; if this process fails, the model is not completely enclosing a volume and a gap exists. Another method is to analyse the edges of the model for any open or 'naked' edges. NURBS-based CAD programs with integrated mesh tools are able to convert NURBS models to mesh models and any gaps (holes) in the mesh can then be filled using mesh repair tools before saving or exporting as an STL file.

Surface normals

Surface normals always point outwards from the surfaces of a solid model. If the surface normals on a CAD model and resulting STL mesh face inwards instead, this means the model is not a solid. Models that are not solid cannot be rapid prototyped. Some CAD programs enable the direction of surface normals on NURBS models and STL meshes to be checked.

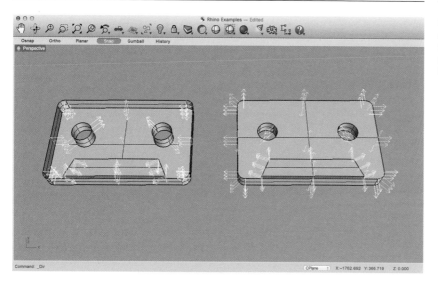

Fig. 102
An open polysurface (left) with surface normals pointing inwards, and a closed polysurface or solid (right) with surface normals pointing outwards.

Invalid models

In some CAD programs, invalid models can be created when, for example, a surface is trimmed using a curve that has one or more microscopically small segments in it. The segments, if smaller than the modelling tolerance (typically 0.01mm/0.00039in), will still enable the surface to be trimmed but will result in a surface that later causes errors when converted to an STL file. Another reason for an invalid model is microscopically small undesired surfaces or solids, which can sometimes be formed during such editing operations as splitting and joining surfaces, combining or subtracting solids using Boolean operations, and adding radii onto the edges of surfaces and solids using filleting. These very small objects can remain invisible to the eye but are part of the model and can cause the subsequent conversion to an STL mesh to fail; they can also result in a 'bad' mesh. Some CAD programs are able to check for invalid models and include tools for helping to repair any invalid surfaces. In some instances, invalid surfaces cannot be repaired using these tools and will require remodelling.

Model position

As a general rule, in CAD programs that enable models to be positioned in relation to the X,Y,Z modelling coordinate system, a CAD model ready for saving/exporting as an STL file should be positioned in the positive quadrant of the coordinate system. This helps to ensure that the STL file is correctly understood by the RP machine control software.

STL file format

CAD models can be saved/exported as two types of STL file, binary and ASCII. While both work with RP machines, the ASCII format creates larger file sizes, which are less efficient and slower to process, so it is better to use the binary format.

File size

To avoid slowing down the build of an RP part unnecessarily, the STL file size should not be too large. CAD models with simple geometry and low levels of detail will require a smaller number of triangles in the STL mesh in order to be represented accurately when built as an RP part. These types of model should result in STL files below 5MB. Complicated CAD models, with complex surface forms and intricate details, require more triangles, which will result in larger STL files. With more complex models, STL file size should be kept as low as possible while retaining a sufficient number of triangles to build an accurate representation of the CAD model as an RP part – where possible, below 50MB. The number of triangles can be adjusted using the methods described in the earlier section on faceting (see page 122).

RESEARCH AND THE FUTURE OF COMPUTER-AIDED DESIGN AND RAPID PROTOTYPING

The future can be hard to predict. However, global trends will certainly continue to influence the way in which computer-aided design, rapid prototyping and additive manufacturing technologies are developed and adopted. Changes in the environment, society and economics will all affect where, how and to what extent these technologies are used in the future.

This chapter explores some of the trends likely to affect how these technologies will impact product design and manufacturing. Several case studies highlight recent developments by companies and individuals pioneering the development and use of these technologies, providing a snapshot of how they are being used now and a glimpse of where they might be leading us.

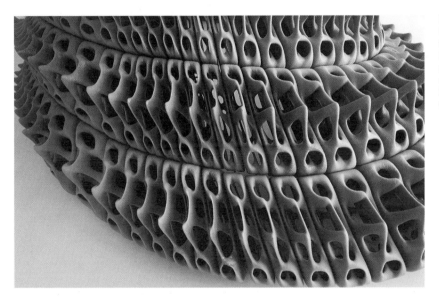

Fig. 1
Pantheon, by Emerging Objects, is a homage to one of the oldest extant concrete structures. It comprises 196 unique 3D printed cement polymer components. Each component is held in compression to create a structural network of individual masonry polymer blocks, each with a compressive strength of 1800psi.

Economics

Development and production costs are a major factor in determining both how and where products are manufactured. In order to achieve the economies of scale necessary to sell products at a reasonable price, companies currently need to make an upfront investment in machine tooling. This investment is a financial risk because it must be recuperated through the production and sale of thousands of identical products. Tooling also adds several months to the time it takes to bring a new product to market, and in increasingly competitive global markets, reducing this time equates to a competitive business advantage. CAD and RP have already significantly reduced development costs and time to market by ensuring greater accuracy, improved communication and faster product development. AM requires no tooling, vastly reducing the upfront cost and risk currently associated with new products, and dramatically reducing time to market.

As AM processes require little labour input, labour costs do not determine production costs as they do with many traditional manufacturing processes. The use of AM to produce ready-assembled products, without the need to join and assemble separate components by hand (or machine) after their manufacture, further reduces labour costs. This represents a paradigm shift in manufacturing economics, hailed by Jeremy Rifkin, author of *The Third Industrial Revolution: How Lateral Power is Transforming Energy, the Economy and the World*, as a fundamental part of a new industrial revolution. Production costs of AM become similar wherever you are in the world, dictated more by local taxation than by labour costs, and enable the manufacturing sector in developed economies to compete on more equal terms with that of developing economies. Barriers to trade become more important, and ease of access to large markets of consumers becomes the main issue for businesses.

Fig. 2
Barbaric Cut, a collection of conceptual kitchen knives designed in 2007 by Chicago-based, Turkish-born product designer Defne Koz.

Fig. 3
Additively manufactured from cement polymer, Seat Slug by Emerging Objects is a biomorphic interpretation of a bench. It is inspired by *Flabellina goddardi* – the newest species of sea slug, discovered in California – and by the infinite tessellations of Japanese *karakusa* patterns. The Seat Slug blurs the lines between biology, technology and furniture. It is constructed of 230 unique rapid manufactured pieces and requires assembly.

Fig. 4
Acetabular cup and finger surgical implants designed by Within Technologies using Within Medical Software and manufactured in titanium alloy using an EOS M280 machine.

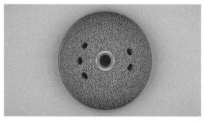

There are several likely implications of the increased take-up of AM processes by the manufacturing sector. As production costs become less dependent on location, in order to reduce the environmental and financial costs associated with transportation and import of goods, to make supply chains more efficient, and to appeal to ethically aware consumers, large businesses will choose to establish manufacturing facilities for their products in countries close to the markets for those products. To minimize logistic costs, manufacture will also be decentralized, located in cities close to consumers, similar to retailing businesses today. Smaller local manufacturing businesses will compete alongside the larger manufacturers.

Traditionally, manufacturers produce in large volumes and retailers hold large quantities of stock. In the future, production and retail in many sectors will combine. Manufacturing facilities will replace retailers' stock rooms, and it will be possible to manufacture many products immediately on demand for either local delivery or collection in store. Some retail stores will disappear altogether, replaced by online retailers able to supply products directly to people's homes from a nearby additive manufacturer. In this scenario, design will also become decentralized, distributing the possibilities, benefits and production more evenly than traditional mass production. Designs that meet the specific needs and desires of local markets will be in demand, and thus an understanding of these local markets becomes more important for product designers.

AM processes are already cost effective for production quantities ranging from one to several thousand, with small, lightweight parts currently the most cost effective. Once technological developments have enabled AM machines to become faster at producing large volumes, thus enabling more cost-effective production, and once the costs of the machines and materials have fallen due to improved economies of scale, the lower upfront costs and low unit costs associated with AM will be highly appealing to businesses developing new products. The lower labour costs associated with AM will further add to this

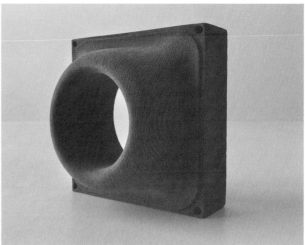

attractive proposition. These reductions in initial capital outlay and financial risk will result in a much greater number of start-up companies developing new products. As more countries become wealthier and their populations become consumers, new markets will develop, resulting in new opportunities for the businesses poised to offer relevant products. Increasingly wealthy markets will also drive demand for high-end customized products.

Materials

Two of the barriers to greater uptake of additive manufacturing are the expense of the materials used and their relatively poor post-production properties, which are not yet able to compete with those of the materials used in such traditional manufacturing processes as injection moulding. For example, polymers used for AM are currently approximately 20 to 100 times more expensive than those used in traditional manufacturing. Wider use of AM machines and further research and development are expected to reduce material costs and enable AM machines to produce parts with material properties that are equal to or better than those created using traditional methods of fabrication. This is already the case for AM processes that use metals, such as direct metal laser sintering (DMLS) and electron beam melting (EBM). Composite materials will continue to be developed for use in multi-material AM machines to enable the manufacture of products with entirely new properties not possible with traditional manufacturing processes.

Polymers

As the scale of production using AM processes increases, oil-derived polymers used for AM processes will need to meet increasingly stringent environmental requirements for recyclability. For companies that utilize AM systems to combine different polymer materials and to combine polymers with ceramics or metals to create composite, functionally graded materials (FGMs), these tougher environmental requirements may be problematic. New methods will be needed to separate these materials back into their constituent base materials to recycle and reuse them within AM or other manufacturing processes.

While the number of materials used in RP and AM has increased dramatically in the last ten years, many materials currently used in AM processes, such as oil-derived polymers (plastics), won't be around forever. It is difficult to predict when oil will run out or, more importantly, just when we will reach 'peak oil', our maximum rate of oil extraction. Some organizations claim we have already reached it; more optimistic estimations predict peak oil to occur soon after 2020. With world demand for oil predicted to grow by 15 per cent by 2030, demand is very soon likely to exceed ability to extract it. The resulting increases in oil price will eventually make it uneconomical to convert oil to polymers for use in

Fig. 5 (left)
Additively manufactured from concrete, Planter Bricks by Emerging Objects are custom-designed masonry units that can hold vegetation. Including plants in a wall can help mediate the temperature of the microclimate surrounding the building, buffer sound and filter the air.

Fig. 6 (right)
Wood Block, designed by Anthony Giannini, is an example of 3D printed wood as a possible building material that can be mass-customized. Wood Block can be used as a curtain wall or as a customized masonry unit; the additive layer manufacturing creates a grain similar to that of natural wood. The 'wood' material is composed of recycled agricultural waste.

Fig. 7
Wood Dish, Emerging Objects. 3D printed
in wood.

Fig. 8
Xylem Reticulate and Peltate Pendants made in
stainless steel, Nervous Systems.

prototyping and in end-use consumer products. AM systems will therefore need
to adopt the use of recycled plastics and plant-based biopolymers.

Metals

Already used in AM processes to produce high-value end-use products in the
aerospace, motorsport, dental and medical sectors, metals have a promising
future in AM. The amount of raw material required and the amount of energy
used to create metal in AM are significantly less than for traditional metal
manufacturing processes. Most metals are currently in plentiful supply, but the
average per-person rate of metal usage is on the rise. As a result of an increasing
population, growing economic development and the rise in the price of polymers
caused by peak oil, metals will be more and more in demand in the future. Some
metals, such as platinum, are already considered scarce and likely to run out this
century, while the possibility of mining asteroids for precious metals is already
being seriously explored. With rising material costs, AM machines will need to be
ever more efficient with their use of metal, and be developed to utilize a greater
proportion of recycled metal.

Advanced materials

We already have machines able to print composite polymer materials, ceramics
and metal alloys. While this creates some AM opportunities, applications are still
limited. The next phase is the development of machines that can print a wider
variety of materials. Current research is focused on this area and will lead to AM
machines being able to print all manner of consumer products, including those
with integral batteries, screens, motors and other electrical components.

Living materials

Researchers in commercial and university science labs are exploring how living
material, such as skin, can be grown from cells; already, entire organs, such as
kidneys and bladders, have been grown. In the future, cells will be taken from
humans and used to additively manufacture replacement body organs and parts.
Similarly, successful experiments to grow edible meat by Columbia-based start-up
Modern Meadow have given rise to the possibility that animal tissues could be
grown into foods in AM food factories to complement traditional agriculture.

The environment

The global population is becoming increasingly aware of the effects of man's
activities on the planet. In turn, this awareness places pressure on governments

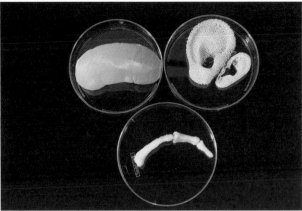

to regulate industry to change the way in which products are manufactured. Reducing the carbon footprint of products is now a major focus of many manufacturers, and this trend is likely to continue to affect how products are manufactured, transported and consumed and what happens to products when they cease to function or are no longer required.

CNC machining of metals to convert blocks of raw material into product components is highly wasteful. Such AM processes as DMLS and EBM can reduce such material wastage by as much as 95 per cent. AM enables designers to further reduce material usage by hollowing out parts, replacing solid material with lightweight yet strong honeycomb lattices. However, when it comes to material wastage it is not all good news; in the SLS process, for example, in order to ensure that the material properties of fabricated parts are reasonably consistent, currently only around two-thirds of unused raw material left in the part build chamber can be reused. With greater requirement for more consistent material properties of products created using AM production processes, the proportion of material reuse is likely to be further reduced. Processes that enable a high proportion of waste material to be reused, or that only consume material required to build the product, provide the greatest potential to reduce carbon footprint.

AM removes the need to mass manufacture products in a location where labour costs are low and then ship them around the planet to consumers. The need to reduce carbon footprint will lead to a greater proportion of manufacturing taking place in widespread locations close to consumer markets for products, thus reducing transportation and energy costs. AM processes also enable products to be made to order; this will mean less surplus stock, reduced costs and less impact on the environment from the disposal of this surplus.

Fig. 9
3D printed kidney and tissue scaffolds created by the Biomaterials Group at the Wake Forest Institute for Regenerative Medicine, Wake Forest Baptist Hospital, Winston Salem, North Carolina, USA.

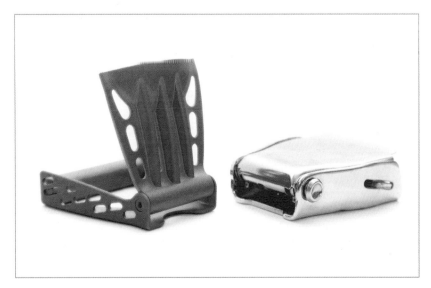

Fig. 10
On the left, a weight-saving titanium airline seat belt buckle by Crucible Design. On the right is a standard buckle.

Fig. 11
Heat exchanger, Within Technologies.

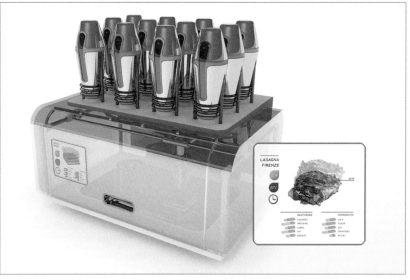

Fig. 12 (left)
Digital Chocolatier, Marcelo Coelho.
Fig. 13 (right)
Digital Fabricator, Marcelo Coelho.

As the world's population continues to grow, there will be increased demand for food but meeting this demand with current methods of food production is already known to be unsustainable. AM technologies offer potential solutions. For example, such foods as beef could be additively manufactured using living cells taken from cattle (see page 132) and produced on a mass scale in automated food factories, reducing deforestation to create farmland, crop growing to feed cattle and methane production from cattle, a significant environmental concern. Converting a wide range of sustainable food crops, small animals and insects into powders that can be stored for long periods and manufactured into any desired shape of food on demand using 3D food printers is another possible solution. This gives rise to the possibility of automated food production in our homes, creating novel eating experiences, with the potential to decrease our dependency on a limited range of unsustainable foods. Just how the media and consumers would react to such options is unknown, but it is likely that any method that offers lower-cost food to consumers without adversely affecting human health will be taken up and promoted by food manufacturers.

Consumers

With AM, making every product different from the next is no more expensive than making every product the same. This fundamental shift in production methods raises the possibility of product designers and manufacturers meeting consumers' specific, individual requirements through the production of entirely personalized consumer products – a process already seen in the production of millions of personalized hearing aids, all of which are now produced on AM machines (see page 68).

An increasing number of consumers use the internet to review and to purchase consumer goods. In response to a growing demand for the option of specifying particular features on products online, manufacturers will continue to explore ways to involve consumers in the process of customization prior to purchase. For product designers, this will mean developing an increasing number of variations of every product they design, creating greater consumer choice.

Further development of interactive interfaces will enable consumers to manipulate 3D computer models of products on screen in real time, adjusting a series of parameters to change the size, shape, materials, patterns and colours of products to their individual preferences. The development of software will enable consumers not only to customize products but also to engage in the design of consumer products themselves to a much greater extent. This intuitive 3D software, quite unlike the CAD software of today, will enable people to create all

Fig. 14
N12 Bikini, Continuum Fashion.

Fig. 15
STRVCT shoe, Continuum Fashion.

manner of products, taking product design out of the realm of the designer and into the hands of the consumer. This will lead to a continued rise in the use of CAD and AM in the hobby sector – already an area of large growth and an important driving force in the development of low-end AM machines. The software will inform those consumers if the features or materials specified for a particular design are too complex for their home-based AM machine, directing them instead to their local 3D printing bureau.

Technology

In the past five years, thousands of patents have been granted to companies and individuals developing CAD and AM technologies. As these technologies become more widely used, the volume of patent applications is likely to increase rapidly.

AM machines will continue to increase in output quality and fall in price. High-end machines will become faster, more accurate, use less energy and be able to work with a wider range of materials. Lower-end machines will develop sufficiently to be able to produce highly accurate prototypes and end-use parts that require no post-process finishing. The largest machines will become significantly larger, able to manufacture the largest of products. Portable machines will be developed to enable manufacture on the move and in remote

Fig. 16
Dragonfly.MGX, WertelOberfell for Materialise.

locations, with potential applications in the military and in disaster relief. With automated packaging and logistics incorporated closely with AM, the production line will become shorter and the supply chain will become more efficient.

Design companies are already purchasing RP machines to prototype products in-house rather than using specialist bureaus, a trend that will continue as the cost and performance of AM machines improve. As a result, some RP bureaus are turning their attention to AM, currently using it for the production of low-volume, high-value engineering and medical parts, and tool inserts with improved internal cooling channels for use in injection moulding and die casting. In the future, as AM replaces many traditional manufacturing processes, RP bureaus will need to further shift their focus from the production of tool inserts to the manufacture of products using highly capable AM machines, or even to the manufacture of AM machines themselves. An example of one such forward-thinking bureau is Materialise, a rapid prototyping service bureau based in Belgium. Since the early 2000s Materialise have worked with a number of leading designers to develop a collection of AM products under the name '.MGX' (see pages 106 and 108). Materialise have also developed their own large-scale RP machines to better service the needs of the automotive industry.

A larger number of companies will offer cloud-based services, including a wide range of ready-to-print products and the conversion of consumers' uploaded sketches into three-dimensional products in a range of materials. Easier-to-learn and easier-to-use 3D modelling software will enable product designers to realize their creative visions in 3D more quickly and intuitively. Developments in software will also make it easier for designers to create highly complex geometries and to optimize product strength and material usage. Modelling software that utilizes eye, gesture and voice control will be further developed and commercialized. CAD software will gain intelligence, using inputted parameters to suggest alternative forms of products to designers in keeping with user requirements or the requirements of the brand for which they are designing. These developments mean that, before long, it might be possible to work in CAD software at the speed and with the fluency of process of sketching ideas on paper.

Design

Designing for manufacture

Designing for traditional tool-based manufacturing processes, such as injection moulding and die casting, currently requires designers to follow a process of design for manufacturability (DFM), whereby they must take into consideration the limitations of the manufacturing process for which they are designing. These limitations mean that the designer is required to design the shape of components

Fig. 17
Interactive interface enabling non-CAD users to engage in the design process, Nervous Systems.

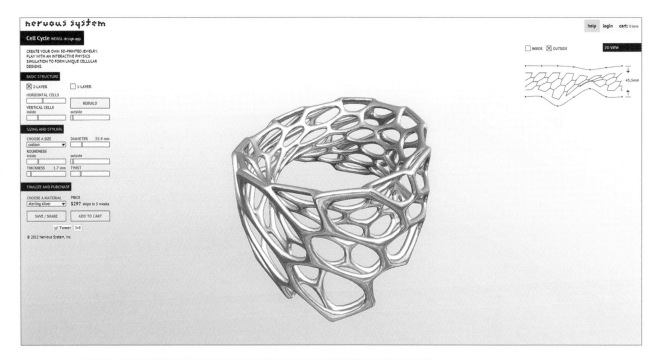

Fig. 18
Additively manufactured bracelets, Nervous Systems.

in such a way that they are easy and low cost to manufacture. It is necessary to specify draft angles and avoid undercuts to ensure that the component can be separated from the tool once it has been moulded or cast. It also means, where possible, reducing the complexity of the part and therefore, by association, both the complexity and cost of the machine tool required to create it.

AM revolutionizes this process, removing these constraints entirely. Parts can be as complex as the designer requires or desires them to be, with no impact on the price of the product. Minimum wall thickness, required part strength and material usage become the main limitations upon design. Functionally graded materials (FGMs) will enable the design and manufacture of products with new and improved performance characteristics, transforming such sectors as sporting goods. These developments will enable product designers to design objects that are far less subservient to the processes by which they are manufactured, and will challenge preconceived notions of product design.

The internet

As mentioned above, the rise of the internet has begun to democratize design, enabling consumers to get in on the act. Products that can be customized online will be in demand from consumers and therefore in demand from product designers by manufacturers. Mass customization, and even mass personalization, where every product produced is unique to the end user, will become the norm. Designers will not only design products but also use computer programs to automatically generate multiple variations of each product. While consumers will be able to manipulate products using online interfaces, the parameters for manipulation for many products will be controlled by product designers, to ensure that the designs can be manufactured, to protect the brand identity of businesses that deem this important and to prevent consumers from creating products that would not perform their intended function sufficiently well. However, enabling consumers to create thousands of different variations of a design in this way also means that the current form of design protection will become meaningless. Focus will need to shift from protecting the design to protecting the software program and interface used to control the on-screen manipulations of a product.

Demand for design

The rise of such crowdfunding websites as Indiegogo, Kickstarter, RocketHub and Quirky has enabled small businesses and individuals to fund the production of new products, enabling demand to be created and sufficient finance to be raised

Fig. 19
Research for an additively manufactured latrine utilizing recycled waste plastics for poor regions in South America, by Washington Open Object Fabricators. Left, the plastic (created by shredding milk bottles) ready for converting into plastic filament used by a 3D printer. Right, the plastic filament.

before production begins. The cloud-based, made-to-order production model made possible by AM and the internet will further reduce risk and increase the number of new products being designed and sold. Online reviews of products by consumers will become increasingly important. Only products that meet genuine needs, perform well and have sufficient appeal will be produced. To differentiate themselves and compete in this increasingly competitive global market, businesses will require creative product designers who are able to make such products.

These designers will be in demand by a growing number of businesses, but their products will be easy for others to copy. With consumers able to use interfaces to manipulate designs, protecting intellectual property is likely to become less important and the competitive advantage created by offering new, original products to the market will become short lived. Offering new products on a regular basis and developing and protecting more sophisticated software to enable consumers to manipulate products will be the only ways by which to stay competitive. This will further increase demand for original, creative, useful and desirable product design. Commerce will not be the only sector in which demand for good design will be strong. Increasing opportunities will exist for product designers to work with socially focused organizations and the millions of not-for-profit non-governmental organizations (NGOs) already in existence to explore how AM technologies could be used to improve the health and lives of people.

Fig. 20
Design by Roy Ombatti for a low-cost additively manufactured shoe sole to help sufferers of jigger fly foot infestation in Africa.

Case Study
RepRap

Product: RepRap self-replicating manufacturing machines
Materials: PLA or ABS, steel
RP process: fused deposition modelling (FDM)
Designer: Adrian Bowyer
Website: http://reprap.org
Awards: Times Higher Education Awards (Research Project of the Year) 2012

Introduction

Born in London in 1952, Adrian Bowyer studied mechanical engineering and completed a PhD in tribology at Imperial College, London. In 2005, while a senior lecturer in mechanical engineering at the University of Bath, Bowyer conceived the global RepRap project, the first general-purpose self-replicating manufacturing machine. He is currently director of RepRap Professional Ltd, which makes and sells kits for RepRap machines worldwide.

Approach

The concept was to create a 3D printer that could print out another 3D printer, and thus become a self-replicating machine. The intention was also to create a 3D printer that could be distributed at low cost to communities around the world, enabling them to create a wide range of complex products, removing the need to purchase those products from retailers.

Process

Bowyer decided to make RepRap an open-source, community project, one that would provide information about how to make the RepRap machine for free and encourage people to create improved versions of his initial design. Each design produced by the project is released under a free software licence, called the GNU General Public Licence.

The instructions for building a machine and the digital models of its parts are freely available. The electronics are based on the open-source Arduino platform. The machines Bowyer initially created utilized the fused deposition modelling (FDM) fabrication process (see page 98). The

Fig. 21
Darwin, the first RepRap machine.

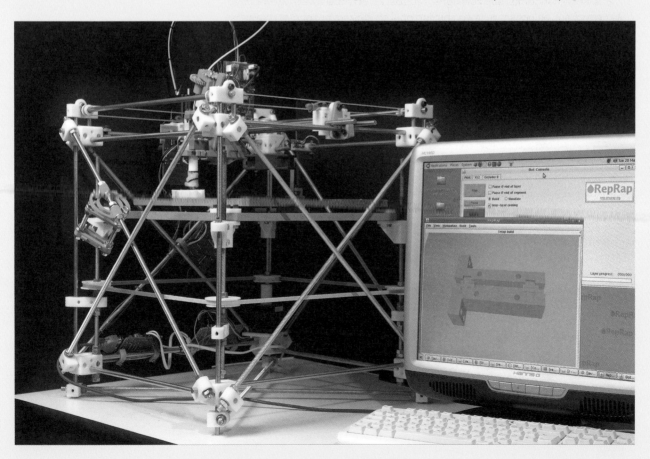

Fig. 22
The second-generation machine, Mendel.

initial RepRap machine, produced in 2007 and named Darwin, was in 2009 replaced by the improved Mendel, then the Prusa Mendel and then in 2010 by Huxley, the third-generation RepRap 3D printer. The design continues to evolve, with the goal of improving its ability to print more of the components from which it is made.

The RepRap Mendel machine is built from a kit of parts that includes several printed components and multiple bought components. Parts are assembled using a spanner to create a frame onto which other parts and subassemblies are added. A guide template provided with the kit, and the use of a set square and ruler, ensure that parts are joined with the correct measurements, and at the correct angles, before further components are added. For those brave enough to take on the challenge, detailed assembly instructions are provided on the RepRap webpage.

Fig. 23
Child's sandals produced on a RepRap machine.

companies. Current RepRap research is focusing on refining the process of printing circuit boards and the use of multiple materials printed via multiple print heads.

The RepRap project has not yet developed a machine able to print out all of its own parts, or an autonomous machine able to operate without human input. However, it is possible to imagine how further developments with the RepRap, alongside developments in artificial intelligence and robotics, will lead humanity incrementally towards the reality of autonomous 3D printing machines.

Result

RepRap was the first of the low-cost 3D printers, and the RepRap project started the open-source 3D printer revolution. It has become the most widely used 3D printer among the members of the Maker Community, a global body of hackers, makers, crafters and DIY enthusiasts, and has inspired the creation of low-cost self-assembly and ready-assembled 3D printers by several other

Case Study
Fab@Home

Product: Fab@Home
Materials: various
RP process: variant of fused deposition modelling (FDM)
Designer: Hod Lipson
Website: www.fab@home.org
Awards: Popular Mechanics Breakthrough Award 2007

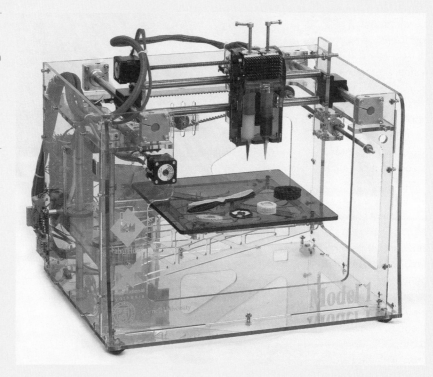

Fig. 24
Fab@Home Model 1.

Introduction

The Fab@Home project was founded by Hod Lipson and Evan Malone in 2006. The project is an open-source mass collaboration and was founded to develop low-cost, open-source 3D printers aimed at bringing personal fabrication into the home. Lipson has led research in such areas as evolutionary robotics, multi-material functional rapid prototyping, machine self-replication and programmable self-assembly.

Approach

While attempting to design a robot that could evolve by reprogramming itself and producing its own hardware, Lipson realized he would need an RP machine. Although these machines existed, they were expensive and utilized a limited range of materials. He and Malone set about creating a low-cost open-source 3D printer, and soon recognized that 3D printing technology held the potential to create almost any conceivable object –

replacement parts, toys, food – on demand and by anyone. In 2006 RP machine manufacturers were focused on expensive high-end commercial machines. Believing that the next phase of the digital revolution would enable people to make, sell or buy fully functional objects, Lipson and Malone conceived the Fab@Home project to help make this vision a reality.

To keep costs for the 3D printer down, the team used off-the-shelf materials and components and designed it for self-assembly. The printer chassis was made mostly from laser-cut acrylic, tool heads and electronics. The first printer – Model 1 – gained widespread interest, and within a year of the project starting the Fab@Home website had received over 17 million hits. A community of engineers, inventors, artists, students and hobbyists engaged with the project helped to develop the design and explore new applications for it, communicating through blogs and online forums. In 2008 the

Fig. 25
Fab@Home Model 2.

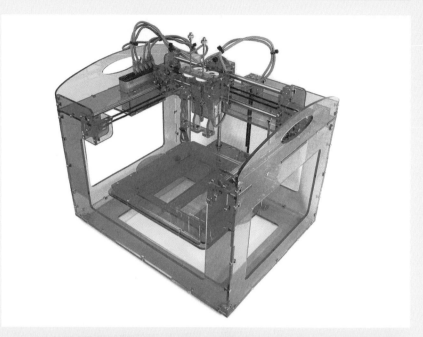

development of Model 2 began – a lower-cost version of the first, designed to be easier to build and modify. Model 2 supports user-developed hardware and software programs, which enable the creation of application-specific software programs.

Fab@Home developed syringe tools for the printer that can make objects out of multiple materials, including silicone, cement, cake frosting, chocolate and cheese. Experiments have been carried out using conductive silver-filled silicone and conductive ink to create electrical circuits, and products produced on the printer include a battery, a torch, a bicycle sprocket, toy parts, pastry moulds and various food products. Members of the Fab@Home project community are currently designing new tools, including a CNC attachment, large-volume reservoirs and an ice deposition tool. Coders are designing a new set of standards, languages and programs to help make personal fabricators become ubiquitous. The project has worked on food printing and has recently been focusing on bio-printing. The current focus is on multi-material printing whereby electric wires, batteries and motors can be integrated into products printed using the machine.

Result

The widespread interest in the Fab@Home project has been instrumental in increasing demand and driving supply of a range of low-cost 3D printers offered by a growing number of companies. Whether the future is one of desktop fabrication in the home for all, or one of a cloud-based manufacturing model where consumers order 3D printed goods online much as they do today, remains to be seen. Whether or not low-cost desktop fabricators will be able to manufacture complicated objects with

integrated electronics or match the quality of objects created using high-end additive manufacturing machines is also unknown. However, the Fab@Home community will continue to evolve the range of materials that can be used and the variety and quality of objects that can be created. The project is perhaps only years away from realizing Lipson's dream of printing a robot able to walk out of the printer.

Fig. 26
Watch casing and strap produced by a Fab@Home machine.

Case Study
AM Research Group, Loughborough

Product: Customized Sprinting Spikes
Client: Team GB Sprinters
Material: Duraform
RP process: selective laser sintering (SLS)
Designers: Diane Gyi, Matt Head, Neil Hopkinson, Sam Porter, Andre Salles, Dan Toon, Andrea Vinet
Modelling software: Dassult Systèmes SolidWorks
Website: www.lboro.ac.uk/research/amrg
Awards: Innovation Award, Professional Engineering Awards 2008, Society of Manufacturing Engineers (Breakthrough Technology), US, 2009

Fig. 27
An athlete taking part in the lab tests.
Fig. 28
SolidWorks CAD model of sprinting spike soles. Many CAD models with varying spike arrangements and sole stiffnesses were created for testing with athletes.

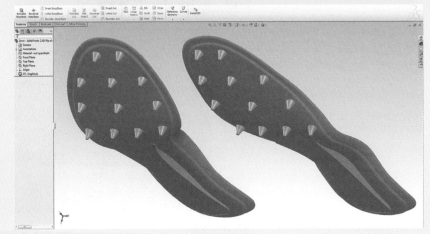

Introduction
The Additive Manufacturing Research Group (AMRG) at Loughborough University is regarded as one of the world's leading centres for AM research. It employs leading academics and a comprehensive AM laboratory, supported by state-of-the-art testing facilities. AMRG aims to push forward the development and application of additive layer manufacturing technologies into mainstream industrial applications.

At the Olympics in Athens in 2004, the difference between winning gold, silver or bronze in the 100-metre sprint was incredibly small – just 0.01 of a second. Loughborough researchers decided to explore ways to redesign sprinting spikes to enable a runner to shave 0.01 of a second from their sprint time.

Approach
The researchers focused on using CAD and additive manufacturing to change the soles of the sprinting spikes, aiming to match the longitudinal bending stiffness of the sole to individual athletes. The soles were attached to standard sprint shoe uppers using cement glue and their stiffness measured through a series of mechanical tests. The shoe was then placed into a sole press that applied 50 to 60psi of equal pressure around the shoe to ensure upper and sole were firmly attached. A cushion insert was then inserted into the shoe prior to physical testing. A series of sprint-related tasks were then performed by elite athletes in sprint shoes of varying stiffness and measured against a control shoe.

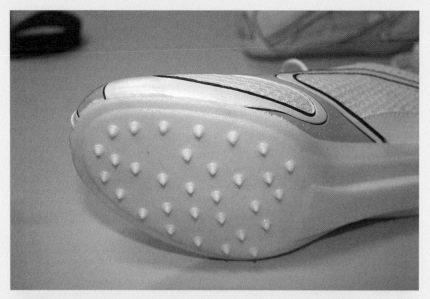

Process

Three-dimensional scans of existing sprint shoe lasts (the solid forms around which shoes are moulded) were taken into SolidWorks. Various designs were created, with varying thickness and longitudinal bending stiffness. Several different options for spike positioning were explored. The SolidWorks files were then saved as STL files ready for output to additive manufacturing.

The soles were manufactured on a Vanguard SLS machine using Duraform plastic, an established material for use with SLS and one that provided the appropriate level of stiffness. Although injection moulding could have been used to manufacture the soles, creating several alternative soles would have required a much more significant investment of time and money.

Elite athletes performed a number of lab tests, including squat jumps and bounce drop jumps, to measure and compare the stiffness and performance of different soles. The testing equipment included a Vicon 3D motion analyser and a Kistler force plate. Track tests were used to measure the influence on joint angles of different soles at the 10-metre and 50-metre stages of a 100-metre sprint. Markers were placed onto the spikes and the bare feet of the sprinters, and high speed (1000 frames per second) digital video recorded the positions of the markers at different points. This information was then used by the researchers to quantify the effects of different soles on the kinematics in the foot during sprinting.

The researchers discovered that by adjusting the sole of the shoe to within a certain stiffness range for each athlete, in some cases the amount of energy that was generated at the ankle could be doubled. The maximum improvement in performance achieved

was 3.5 per cent, which for an athlete able to run 100 metres in 10 seconds represents a 0.35-second improvement. At the 2012 London Olympic Games 100-metre sprint final, seven of the eight finalists were within a 0.35-second window.

The research is now being used to develop the concept of customized sports footwear for the consumer. It is anticipated that footwear customization will move beyond specifying just colour and will enable a choice of materials, flex characteristics, external shape and personalized internal shape, banishing to the past the problem of finding a pair of shoes that fit perfectly and look good too.

Fig. 29
Two variations of spike layout on the soles.

Case Study
Growthobjects

Products: Broccoli (research model), Lily lamp
Materials: Broccoli: epoxy resin; Lily: polyamide
RP processes: Broccoli: stereolithography apparatus (SLA); Lily: selective laser sintering (SLS)
Dimensions: Broccoli: 340 x 310 x 200mm (13.39 x 12.20 x 7.87in); Lily: 320 x 320 x 210mm (12.60 x 12.60 x 8.27in)
Designers: Jordi Bayer, Katia R. Glossmann, Xavier Tutó
Modelling software: Robert McNeel & Associates Rhinoceros 3D with Grasshopper plug-in
Website: www.growthobjects.com

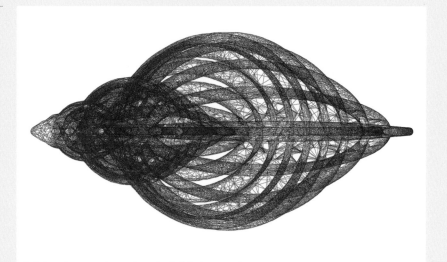

Introduction
Growthobjects is a collaborative research project between KXDesigners (Katia R. Glossmann and Xavier Tutó) and CloneNature (Jordi Bayer). Their research looks at the generation of complex geometries inspired by nature and the production of objects using AM technologies. Since 2009 Growthobjects has collaborated on projects focusing on the generation of design solutions based on principles of biomimicry, highly complex natural geometries (HICONG), morphogenesis, fractals, algorithmic programming, AM technologies and customization.

Approach
In nature, highly complex geometries result from the evolutionary process of organisms becoming optimized for their environment. Until very recently, it has been difficult for man to achieve a similar level of functional optimization due to the restrictions placed on designers and engineers by traditional manufacturing processes. Identifying that AM makes it possible to recreate any form found in nature, but only if it can first be created in a CAD program, Growthobjects promotes the development of new CAD tools, based

on parametric and algorithmic design and scripting, to make this process easier for designers.

Process
One of Growthobjects' observations is that almost every animal or vegetable that interchanges energy with the environment is using a relationship between surface area and volume to solve a problem. For example, hibernating bears curl into a ball in order to minimize the area of surface exposed to the air and avoid energy loss. To explore this relationship in fractal patterns and in HICON geometries, Growthobjects studied the Brassicaceae family of vegetables. Modelling broccoli in CAD revealed that it had a surface-area-to-volume ratio approximately 48 per cent higher than a smooth conical shape of the same dimensions. Their proposal was that the increased surface area of this form had potential applications within such heating or cooling products as heat exchangers, making them more efficient and smaller, or reducing manufacturing costs.

Growthobjects uses a mixture of standard CAD software and programmed mathematical algorithms based on fractals (self-similar patterns

Fig. 30
Recreation of the Fibonacci sequence found in shells as a CAD model.

Clockwise from top left:
Fig. 31
Computer rendering of a CAD model recreating the highly complex geometries found in broccoli.
Fig. 32
Wireframe view of a CAD model of broccoli.
Fig. 33
Experiments with fractal patterns during the development of the Lily wall lamp.
Fig. 34
Additively manufactured Lily wall lamp, showing fractal sequences similar to those in nature.
Fig. 35
CAD model of broccoli, suggesting that additively manufactured objects, perhaps even 3D printed food, will one day recreate the highly complex appearance of natural foods.

that appear the same from near as from far) and Lindenmayer systems (L-systems), rewriting systems used to model the growth processes of plant development and able to model the forms of a variety of organisms. The objects are created using such scripting-based CAD tools as the Grasshopper plug-in for Rhinoceros 3D.

Growthobjects' processes often identify weaknesses in current design tools, in particular CAD software. An example is the STL file format. STL files represent 3D surfaces using tens, hundreds or thousands of very small, flat-faced triangles. For highly complex objects that replicate natural forms, the process of saving in this format results in extremely large files, which then take a long time for AM machines to translate. The computer model of broccoli, for example, resulted in a 200MB file (STL files over 10MB are currently considered to be large). While current systems enable files of this very large size to be printed, additional time is required to process the information, resulting in poor efficiency.

Result
As a result of the methods currently used to mould, form and machine mass-manufactured products, many products display smooth surfaces with relatively simple geometries. Visual complexity, unevenness and asymmetry exist in the natural world but the majority of man-made objects do not reflect this. Growthobjects' research aims to promote a more efficient, less wasteful and more visually complex future, where the design of many products can be optimized for both their intended environment and given function, based on principles that have evolved in nature over millions of years.

Case Study
Future Factories

Product: Entropia lamp
Client: Kundalini
Material: polyamide
RP process: selective laser sintering (SLS)
Dimensions: diameter: 120mm (4.72in)
Designer: Lionel Theodore Dean
Design to production: 3 months
Modelling software: Alias Studiotools and Virtools to create the generative script; Alias Studiotools and Imagestudio (discontinued) for rendering
Website: www.futurefactories.com

Fig. 36
Entropia table lamp.

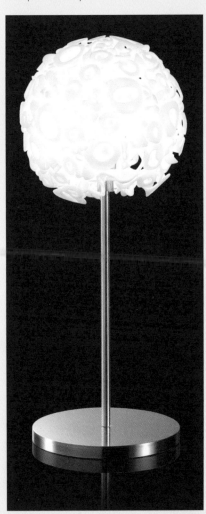

Introduction

FutureFactories is the studio of product artist Lionel Theodore Dean. What began as a university research project in 2002 expanded into a PhD thesis and from there into a commercial practice that now focuses exclusively on AM technologies applied to the creation of end-use products. A key area of research is computational design: the combination of CAD and programming. FutureFactories sell several AM products. In 2005 one of these, Tuber9, was acquired by the Museum of Modern Art in New York for its permanent design collection.

Approach

FutureFactories' concept of mass-individualization involves the creation of parametric CAD models that update and maintain their integrity as elements within them are adjusted. Combining computer scripts and CAD to create meta-designs with the capacity to transform over time, they aim to enable the customization of designs. When changes to the CAD models are driven by scripts, a large number of one-off variations of a design become possible. However, manufacturers and the market are not always ready to experiment in this way.

Kundalini founder Gregorio Spini commissioned from FutureFactories a mass-manufactured, serially produced design, to be manufactured by SLS. The brief was for an 'Eden flower'. Spini wanted no hint of man-made design and no clues as to how the parts were manufactured – a design that would both intrigue and baffle. At the same time, Spini desired evidence of creative process rather than merely the design of a random form.

Process

The concept was for 'a natural growth of organic floral forms surrounding a light source'. To satisfy both the need for complexity in the design and his own desire to explore individualization principles, Dean created rule- or script-driven CAD building blocks for 'leaf' and 'flower' elements that were then assembled manually into chains around a sphere. Each time an element was required it would be generated by the CAD tool and be different to any other. If it didn't fit, the element would be regenerated. Approximately 1000 elements were arranged in the 100 chains that make up the form. No sketching was done – 3D patterns that were too complex to comprehend would have been impossible to draw. Instead, Dean experimented with CAD geometries and crude digital mock-ups.

Being an expensive process, the efficient use of SLS was crucial. The more products that could be packed into the build chamber of the SLS machine, the more viable the project. Production costs were also linked to build time and to the height of the product and therefore the number of layers built. It was determined that a spherical lampshade diameter of 110mm (4.33in) would enable a sufficient number of shades to fit into the build chamber to achieve the target production price. For final production, 120mm (4.72in) resulted in a lamp with higher perceived value, albeit with reduced production efficiency.

To maximize the visual impact of the modestly sized SLS shade, a slender chromed steel stand, 5mm (0.2in) in diameter, was sourced to carry the mains cable for the table lamp, and a clear mains cable was sourced for the pendant version. A G9 halogen fitting that required no transformer was used. A threaded fitting was designed into the SLS to accommodate both pendant and table orientations. The first test batch produced was used for photography and exhibition as well as testing. The second batch produced

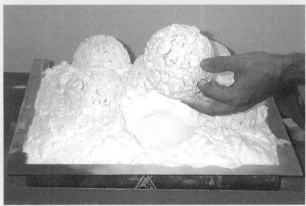

Was acceptable for sale but the design development continued.

Result

Apparently the first direct-manufactured consumer product produced by a manufacturer other than an RP bureau, Entropia (2006) represents an early and significant step. One of the advantages of using AM processes is that every object produced can be different from the next. The lack of a need for tooling for AM processes also enables designs to be continually updated and improved without the cost of new tooling.

Such companies as Nervous Systems and Continuum are currently pioneering the use of script-driven interfaces, enabling consumers to interact with, and tailor, 3D CAD models of jewellery, home accessories and fashion designs prior to ordering. It is likely others will begin to offer similar services, and thus realize the concept of mass-individualization of consumer products proposed by FutureFactories.

Clockwise from top left:

Fig. 37
Completed CAD model of Entropia, consisting of 1000 elements arranged into 100 chains.

Fig. 38
Close-up wireframe view of the script-driven 'leaf' and 'flower' building blocks.

Fig. 39
Close-up rendered view of the building blocks.

Fig. 40
Partial assembly of the building blocks. Each time the feature is repeated within the form, there is a slightly different outcome, resulting in the impression of organic growth.

Fig. 41
A fabricated Entropia lampshade being removed from the SLS machine.

Fig. 42
Completed CAD model of Entropia. The form of the shade appears to have been grown rather than constructed.

Case Study
Bespoke Innovations

Product: bespoke prostheses fairings
Client: various
Materials: polyamide substrate, various finish materials
RP process: selective laser sintering (SLS)
Dimensions: varied, according to client
Designer: Scott Summit
Modelling software: Autodesk 123D Catch (photogrammetry)
Website: www.bespokeinnovations.com

Introduction
Founded in 2009 by an industrial designer and an orthopaedic surgeon, Bespoke Innovations aim to bring greater humanity to people with congenital or traumatic lower limb loss. They operate at the forefront of personalized design made possible by AM processes.

Approach
Bespoke Innovations design durable and lightweight personalized fairings that attach to and surround an existing prosthetic limb, recreating the form of the lower leg using a process that involves 3D scanning, CAD and AM. Working with individual customers offers them unprecedented opportunities to co-create. They have discovered that their customers usually prefer limited choice and often revert to a safe, existing model over any attempt to become the designer.

Process
The design process begins with a 3D scan of both the existing prosthetic and the 'sound side' leg of the wearer, using structured light, lasers or Kinect-based scanners. (If an amputee has lost both legs, leaving no 'sound side' leg to be scanned, a volunteer of the approximate age, size and athletic level is scanned as a surrogate.) When necessary to travel light, a standard digital camera is used and the images taken turned into a 3D database using 123D Catch, photogrammetric software created by Autodesk. The resulting 'point cloud' data is then cleaned and turned into a surface model. The surface is then mirrored and carefully superimposed over the prosthetic limb.

An appropriate parametric template model is introduced into the CAD assembly, and a series of Boolean operations create the basic bounding geometry. This template can be modified extensively to allow a close fit, and to capture the personality of the wearer. The contours must recreate the human form as honestly as possible, while avoiding any protrusions coming from the underlying prosthetic, which can sometimes fall out with the geometric volumes of the human leg. Patterns or other style elements are then added to the geometry, using various 3D CAD modelling techniques. At this point, the

Fig. 43
James lost his leg in a motorcycle accident in San Francisco. Bespoke Innovations created a custom polyamide and chrome-plated polyamide prosthesis fairing that expresses James's personality and, of course, his motorcycle.

wearer may even provide their own unique artwork for a pattern to be reflected in the design.

Final fabrication is often done using SLS, since it is capable of creating large, durable and complex parts, and typically uses polyamide, which is both resilient enough to endure abuse and structural enough to hold a screw thread. Parts created this way are even dishwasher-safe.

Result

Taking full advantage of 3D scanning, CAD and AM allows the company to create highly personalized products. Attracting admiring interest from passers-by, the fairings enable amputees to express confidence, creativity and individuality, and remove the awkwardness felt as a result of the appearance of traditional prostheses. The involvement of the user in the design process enables an expression of personality and individual preference in the end product in an entirely new way.

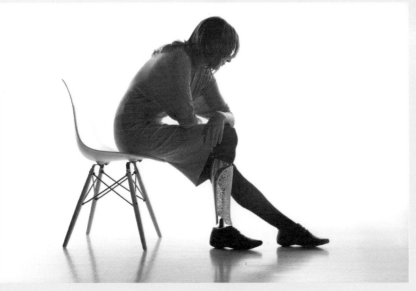

Fig. 44 (above)
At age 33 Chad, an avid athlete, was diagnosed with synovial sarcoma on the bottom of his right foot. Faced with the choice of losing a large section of his foot and having a limp or losing his leg mid-shin, he made the difficult decision to amputate. Bespoke Innovations designed a prosthesis that would allow him more normality in his athletic and daily life.

Fig. 45 (left)
In 2004 Deborah lost her lower leg in a motorcycle accident and was fitted with a standard prosthetic limb. In 2010 she met with Bespoke Innovations, who designed a custom fairing that expresses Deborah's personal style.

Case Study
Exstent

Product: ExoVasc
Materials: Former: polyamide; implant: polyester
RP process: selective laser sintering (SLS)
Designer: Tal Golesworthy
Modelling software: Bespoke software created by Warren Thornton at Imperial College London
Website: www.exstent.com

Introduction

Tal Golesworthy is the founder of Exstent, developer of the ExoVasc. Golesworthy suffers from Marfan syndrome, an inherited disorder of the body's tissues caused by a deficiency of the structural protein fibre fibrillin. The disorder has widespread effects, most seriously in the ascending aorta, the main artery leading from the heart. Around 30mm (1.18in) in diameter, the ascending aorta transports around 5 litres of blood per minute from the heart to a network of arteries. In sufferers of Marfan syndrome, the ascending aorta gradually dilates and can eventually split and rupture, with fatal consequences.

Approach

In 1992 Golesworthy learnt that his ascending aorta was dilating; by 2002 it had dilated to around 50mm (1.97in) in diameter, the size at which surgery was required. This six-hour procedure involved a general anaesthetic, a surgical incision to open the chest, connection to an artificial heart and lung machine, lowering the body temperature, stopping the heart, grafting an artificial membrane onto the aorta and replacing the aorta's valve with an artificial one.

Questioning these existing procedures, Golesworthy considered a possible alternative solution. Aware of magnetic resonance imaging (MRI) and X-ray-based computer tomography (CT), he developed a proposal to use medical imaging combined with CAD and RP to manufacture a bespoke external supporting sleeve for the ascending aorta.

Process

London-based cardiothoracic surgeons Tom Treasure and John Pepper were enlisted into the project. The process of acquiring images of Golesworthy's ascending aorta was developed with the MR unit at the Royal Brompton Hospital, and a method of generating CAD models from these images was developed by Warren Thornton at Imperial College. After exploring various approaches to scanning, several parallel 2D slices viewed in a number of planes were taken as part of a conventional MR scan. Averages were taken of multiple images for each position in space to provide usable image data from which to

Fig. 46
ExoVasc former created using the SLS RP process and over which the textile sleeve implant is formed.

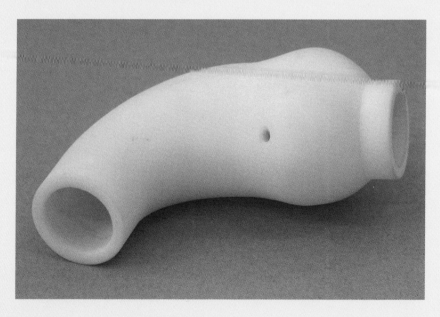

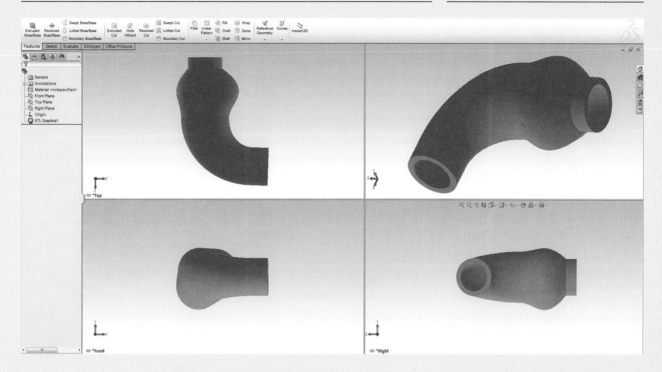

calculate dimensions for the CAD modelling process.

A bespoke CAD approach was developed to analyse a number of known morphological features associated with the ascending aorta – it managed the varying image quality produced by the scanning process while providing an acceptable dimensional accuracy on the finished CAD model. Several models were created, and the final one was assessed by the operating surgeon to validate its suitability. The CAD model was then converted into a solid polymer model using SLS, solid polymer being the most suited to withstanding the various solvent cleaning and sterilization processes to which the product would later be subject. An STL triangle side length of typically 1mm (0.04in) was determined to be acceptable for creating an accurate model.

The next stage was to form a medical polyester textile around the SLS former using a heat-shrinking process in a sterile environment. In surgery, the SLS former with textile implant on it could be easily aligned with Golesworthy's aorta; the textile implant was then removed from the former and stitched around the aorta. The process of forming the textile onto the SLS former stabilized its form so that it retained its shape once

removed. The textile was then sufficiently flexible to wrap around the aorta and sufficiently strong to prevent the aorta from expanding.

Result

Golesworthy was implanted with the device in an operation in May 2004, proving its feasibility. Since then the textile sleeve – ExoVasc – has been used successfully to treat 30 patients. The current manufacturing procedure will remain unchanged until the project reaches 50 patients. Thereafter the entire manufacturing process will be reviewed, including the imaging protocol and method, the CAD routine, and the method used to manufacture the former.

ExoVasc highlights the value of forming multidisciplinary teams to develop innovative solutions to critical health problems. With the potential to help hundreds of thousands of sufferers, this design is also an outstanding example of the way such technologies as CAD and RP can be used to develop practical solutions that transform lives for the better.

Fig. 47
Screen grab of the CAD model file created from the MRI scans of Golesworthy's ascending aorta.

Fig. 48 (below)
Former and ExoVasc textile sleeve implant pre-forming.
Fig. 49 (bottom)
Close-up showing the ExoVasc textile sleeve implant shaped over the SLS former.

Case Study
Southampton University

Product: Laser Sintered Aircraft
Material: poylamide
RP process: selective laser sintering (SLS)
Dimensions: wingspan: 1200mm (47.24in)
Designers: Mario Ferraro, Andy Keane, Jim Scanlan, Jeroen van Schaik
Design to production: 6 weeks
Modelling software: Dassault Systèmes SolidWorks
Website: www.southampton.ac. uk/~decode

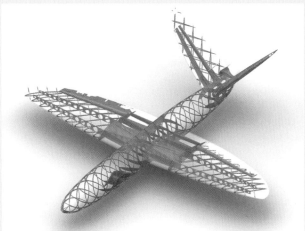

Fig. 50 (top)
SULSA in flight.
Fig. 51 (above left)
CAD model.
Fig. 52 (above right)
Render of CAD model.

Introduction

Southampton University Laser Sintered Aircraft (SULSA) is the world's first additively manufactured unmanned aerial vehicle (UAV). Designed and flown by a team from the university's Computational Engineering and Design Research group led by Jim Scanlan and Andy Keane, the aircraft is equipped with a miniature autopilot, is electrically powered and has a top speed of close to 100mph (161kph). SULSA is part of an Engineering and Physical Sciences Research Council (EPSRC)-funded research project named DECODE, which is researching the use of leading-edge manufacturing techniques, such as SLS, in the design of UAVs.

Approach

The design brief created by Scanlan and Keane specified a strong, lightweight aircraft built from just four parts: main fuselage, rudder fins, nose cone and wings. Assembly had to be quick and easy, with no need for time-consuming post-processing. Both the aircraft fuselage and the wings had to house a number of internal

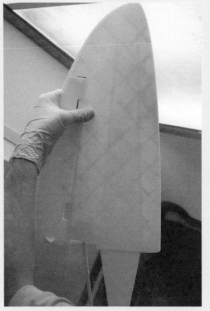

mechanical components, and a simple method was needed to fit them.

The team initially revisited historical design ideas that were highly effective but prohibitively expensive to use on modern aircraft due to their complexity of assembly: the complex geodesic structural design developed by Barnes Wallis for the Vickers Wellington bomber (1936); the drag-reducing elliptical wings of the Heinkel HE 70 (1932); and the Supermarine Spitfire (1936) designed by Reginald Joseph Mitchell. Combining these ideas, the team set out to create an aircraft that would have both strength and structural rigidity but would also be lightweight and aerodynamically efficient.

Process

Three-dimensional computer models were created using SolidWorks and then sent to AM bureau 3T RPD. SLS was the ideal process to manufacture the aircraft as the polyamide material used offered tremendous strength despite the weight of the plastic parts being less than 2kg (4.4lb). The entire structure of the aircraft, including the wings, fuselage, integral control surfaces and access hatches, was printed on an EOS EOSINT P730 SLS machine.

CAD engineers at 3T incorporated the snap fittings required to hold the four nylon parts together to form the overall aircraft. They also designed mountings and channels to hold the ten internal components, enabling the motor, battery, avionics and controls to be clipped into place inside the main fuselage, and two servos, one in each wing. The wings featured two ailerons with integral hinges, and similar large hinged flaps were located on the rear control surfaces. All these features were incorporated into the aircraft's design, and the ability of SLS to create hinge features and clips meant that they could be built as integral parts to the main components, thereby increasing their functionality and reducing the need for additional parts to be fitted post-build. So that the entire aircraft could be put together without tools in minutes, no screws or other fasteners were used – all equipment was attached using channel and snap-fit techniques.

Result

SULSA is very stiff and lightweight, but also very complex. If it had been manufactured using conventional processes it would have required a large number of individually tailored parts, bonded or fastened at great expense. By using an AM technique, the number of separate parts could be minimized, both part complexity and shape were unrestricted, and the complex internal structure and elliptical wing did not add to the cost of fabrication.

Unmanned aircraft are currently used primarily by the military, but will be increasingly used in scientific research and in humanitarian-focused disaster and emergency situations. The flexibility of form creation and the possibility of the economic manufacture of one-off design solutions using AM processes will therefore enable not only UAVs but also a wide range of other products to be developed to help a growing number of organizations solve specific problems.

Left to right:
Fig. 53
SLS fuselage component showing complex internal geometric structure.
Fig. 54
SLS wing component showing internal structure.
Fig. 55
SULSA being assembled.

Case Study
EADS

Product: Airbike
Material: polyamide
RP process: selective laser sintering (SLS)
Dimensions: height: 1750mm (29.53in); length: 1600mm (62.99in); handlebar width: 600mm (23.62in)
Designers: Andy Hawkins and Chris Turner
Design to production: 6 weeks
Modelling software: Dassault Systèmes CATIA V5
Website: www.eads.com

Fig. 56
SLS fabricated Airbike, an application of AM technology to an everyday product. The Airbike demonstrates the potential for AM technologies to transform manufacturing.
Fig. 57
Close-up of the clean Kevlar belt drive system, crankset, wheel spokes and integrated truss structure.

Introduction

EADS is a global leader in aerospace, defence and related services. The group, consisting of Airbus, Astrium, Cassidian and Eurocopter, operates in 48 countries, generates revenues in excess of €45 billion and employs a workforce of around 122,000. In March 2011 EADS produced the world's first additively manufactured bicycle – named the Airbike because Airbus was the first EADS company to use the technology.

Approach

A bike was chosen as a suitable item with which to explore the application of AM technologies to a product that everyone could understand. This, however, required a complete rethink of bicycle design. Conventional bicycle frames are typically manufactured from welded tubular sections of steel or aluminium. To make the plastic frame of the Airbike sufficiently strong, it needed to be larger and use a different cross-sectional profile. The wheel spokes, rims and bearings presented further design challenges.

Fig. 58
Testing the Airbike prototype.

processes, AM processes use around one-tenth of the material and reduce waste by up to 90 per cent. Metal parts produced by AM processes are up to 65 per cent lighter but still as strong as parts made using conventional techniques. Studies show that for every 1kg (2.2lb) reduction in weight, airlines can save around US$3500 worth of fuel over the lifespan of an aircraft, with corresponding reductions in carbon-dioxide emissions.

Process

The bike design was first modelled and tested in CAD. Several unique design features were incorporated, such as the flexible structure to provide saddle cushioning and the integrated bearings encased within the wheel hubs. The bike was designed to require no conventional maintenance or assembly. SLS was selected to create the prototype. The unique frame design, which integrated a truss structure to reduce weight but maintain stiffness, was made from polyamide (nylon), replacing the steel or aluminium used for conventional bicycle frames. Replacing a standard bicycle chain was a clean Kevlar belt drive system.

The design of the wheel spokes mimicked the eight-bladed scimitar propeller design found on the Airbus Military A400M. Complete sections of the bike were built as one piece, the wheels, bearings and axle being incorporated within the SLS process and built at the same time. Once the build was complete, excess build powder was blown out from recesses using compressed air. Certain components, such as the wheels, required more than one prototype to

perfect. Successive refinements were made to the CAD model of the wheels to adjust the space around the bearings to prevent the wheels from wobbling, and to refine the thicknesses of the wheel rims to ensure they were strong enough to withstand the pressure of the inflated tyre inner tubes.

Result

Requiring no assembly or maintenance, the Airbike is also built to rider specification and thus requires no adjustment. The design of the prototype bike was created in a short timeframe and has not been developed further, but it demonstrates the potential of additive processes to transform manufacturing around the globe. EADS has recently collaborated with UK bicycle manufacturer Charge Bikes to fabricate titanium drop-outs for some of their cyclocross frames using another AM process, electron beam melting (EBM).

With the potential to help the aerospace sector reduce its waste and carbon emissions, AM technologies are likely to be employed by EADS in a wide range of aerospace applications. Compared to traditional machining

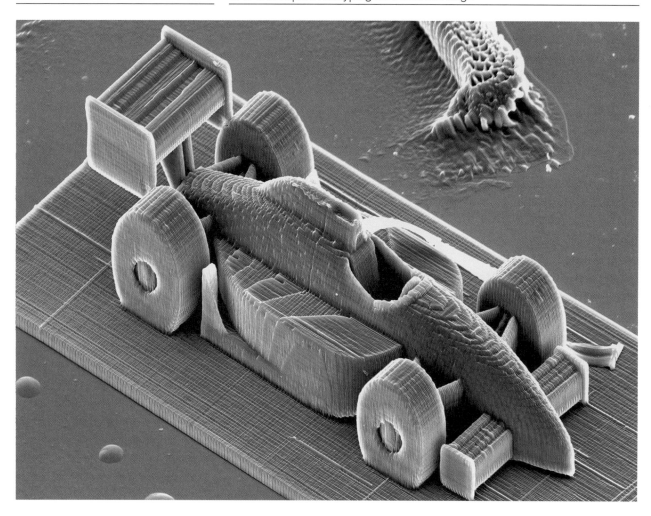

Fig. 59
0.285mm nano printed Indy Race Car, Jan
Torgersen, Vienna University of Technology.

Conclusion

Will the future be one in which product design breaks free from business
and commerce? Will developments in software and AM enable individuals
disillusioned with trends, brands and mass consumer-oriented products to create
individualized products on demand? How complex will these objects be and what
variety and combinations of materials will be used? Will the manufacture and
distribution of products alter radically as a result?

In the future, product design and development will certainly look very
different. Ever since the first industrial revolution began in the UK in the late
eighteenth century, manufacturing has become ever more efficient, less reliant
on manual labour and more reliant on machines. To reduce costs, factories will
become even more reliant on CAD, autonomous computer-controlled machines
and robots, replacing much of the manual work still undertaken in factories today.
AM factories will employ only a few people, requiring a minimum of sufficiently
skilled employees to ensure constant supplies of powdered or liquid materials to
feed the machines and to man the computer software controlling the machines.

Computers and additive layer manufacturing systems will be used to
automatically manufacture all manner of complex products comprising different
materials and components without the need for tooling or assembly. The inputs
required for manufacture will simply be CAD data and raw materials. We are
perhaps only 10 to 20 years away from this scenario becoming a widespread
reality, and it will transform the landscape of consumer product design. The
concept of the replicator, first introduced in the television series *Star Trek* and able
to reproduce almost any product at the touch of a button, will soon no longer be
the realm of science fiction.

Contour Crafting
Simulation Plan for Lunar Settlement Infrastructure Build-Up
PI: Behrokh Khoshnevis
Professor of Engineering
University of Southern California

Lunar Contour Crafting Prototype

Structure Prototype Small Scale

Variation Prototype

Wall Prototype

Machinery Detail

Nozzle

Fig. 60
Additively manufactured lunar settlement
concept for NASA by Professor Behrokh
Khoshnevis, University of Southern California.

Just as millennia ago, the number of hand tools grew to enable man to work raw materials more quickly and in more specialized and complex ways, AM systems are likely to become much faster and ever more specialized at particular manufacturing functions, producing particular types and sizes of product, from those on a nano scale up to those on the scale of aircraft and buildings.

As the barriers to using CAD for the creation of 3D models are removed through the provision of easier-to-use software, a larger number of individuals and businesses will be able to design, create and sell products. As more businesses are able to afford the machines required to produce products, manufacturing will take place in the hands of a much larger number of smaller companies, spreading the production base more evenly, and enabling companies to respond to consumers' needs more quickly. As more businesses develop new customizable and personalized products, consumers will enjoy greater choice than ever before. Large manufacturing brands will undoubtedly adopt AM technologies as it becomes economically attractive to do so, but will be challenged in their dominance and control over markets. However, a potential social implication of the shift in the design, production and sale of products from designers, large manufacturers and retailers to individuals is the reduction in organizational and legislative control over the type and safety of products available, and new forms of protective legislation will likely be required to address this. As protecting brand and design becomes less important, the design, production and marketing of new, useful, desirable and reliable designs and interfaces becomes an even more important means of creating consumer desire and retaining and growing market share. AM will enable businesses to take advantage of developing opportunities in both existing and emerging markets, and production and supply will become local to these markets.

Companies that produce AM machines will continue to grow rapidly, supplying their ever more capable and diverse machines to an ever expanding

Fig. 61
Xilloc Medical Mandibula, Sirris, the first additively manufactured full lower jaw implant used in surgery. Additive manufacturing by LayerWise, Leuven, Belgium.

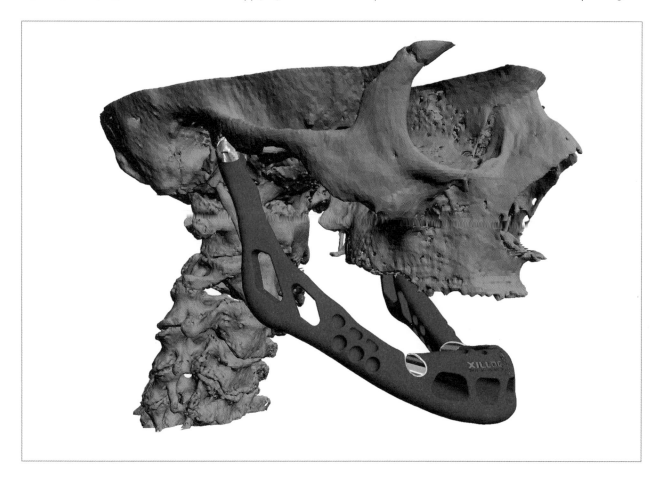

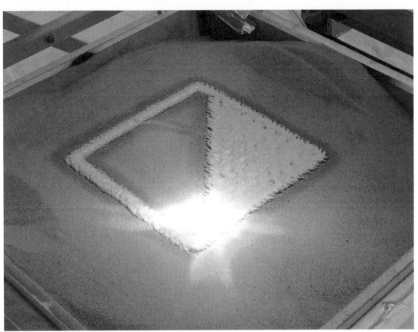

Fig. 62
Solar Sinter, a project conceived by product designer Markus Kayser to explore the potential of desert manufacturing, where energy and material occur in abundance. In this experiment sunlight and sand are used as raw energy and material to produce glass objects using 3D printing. The aim was to raise questions about the future of manufacturing and the production potential of one of the world's most abundant energy resources, the sun. Testing was carried out over two weeks in the Sahara Desert near Siwa, Egypt.

number of manufacturing companies, organizations and individuals. More companies developing products to make use of AM machines and greater need for customization and personalization will mean more opportunities for product designers. Designers will need to know how to use highly capable CAD software to create customized families of products for engaging consumers in the cloud. They will also need to use CAD to design products suited to personalization, products optimized for particular functional requirements and products of any conceivable form.

Contemporary product design is a reflection of the time in which we live and of the tools, materials and processes currently available. The design of products in the future will not always require a high-tech approach using AM. Indeed, widespread use of AM may well evoke consumer demand for products produced using traditional materials and handcraft processes. However, visionary, progressive designers will continue to learn and keep pace with advances in the capabilities of CAD and manufacturing technologies. These designers will use their knowledge, imagination, creativity and intuition to question and challenge existing ways of doing things, to push frontiers and to take advantage of these tools to create competitive advantage for businesses and to enrich our lives.

CAD AND RAPID PROTOTYPING FOR PRODUCT DESIGN

GLOSSARY

3D MODELLING, RENDERING AND ENGINEERING SOFTWARE

COMMON TYPES OF 3D FILE

FURTHER READING

INTERNET RESOURCES

INDEX

PICTURE CREDITS

ACKNOWLEDGEMENTS

Glossary

3D printing
Commonly used to describe all rapid prototyping and additive manufacturing processes, 3D printing (3DP) is also the name of a specific rapid prototyping process, in which prototypes are created from layers of fine plaster, corn starch or polymer powder, bonded together with a liquid adhesive deposited onto the powder from an inkjet print head. Methods of 3D printing using ceramic powders and metal powders have also been developed.

Additive manufacturing (AM)
The making of product components using additive rapid prototyping processes. May be referred to as additive layer manufacturing (ALM), solid freeform fabrication or 3D printing.

Anti-aliasing
An adjustable parameter in rendering programs used to help diagonal edges of objects seen in renderings, which consist of square pixels, to appear smooth and not jagged or stair-stepped. It is also used to filter image maps used to create the appearance of materials, in order to eliminate visible pixelation of the images used as maps.

Appearance prototype
A product prototype mimicking the intended manufactured appearance of the product, including form, colours, materials and surface finishes but not necessarily the functional attributes of the product. Appearance prototypes are used for design validation and for marketing purposes.

Assembly model
A CAD model consisting of two or more separate part models assembled together. Assembly models are used to ensure that parts will fit together as intended prior to manufacture.

Background
The space that surrounds a CAD model, which for the purposes of rendering can be specified as a colour, a gradient between colours or an image of a suitable context for the product.

Bill of materials (BOM)
A list of the parts, and the quantities of each, needed to manufacture a product. It includes part numbers; part names; part descriptions; part materials; part quantities; and part measurements. The bills of materials for a complex product may also include information about subassemblies (a collection of parts assembled together to be used with a larger assembly) and subcomponents (a component-like part within a component).

Bump map
A digital image, normally greyscale and consisting of 256 levels of grey from black to white, used to create the effect of surface roughness on materials in product renderings. Grey pixels are assigned height values, with black pixels representing the troughs, white pixels the peaks and shades of grey heights in between.

Camera
The theoretical lens through which you view a model in CAD, the position of which determines your view of the object, and the settings of which can often be adjusted to provide various differences within rendered images, such as the perspective of the model and the area in focus within the render.

Class A surface
The surface of a CAD model that the end-user will be able to see and touch once the product has been manufactured.

Closed polysurface
Several CAD surfaces joined together to create a model with thickness and volume – also known as a solid model and referred to as a watertight model. Models for output to additive RP processes must be closed polysurfaces.

Closed surface
A single CAD surface completely enclosing a volume, thus giving it thickness and thus also making it a solid model. In NURBS modelling programs the shape of closed surfaces can be manipulated using control points sitting off the surface.

Computational fluid dynamics (CFD)
Software related to finite element analysis (FEA) that is used to test the movement of air and liquid through the internal or over the external surfaces of a product, as well as, for example, the flow of plastic into a virtual injection mould cavity.

Computer-aided design (CAD)
The use of the computer to create design, generally used with reference to the creation of virtual three-dimensional models and two-dimensional drawings as an aid in the process of designing products, engineering components and buildings. Also used with reference to the use of the computer to design 2D graphics and animations.

Computer-aided engineering (CAE)
The use of the computer as an aid in the process of testing and evaluating product components virtually, prior to their manufacture to ensure optimum performance and manufacturability.

Computer-aided manufacture (CAM)
The use of the computer in preparation for the manufacture of components.

Computer numerical control (CNC)
The control of machining processes by computer. Computer operated machining processes that remove material from a workpiece are known as computer numerical control (CNC) machining processes, and include milling, routing and lathe operations. Depending on the machine, the process can be 2-axis, 3-axis, 4-axis, 5-axis, 6-axis or 7-axis.

Construction planes
Two-dimensional planes within the CAD modelling environment, on which drawings are constructed as part of the process of creating a CAD model. In parametric CAD programs, drawings must be made on construction planes.

Continuity
A term used in CAD to describe the smoothness between separate splines or separate surfaces that have been joined together to make a longer curve or surface. Four types of continuity can be applied when matching splines or surfaces according to the desired level of smoothness at the point of juncture: Positional (G0), Tangential (G1), Curvature (G2) and Acceleration (G3).

Control points
Points in NURBS CAD programs used to control the shape of splines and surfaces.

Degree
An adjustable parameter in NURBS CAD programs used to control the deformation of the curves and surfaces of a model.

Design history
A feature available in some CAD programs providing a list of operations performed during the process of creating a CAD model. In parametric CAD programs the design history enables you to revisit and make changes to parts and features.

Diffuse map
A colour image map used to recreate the appearance of real-world materials within computer renderings.

Direct light processing (DLP)
A relatively fast additive RP process that cures parts as they are being built from a photo-curable resin. Used to create small parts with a very good surface finish from a range of materials, including wax-like materials.

Direct manipulation
Editing the shape of a surface of a CAD model by manipulating control points.

Direct metal laser sintering (DMLS)
An additive RP process that uses a high-powered laser to sinter (fuse) a fine metal powder, and can be used to additively manufacture end-use products from a variety of metals.

Draft angle
The angle of taper, perpendicular to the parting line, of surfaces on a part in CAD intended to be manufactured as either a moulding or a casting.

Drawing
An entity in CAD consisting only of splines which are later used to create surfaces and solids. The term is also used to describe a dimensioned two-dimensional representation of a three-dimensional object. These types of drawings are often referred to as technical drawings, engineering drawings or manufacturing drawings.

Export
Most CAD applications allow you to save files in formats that can be opened and read by other computer programs. This process is known as exporting.

Fillet
In solid CAD modelling, a rounding of an interior or exterior corner or edge of a CAD part. In surface CAD modelling, a curved surface created between two adjoining surfaces.

Finite element analysis (FEA)

Functionality provided within some CAD programs, and within specialist FEA software, used to predict whether a product will break, wear out or work the way it was intended to when it is used. FEA is also able to determine how a product reacts to real-world forces, vibration, heat, fluid flow and other physical effects.

Frame

A single image from an animation, representing one stage of movement. For every second of animation there are typically between 12 and 30 frames. More frames create smoother movement.

Fused deposition modelling (FDM)

A relatively slow but clean additive RP process in which a thin filament of thermoplastic polymer is heated above its melting point and fed through a small nozzle, which deposits the semi-liquid plastic onto the appropriate places on a build platform layer-by-layer to create the part.

Fused metal deposition

Additive RP processes used to fabricate fully dense metal parts by feeding metal powder through a nozzle into the path of a laser beam, which melts the metal powder, depositing it onto the build platform.

Global illumination

A type of illumination used in some CAD and rendering programs that recreates the way light bounces between surfaces, creating additional indirect light and transferring colour between surfaces. Radiosity and photon mapping are two processes used by rendering programs to calculate and produce global illumination.

Ground surface

A surface positioned underneath a CAD model prior to rendering, in order to create a shadow and/or reflection and to help ground the model, preventing it from appearing to float in space, which for most products would look unnatural.

Haptic

Tactile feedback technology that applies forces, vibrations or motions to the user. In some CAD software, this mechanical simulation can be used to assist in the creation of virtual objects.

High dynamic range (HDR)

When creating an order of a model, an HDR images can be used in high dynamic range image-based (HDRI) lighting to create physically accurate lighting, and to create accurate reflections in the reflective surfaces of a model.

Hot-wire cutting

A fabrication process used to cut foams with relatively low melt temperatures, commonly expanded polystyrene, extruded polystyrene and expanded polypropylene, using a thin, taut nickel chromium or stainless steel wire heated to around 200°C (392°F).

Image-based lighting

A method used to create realistic lighting within some CAD and rendering programs by mapping images of real interior or exterior environments onto the background environment sphere surrounding the CAD model.

Image map

Digital images used to create the appearance of materials when rendering a CAD model. Image maps can be used to create material colour, texture, roughness, surface highlights, transparency and luminosity.

Jetting systems

Relatively fast additive RP processes that use multiple inkjet-based print heads to print parts using photo-curable liquid resins. They create accurate parts with a very good surface finish. Unlike SLA, parts are cured as they are created.

Keyframe

A single animation frame in which information is stored as a reference. Subsequent frames store only changes in the frame, not the whole frame, which helps to keep animation files much smaller.

Laser cutting

A CNC prototyping and manufacturing process that uses a laser beam to cut a wide range of sheet materials ranging from 0.2 to 40mm (0.0079 to 1.57in) thick, by melting, burning or vaporizing them.

Non-uniform rational basis spline (NURBS)

NURBS CAD programs use mathematically defined curves (splines) and surfaces, the shape of which are controlled by control points sitting off the curves/surfaces.

Open polysurface

Several CAD surfaces joined together to create a model with no thickness or volume, that may be used for visualization but cannot be output to RP processes.

Open surface

A single CAD surface that does not have thickness or enclose a volume.

Parameter

Any variable setting in a CAD program. The dimensions of a part, for example, define its parameters and can be varied to change the shape and size of the part.

Parametric

A parametric CAD modelling program is one that enables the parameters (shapes/dimensions) of a part to be changed at any time during the process of modelling the part, without starting the modelling process from scratch.

Parting line

The line, sometimes visible on the surface of product parts, created during moulding or casting processes where the separate parts of the mould used in the manufacture of the part meet together to form the mould cavity. The parting line is where the parts of the mould separate. In a simple mould this line will be straight; however, more complex parts sometimes require moulds that result in stepped or curved parting lines.

Pixel

Digital images consist of hundreds of thousands of very small squares called pixels, the smallest controllable elements of a picture represented on a computer screen.

Plasma cutting

A means of cutting metal sheet and plate – usually steel or aluminium – using an inert gas blown through a small, water-cooled nozzle onto the surface of the workpiece. Some of the gas is converted to a very high-temperature plasma when it comes into contact with an electrical arc created between a negatively charged electrode located in the gas nozzle and the positively charged surface of the workpiece.

Plotter cutter

A CNC machine that uses a knife to cut sheet materials into designs specified in 2D CAD files.

Plug-in

Software, usually developed by a third party, designed to work within a larger computer program in order to add functionality. Many popular rendering programs are available as plug-ins to CAD modelling programs.

Polygon

A three- or four-sided face, several of which joined together create an element known as a polygon mesh.

Polygon mesh

Models in polygon mesh modelling programs, and solid models exported from CAD programs as STL files, consist of triangular or quadrilateral (quad) polygons connected together to form a polygon mesh.

Polymer

A natural or synthetic compound, also known as resin and more commonly known as plastic. Polymers are either produced by polymerization or extracted from plants.

Polysurface

Two or more CAD surfaces joined together.

Post processing

Finishing processes that take place after fabrication of a part, often to improve surface finish.

Product lifecycle management (PLM)

The process of managing the design, manufacture, service and disposal of a product. PLM software helps manufacturers to cope with the increasing complexity and challenges of developing new products. Software includes CAD, CAE, CAM and maintenance software. Some software covers the whole PLM range, while others offer single niche applications.

Production drawing

A 2D drawing specifying the shape and dimensions of a part to be manufactured.

Rapid manufacturing (RM)

The use of RP processes (both subtractive and additive) for the manufacture of product components.

Rapid prototyping (RP)

A variety of processes used to fabricate models and prototype parts for products using CAD data from computer models. RP most commonly refers to the use of 3D CAD data to create three-dimensional prototype parts, but the term can also refer to automated processes that utilize 2D CAD data to create prototype parts from sheet materials. RP processes are either subtractive, whereby a design is cut from a sheet or block of material, or additive, whereby a design is built layer by layer.

Raytracing

An optional function within rendering programs used to simulate natural reflections in reflective surfaces, refraction of light through transparent and semi-transparent materials, and shadows.

Rendering

The process of creating a computer-generated image of a CAD model. Renderings (or renders) often include lifelike representations of colours, materials and surface finishes of products, and can also include realistic background scenes.

Resolution

The image quality of a rendering is determined by its resolution, an adjustable parameter that controls the number of horizontal and vertical pixels in the rendered image. More pixels are required to print an image (typically 300 x 300 pixels per inch) than to view it on the computer monitor (typically 72 x 72 pixels per inch).

Reverse engineering

The process of discovering the technological principles of a device or object through analysis of its structure and function, in order to duplicate or enhance it. Laser scanners can be used to digitize a physical model of a product in order to assist with reconstructing the physical model as a virtual model within a CAD modelling program.

Rib

A feature, normally added to the inside surface of a CAD part, used to improve the load-carrying ability or the stiffness of a plastic component, in order to obtain the required strength at an acceptable wall thickness. Ribs offer structural advantages, but if designed incorrectly they can cause warping and appearance problems. Specific guidelines must be followed to avoid this.

Screw boss

A feature added to CAD parts, allowing self-tapping screws (thread cutting or thread forming) to be used to assemble the parts post-manufacture. Screws are inserted into a through clearance boss on one part and into a boss with a pilot hole on the other. The pilot hole can be either moulded in or drilled post-moulding.

Selective laser sintering (SLS)

An additive RP process that uses a laser to sinter (fuse) a fine thermoplastic powder, and which is often used to create functioning prototypes.

Selective mask sintering (SMS)

An additive RP process similar to SLS that creates parts from powdered polymer materials. However, instead of a single laser beam, it uses an infrared lamp to fuse each layer of the part in one flash. Various materials can be used to create functional prototypes and end-use parts.

Shader

An adjustable setting in rendering programs that determines how a material will reflect light.

Solid model

Several CAD surfaces joined together to create a model with thickness and volume, also known as a closed polysurface and referred to as a watertight model. Models for output to additive RP processes must be solid.

Solid modelling

The process of creating solid models in CAD programs. Solid models can be created directly from splines using such processes as extrusion, or by creating surfaces from splines and then combining the surfaces together to create closed polysurface models with thickness and volume.

Spline

A mathematically defined curve that has its shape controlled by control points sitting off the curve. Splines can be used in CAD modelling programs to create both surface models and solid models.

Stair-stepping

The jagged appearance of diagonal edges of objects in low-resolution renderings or renderings in which insufficient anti-aliasing has been applied. Stair-stepping is also used to describe the stepped finish created on the surfaces of parts oriented at shallow angles to the horizontal, and on curved surfaces, particularly in such additive RP processes as FDM and 3DP, in which the layer thickness is greater than in other RP processes. Orientation of the STL model file by the RP machine operator is critical to minimizing stair-stepping on curved or flat surfaces. To achieve a smooth finish, stair-stepped surfaces on RP models require sanding by hand.

Stereolithography apparatus (SLA)

An additive RP process that creates accurate parts with very good surface finish from a UV curable liquid resin.

Subdivision

The process used in polygon mesh modellers to represent smooth curved surfaces from low density polygon mesh models without creating a more memory intensive model, by subdividing each polygonal face of the model into smaller faces that better approximate a smooth curved surface.

Support material

Material used in some additive RP processes to support thin overhanging sections on parts to prevent them from bending or breaking off during the build process. This material is later broken off or washed off using either water or a caustic solution.

Surface modelling

CAD modelling involving the use of splines to create open surfaces and closed surfaces (solid models). Surfaces can be combined to create open polysurfaces and closed polysurfaces (solid models).

Surface normal

A line perpendicular to a point on the surface of a CAD model, which always points outwards from the surface of a solid model.

Surface triangulation language (STL)

An STL file, also known as a surface tessellation language file or a stereolithography file, the current industry standard file type for export from CAD programs to additive RP processes.

Thermoplastic

Also known as thermosoftening plastic, a polymer that becomes pliable or mouldable above a specific temperature, and returns to a solid state on cooling. Thermoplastic can be remoulded, unlike thermoset plastic, which is cured through heat, a chemical reaction or irradiation and cannot be remoulded.

Undercut

An angled surface, protuberance or indentation that prevents a moulded plastic part, or a die-cast metal part, from being directly ejected from the mould tool or tool dies. Undercuts can be either internal or external, depending on whether they exist on inside or outside surfaces of a part. Undercuts can still be moulded or cast, but require a side action, an extra part of the tool that moves separately from the two halves. These add to the cost of the tooling and therefore increase the cost of the part.

Voxel

A volumetric pixel. In parts created by the direct light processing RP process, each thin layer of build material consists of voxels, which are cured using UV light reflected from multiple mirrors.

Water-jet cutting

A CNC process used to prototype and manufacture parts from thick sheet materials, typically mild steel, stainless steel, glass and stone, using a fine high pressure jet of cold water mixed with a fine abrasive silicate powder to cut through the material.

Watertight

A term used to describe CAD models that are solid, and therefore have no gaps or holes in their surfaces and thus have thickness and volume. A good way to check whether your CAD model is watertight is to analyse its volume; if a volume cannot be calculated, the model is not a solid and therefore not watertight.

Wire electrical discharge machining (EDM)

A highly accurate prototyping and manufacturing process similar to hot-wire cutting, used to make deep or intricately shaped cuts through metals using rapid electrical discharges (sparks) created between a high voltage, negatively charged, thin copper or brass wire and a positively charged metal workpiece.

Working prototype

A product prototype with the intended functionality of the end product, but not necessarily the appearance, created for usability testing and to obtain user feedback.

Zebra Analysis

A method used in CAD in which black and white stripes are applied to surfaces and polysurfaces in order to provide a visual indication of their smoothness, and to help analyse continuity across transitions between surfaces.

3D modelling, rendering and engineering software

2D sketching software

Autodesk www.autodesk.com
  SketchBook Designer (digital sketching of design concepts)

PTC www.ptc.com
  Creo Sketch (2D freehand sketching)

2D drafting software

Ashlar Vellum www.ashlar.com
  Graphite (2D/3D drafting)

Autodesk www.autodesk.com
  AutoCAD (2D drafting and 3D modelling)

IMSI/Design www.imsi.com
  TurboCAD Designer 18 (2D drafting)
  DesignCAD (2D drafting)
  TurboCAD Mac Designer 2D (2D drafting)
  TurboCAD LTE (full-featured 2D drafting)
  TurboCAD LTE Pro (as above with additional pro tools)

IronCAD www.ironcad.com
  IRONCAD DRAFT (2D drafting compatible with a large range of file types)

PTC www.ptc.com
  Creo Schematics (2D systems diagrams)
  Creo Layout (2D conceptual engineering)

3D modelling and rendering software

Alibre www.alibre.com
  Alibre Design Pro (parametric solid modeller)
  Alibre Design Expert (as above, but with added surface modelling capability, advanced sheet metal tools and direct editing when design history not available)

Altair www.solidthinking.com
  solidThinking (associative 3D NURBS modelling and rendering with some polygonal and solid modeller features)
  solidThinking Inspired (3D modelling with morphogenesis form generation adapted to suit structural requirements and promote minimal material use)

Ashlar Vellum www.ashlar.com
  Argon (history-free 3D modelling)
  Cobalt (parametric 3D modelling)
  Xenon (associative 3D modelling)
  Alchemy:Essential (file translation)
  Alchemy:Adept (file translation, additional compatibility with PTC Creo and Dassault Systèmes CATIA files)

Autodesk www.autodesk.com
  Alias Design (3D NURBS modelling and rendering)
  Alias Surface (3D NURBS modelling and rendering with advanced class A surface modelling tools)
  Alias Automotive (3D NURBS modelling for automotive design)
  Inventor (parametric modelling, design visualization, engineering simulations and animation of products)

  Inventor Professional (full-featured version)

AutoDesSys www.formz.com
  Bonzai3d
  Form Z (3D modelling and rendering)

BRICSYS www.bricsys.com
  Bricscad (low cost solid modeller)

Dassault Systèmes www.3ds.com
  SolidWorks (3D modelling and simulation) (1.4 million users)
  CATIA (parametric 3D surface and solid modelling and simulation)
  ICEM Surf (class A surface modelling and analysis)
  3DVIA Composer (documentation, exporting, file sharing and viewing of 3D models and animations that can be opened, viewed and played on a wide range of other software, including Word and PowerPoint)

DAZ 3D www.daz3d.com
  Carrara 8 (3D modelling, animation and rendering)
  Carrara 8 Pro (3D modelling, animation and rendering)

DeskArtes www.deskartes.com
  3Data Expert
  Dimensions Expert
  View Expert
  Design Expert
  Render Expert
  Import Package
  Industrial Design System (IDS)

Encore Software www.punchcad.com
  ViaCAD 2D (2D drafting)
  ViaCAD 2D/3D (2D drafting and 3D modelling)
  ViaCAD Pro (drafting, modelling and rendering)
  Shark LT (2D drafting)
  Shark (2D drafting and 3D modelling)
  Shark FX (drafting, modelling and rendering)

Genesis www.right-toolbox.com
  Integral Object Designer (basic 3D modeller)

IMSI/Design www.imsi.com
  TurboCAD Deluxe 18 (2D drafting, 3D modelling and rendering)
  TurboCAD Mac Deluxe 2D/3D (2D drafting, 3D modelling)
  TurboCAD Mac Pro (2D drafting, 3D modelling, rendering)
  TurboCAD Pro 18 (2D drafting, 3D modelling, rendering)
  TurboCAD Pro Platinum 18 (as above with some added features)

Inivis www.inivis.com
  AC3D (introductory 3D software)

IronCAD www.ironcad.com
  IronCAD (history-free parametric 3D modeller)
  INOVATE (low cost 3D modeller and viewer)

Kubotek www.kubotekusa.com
  Key Creator (history-free parametric solid modeller with surface modelling capability)

Maxon www.maxon.net
  Cinema 4D Prime (aimed at graphic designers looking to add 3D modelling to their toolset)
  Cinema 4D Studio (high end 3D modelling and rendering for 3D artists)

Moment of Inspiration http://moi3d.com
  (3D modelling software aimed at designers and artists)

Nemetschek www.vectorworks.net
  Vectorworks Designer (2D drafting, 3D modelling and rendering)

Nevercentre www.nevercentre.com
  Silo (3D sculpting polygon mesh modeller)

OmniCAD http://omnicad.com
  (2D and 3D modelling for mould and die design and complex 3D models)

PTC www.ptc.com
  Creo Direct (designed for fast and easy 3D modelling for casual users)
  Creo Parametric (formerly ProEngineer, parametric modelling software with a variety of add-ons available to analyse fatigue, plastic flow within injection moulds, clearance and creepage analysis for electromechanical designs, analysis of human–product interactions within virtual manikins, simulation of forces and accelerations in systems with moving components, animation of moving components, analysis and control of tolerances)

Radan www.radan.com
  Radan 3D (software for sheet metal design and engineering assembly modelling capable of unfolding sheet metal designs created in its own and other 3D software)
  Alphacam (CAD/CAM software compatible with any CNC machine)

Robert McNeel & Associates www.rhino3d.com
  Rhinoceros 3D (free-form NURBS 3D modelling software with built-in renderer)

Siemens www.plm.automation.siemens.com
  Solid Edge (2D drafting, 3D modelling, motion simulation, rendering)
  NX8 (CAD, CAE and CAM – 3D modelling, FEA simulation and component manufacturing)

Spaceclaim Corporation www.spaceclaim.com
  Spaceclaim Engineer (parametric solid modeller with compatibility with a variety of different 3D model files)

3D polygonal modelling and rendering software

Autodesk www.autodesk.com
  Mudbox (polygonal digital sculpting and digital painting)
  3ds Max Design (polygonal 3D modelling, animation and rendering)
  Maya (3D polygon sculpting and visual effects)
  Softimage (3D character animation and visual effects)

Pixologic www.pixologic.com
ZBrush (3D sculpting, painting and rendering)

3D voxel-based modelling and rendering software

3D Coat www.3d-coat.com
(3D sculpting, painting and rendering using voxel-based sculpting techniques, able to import 3D files from a variety of other 3D modelling programs)

Freeware 3D modelling software

Art of Illusion www.artofillusion.org
(open-source modelling, animating and rendering package)

Blender www.blender3d.com
(open-source modelling, animation and rendering package)

Dassault Systèmes www.3ds.com
DraftSight (free 2D drafting software to create, edit and view .dwg and .dxf files)
3D Via Shape (free 3D modelling software) (www.3dvia.com)

Google www.sketchup.google.com
SketchUp (free basic 3D modelling package)

K3DSurf http://k3dsurf.sourceforge.net
(free mathematically based 3D modelling package)

PTC www.ptc.com
Creo Sketch (2D freehand sketching)
ProDESKTOP (3D solid modelling, engineering drawing and basic rendering)

Haptic 3D modelling software

Anarkik 3D www.anarkik3d.co.uk
Cloud 9 (haptic sculpting software that requires a Flacon input device, which replaces the mouse to provide touch feedback from virtual 3D models)

Sensable www.sensable.com
FreeForm (3D modelling software using Phantom force feedback haptic modelling input, enabling users to touch and manipulate the 3D model)
ClayTools (3D freeform sculptural modelling software using Phantom force feedback haptic modelling input enabling users to touch and manipulate the 3D model)

Dedicated CAE software

Autodesk www.autodesk.com
Moldflow (injection moulding simulation for part optimization)

Dassault Systèmes www.3ds.com
SIMULIA (a suite of software for virtual testing of product performance, e.g. structural analysis of parts and assemblies, within the CATIA modelling software)

Next Limit Technologies www.nextlimit.com
RealFlow (fluid simulations) www.realflow.com

XFlow (engineering simulations) www.xflowcfd.com
EasyKinematics (motion simulation plug-in for Autodesk 2D and 3D software products) www.right-toolbox.com

PTC www.ptc.com
Creo Simulate (structural, thermal and vibration analysis)

Reverse engineering software

Geomagic www.geomagic.com
Geomagic Studio (transforming 3D scan data into polygon mesh models for design analysis and prototyping)
Geomagic Wrap (transforming 3D scan data into polygon mesh models for design analysis and prototyping)
Geomagic Qualify (checking scans of production parts for quality comparisons and to compare with original design)

Sycode www.sycode.com
Point Cloud (reverse engineering software for draping surfaces or wrapping meshes around point cloud data from 3D scanned objects. Outputs in .3dm, .dwg, .dxf, .3ds, .stl, .obj, .skp and .vtk file formats)

File conversion software

Ashlar Vellum www.ashlar.com
Alchemy:Essential (file translation for Ashlar Vellum files to make them compatible with other software)
Alchemy:Adept (file translation for Ashlar Vellum files with additional compatibility with PTC Creo and Dassault Systèmes CATIA)

AutoDWG www.autodwg.com
(converts .dwg files to .dxf files and vice versa, and is also used for updating versions of these files)

Delcam www.delcam.com
Exchange (stand-alone CAD translator program capable of translating from many popular CAD input formats to many output formats)

nPower www.npowersoftware.com
Power SubD•NURBS (plug-in for 3ds Max for converting polygon subdivision surfaces into NURBS surfaces)
Power Rhino (plug-in for Rhino that adds more solid modeller features to Rhino toolset)
PowerNURBS Pro (plug-in for 3ds Max that enables NURBS modelling within 3ds Max)

Okino www.okino.com
PolyTrans (industry standard 3D file conversion/translation)

Softpedia www.softpedia.com
IGES STEP Converter (converts STEP files to IGES files and vice versa)
Mesh Converter (converts between different types of mesh files – .dxf, .dwg, .3ds, .3dm, .stl, .obj)
MeshtoSolid (imports polygon mesh files – .stl, .obj, .3dm – and converts them into solid data files: .sat and .3dm)

Add-on software

Sycode www.sycode.com
(wide variety of stand-alone, plug-in and add-on software to add modelling functionality and import and export capability to popular 3D modelling programs)

Rapid prototyping software

Materialise www.materialise.com
Magics (3D file checking and preparation for rapid prototyping, tooling and manufacturing)

CAD/CAM software

Delcam www.delcam.com
PowerShape (software used for a variety of applications, including 3D modelling for manufacture, electrode design for EDM, mould and tool making)
PowerMill (software for creation of reliable NC code and editable tool paths for multi-axis machining and high-speed finishing of complex parts)
ArtCAM (software for the production of 3D models, 3D sculpted reliefs and moulds quickly and easily. Enables the creation of personalized or custom 3D models from 2D sketches or photographs)
FeatureCAM (software to automate machining and minimize programming times for parts on mills, lathes and wire EDM)
PartMaker (CAM system for automating the programming of multi-axis Turn-Mill centres and Swiss-type lathes)
CRISPIN (software to assist design, engineering and manufacturing of footwear)

Radan www.radan.com
Alphacam (CAD/CAM software compatible with any CNC machine)

Rendering and visualization software

3D Coat http://3d-coat.com
(sculpting, painting and rendering for 3D artists)

ArtVPS www.artvps.com
Shaderlight Pro (rendering plug-in for Google SketchUp)

Autodesk www.autodesk.com
Showcase (renderer supporting many 3D file formats)
Turtle (plug-in for Maya used for converting lighting into texture maps in game development)

Bunkspeed www.bunkspeed.com
Shot (physically accurate renderer for the Windows platform)
Move (all features of Shot plus the ability to animate)
Pro (all the features of Shot and Move plus additional materials, rendering, animation, camera and productivity features/benefits)

Cebas Visual Technology www.cebas.com
finalRender (plug-in renderer for Autodesk 3ds Max and Autodesk Maya)

Chaos Group www.chaosgroup.com
  V-Ray (plug-in renderer for Autodesk 3ds Max, Autodesk Maya, Autodesk Softimage, Rhinoceros 3D and Google SketchUp)

Indigo Renderer www.indigorenderer.com
  (stand-alone renderer)

Luxion www.keyshot.com
  KeyShot (stand-alone renderer with 4.1 megapixel maximum render resolution)
  KeyShot Pro (stand-alone renderer with unlimited render resolution)

Luxology www.luxology.com
  Modo (3D modelling, sculpting and rendering software)

Maxon www.maxon.net
  Cinema 4D Visualize (aimed at architects, designers and photographers for rendering and animation)

Motiva www.motivacg.com
  Colimo (post-production editing of materials, lighting, camera lens effects of renders)

NewTek www.newtek.com
  Lightwave 3D (VFX, rendering and animation aimed primarily at film, TV and games production artists)

Next Limit Technologies www.nextlimit.com
  Maxwell Render www.maxwellrender.com

NVidia www.mentalimages.com
  Mental Ray (stand-alone or plug-in renderer to a range of 3D software, including Autodesk 3ds Max, Autodesk Maya, Autodesk AutoCAD, PTC Pro/Engineer, Dassault Systèmes CATIA, Sensable FreeForm and Maxon Cinema 4D)

NVidia Gelato Pro
www.nvidia.co.uk/page/gelato

PiVR www.pi-vr.com
  VRED Essentials (stand-alone real time ray tracing renderer)
  VRED Essentials Plus (as above but with animation capability)

Pixar http://renderman.pixar.com
  RenderMan for Maya (high-end rendering of 3D animations and visual effects plug-in for Maya)
  RenderMan Studio (high-end rendering of 3D animations and visual effects)
  RenderMan Pro (high-end rendering of 3D animations and visual effects)

Pixologic www.pixologic.com
  ZBrush (digital sculpting and painting program, industry rival to Autodesk Mudbox)

PTC www.ptc.com
  Creo View MCAD (viewing of drawings, models and documents)
  Creo View ECAD (visualizing PCB-related designs)
  Creo Illustrate (creating 3D illustrations from 3D models)

RandomControl www.randomcontrol.com
  Arion (stand-alone renderer also available as a plug-in for Autodesk 3ds Max, Autodesk Maya, McNeel Rhinoceros 3D, NewTek Lightwave 3D, Maxon Cinema 4D, Google SketchUp, SoftImage XSI, Luxology Modo)
  fryrender (stand-alone renderer also available as a plug-in for Autodesk 3ds Max, Autodesk Maya, McNeel Rhinoceros 3D, NewTek Lightwave 3D, Maxon Cinema 4D, Google SketchUp, SoftImage XSI, Luxology Modo)

Refractive Software
www.refractivesoftware.com
  Octane Render (stand-alone renderer)

RenderZone www.formz.com
  (plug-in for AutoDesSys modelling software Bonzai3d and FormZ)

Robert McNeel & Associates
www.flamingo3d.com
  Flamingo3d (rendering plug-in for Rhinoceros 3D modelling software)

Sitex Graphics www.sitexgraphics.com
  Air (plug-in for Maya, Rhinoceros 3D and Cinema 4D Prime)

Solid Iris Technologies www.thearender.com
  Thea Render (stand-alone renderer also available as a plug-in for some popular 3D modelling software packages)

SplutterFish www.splutterfish.com
  Brazil (renderer available as plug-in for 3ds Max and Rhinoceros 3D)

Freeware rendering software

3Delight Studio Pro www.3delight.com
  (free renderer, stand-alone or as a plug-in to Autodesk Maya or Autodesk Softimage)

Aqsis www.aqsis.org

ArtVPS www.artvps.com
  Shaderlight (rendering plug-in for Google SketchUp)

Freestyle http://freestyle.sourceforge.net
  (creates sketches and technical illustrations from your 3D model [for Windows and Linux])

Kerkythea www.kerkythea.net
  (free stand-alone renderer)

LuxRender www.luxrender.net
  (free stand-alone renderer, also available as a plug-in for Blender, Autodesk 3ds Max, Google SketchUp, Cinema 4D, Daz Studio, Autodesk Softimage and Poser)

Motiva www.motivacg.com
  Motiva SOAP (free post-production software for changing colours, materials and lighting after rendering a scene)
  Motiva RealCamera (free post-production software for changing camera lens effects after rendering a scene)
  Material Convertor (converts materials so scenes can be transported between some popular rendering software packages)

NVidia Gelato www.nvidia.co.uk/page/gelato
  (free renderer)

Pixie www.renderpixie.com
  (free renderer)

Povray www.povray.org
  (free command line renderer)

Yafray www.yafray.org
  (free renderer with blender integration)

Animation and simulation software

Dassault Systèmes www.3ds.com
  3DVIA Studio Pro (authoring and publishing lifelike 3D simulations)

eias3D www.eias3d.com
  (animation and rendering package)

Hash www.hash.com
  Animation:Master (modelling and animation)

Maxon www.maxon.net
  Cinema 4D Broadcast (aimed at motion graphic artists)

PMG www.projectmessiah.com
  Messiah Studio Basic (animation and rendering package available stand-alone and as a plug-in for Autodesk Maya, Autodesk 3ds Max, Autodesk Softimage, Luxology Modo, NewTek Lightwave 3D and Maxon Cinema 4D)
  Messiah Studio Pro (as above but with added high-end animation and rendering features)

Robert McNeel & Associates www.rhino3d.com
  Bongo3D (plug-in for Robert McNeel & Associates Rhinoceros 3D)

Side Effects Software www.sidefx.com
  Houdini Escape (modelling, lighting and animation)
  Houdini Master (high-end modelling, lighting, rendering and animation)

Common types of 3D file

File Type	Format Name	Organization	Program
.3dm		Robert McNeel	Rhinoceros 3D
.3ds		AutoDesk	3ds Max
.amf	Additive Manufacturing Format	ASTM International	
.asm	Assembly Model	PTC	Creo (Pro/Engineer)
.blend		Blender Foundation	Blender 3D
.c4d		Maxon	Cinema 4D
.catpart	CATIA Part Model	Dassault Systèmes	CATIA
.catproduct	CATIA Assembly Model	Dassault Systèmes	CATIA
.dwg	Drawing File	Autodesk	AutoCAD
.dxf	Drawing Exchange Format	Autodesk	AutoCAD
.fbx	Film Box	Autodesk	Various
.iam	Inventor Assembly Model	Autodesk	Inventor
.iges			
.ipt	Inventor Part Model	Autodesk	Inventor
.lwo	Lightwave Object	NewTek	Lightwave 3D
.lxo		Luxology	Modo
.ma		Autodesk	Maya
.max		Autodesk	3ds Max
.obj		Wavefront Technologies	
.par	Part Model	Siemens	SolidEdge
.prt	Part Model	PTC/Siemens	Creo/NX8
.raw	Raw Mesh		
.sldasm	SolidWorks Assembly	Dassault Systèmes	SolidWorks
.sldprt	SolidWorks Part	Dassault Systèmes	SolidWorks
.step	Standard for Exchange of Product Model Data		
.stl	Surface Triangulation Language	3D Systems	
.u3d	Universal 3D	ECMA International	
.wrl	Virtual Reality Modelling Language (similar to .stl but includes colour)		

Further reading

Anderson, Chris, *Makers: The New Industrial Revolution*, Random House, 2013

Birn, Jeremy, *Digital Lighting & Rendering*, New Riders, 2nd edition, 2006

Brynjolfsson, Erik and Andrew McAfee, *Race Against the Machine: How the Digital Revolution is Accelerating Innovation, Driving Productivity, and Irreversibly Transforming Employment and the Economy*, Digital Frontier Press, 2012

Chua, Chee Kai, Kah Fai Leong and Chu Sing Lim, *Rapid Prototyping: Principles and Applications*, 3rd edition, WSPC, 2010

Danaher, Simon, *The Complete Guide to Digital 3D Design*, Ilex, 2004

Demers, Owen, *Digital Texturing and Painting*, New Riders, 2001

Gebhardt, Andreas, *Understanding Additive Manufacturing: Rapid Prototyping – Rapid Tooling – Rapid Manufacturing*, Hanser Fachbuchverlag, 2011

Gibson, Ian, David W. Rosen and Brent Stucker, *Additive Manufacturing Technologies: Rapid Prototyping to Direct Digital Manufacturing*, Springer, 2009

Hallgrimsson, Bjarki, *Prototyping and Modelmaking for Product Design*, Laurence King Publishing, 2012

Hopkinson, Neil, Richard Hague and Philip Dickens, *Rapid Manufacturing: An Industrial Revolution for a Digital Age*, Wiley-Blackwell, 2005

Hutchings, Ian M. and Graham D. Martin (eds.), *Inkjet Technology for Digital Fabrication*, Wiley-Blackwell, 2012

Jorge, Mateus Artur et al., *Virtual and Rapid Manufacturing: Advanced Research in Virtual and Rapid Prototyping*, Taylor & Francis, 2007

Kamrani, Ali K. (ed.) and Emad Abouel Nasr, *Rapid Prototyping: Theory and Practice*, Springer Verlag, 2006

Lefteri, Chris, *Making It: Manufacturing Techniques for Product Design*, Laurence King Publishing, 2nd edition, 2012

Lipson, Hod, *Fabricated: The New World of 3D Printing*, John Wiley & Sons, 2013

Marsh, Peter, *The New Industrial Revolution: Consumers, Globalization and the End of Mass Production*, Yale University Press, 2012

Megachange: The World in 2050, Economist Books, 2012

Noorani, Rafiq I., *Rapid Prototyping: Principles and Applications*, John Wiley & Sons, 2005

Pipes, Alan, *Drawing for Designers*, Laurence King Publishing, 2007

Rifkin, Jeremy, *The Third Industrial Revolution: How Lateral Power is Transforming Energy, the Economy, and the World*, Palgrave Macmillan, 2011

van Santen, Rutger, Djan Khoe and Bram Vermeer, *2030: Technology That Will Change the World*, OUP USA, 2010

Smith, Laurence, *The New North*, Profile Books, 2012

Thompson, Rob, *Prototyping and Low-Volume Production*, Thames & Hudson, 2011

For further information about CAD modelling and rendering techniques, there are many books that complement the training manuals provided with CAD software.

For reviews of software used for visualization, see magazines such as *3D World* and *Computer Arts*.

Internet resources

3D modelling and rendering

www.cardesignnews.com/site/home Car design news. Information about designers, design process and discussion forums.

www.develop3d.com Magazine and website from X3DMedia that tracks all the essential technologies used in product development.

www.doschdesign.com 3D models and resources including textures and HDR images.

www.hdrlabs.com/news/index.php HDRI information.

www.hdrsource.com Source for HDRI files.

www.mcadcafe.com Industry news and resources.

www.productdesignforums.com Tutorials and advice from product designers about CAD modelling and visualization.

http://students.autodesk.com Autodesk education community website where trial copies, chat rooms and digital folder facilities are available. Free educational (individual) licences are available for Autodesk CAD programs for faculty and students of degree-granting or certificate-granting educational institutions.

www.the3dstudio.com 2D and 3D resources.

www.3dcadtips.com Information about CAD programs, CAD hardware, industry news, and links to user forums for popular CAD programs.

www.3drender.com Information on lighting and rendering and computer graphics.

www.ucodo.com UCODO stands for User Co-Designed Objects. The platform allows professional product designers and design-orientated businesses to set up an online business for mass customization without needing developers, and without the costs associated with setting up a new business.

RP/AM industry news

www.additive3d.com Castle Island's World Wide Guide to Rapid Prototyping. Information and links to further resources.

www.candyfab.org Site coordinating development of the open source CandyFab Project.

http://www.crucibleid.com/3d-printing Useful truths about designing for 3D printing.

www.dtm-corp.com Directory of RP services and companies.

www.econolyst.co.uk and www.youtube.com/user/Econolyst Consultancy in RP and AM. Informative material in the publications section.

http://fabbaloo.com Personal manufacturing and 3D printing with links to further resources.

http://www.manufacturingthefuture.co.uk/design-guidelines Excellent set of design guidelines for SLS and DMLS created by Mike Ayre of Crucible Industrial Design.

http://www.paramountind.com/selective-laser-sintering.html Paramount Industries, a 3D Systems company, are selective laser sintering research and product development specialists.

www.rapidtoday.com Independent resource for users of RP and AM.

www.theengineer.co.uk Technology and innovation news.

www.thingiverse.com Sharing of anything using RP processes.

http://wohlersassociates.com RP/AM industry news, reports and links to useful resources.

Laser cutting and CNC milling and routing

www.bigbluesaw.com Online laser and water-jet cutting service.

www.emachineshop.com Online service for custom part fabrication using laser cutting, CNC milling, water-jet cutting, blanking, pressure die-casting, injection moulding, compression moulding, extrusion, punching, lathing, wire EDM and a variety of secondary processes. Get one part made and if the part is useful to others, sell additional parts to recoup your costs.

www.ponoko.com Laser cutting/engraving and CNC routing/engraving service bureau. Offer designs for sale in your own showroom.

RP/AM bureaus and 3D object services for designers

www.fluidforms.at Service allowing you to create a variety of additively manufactured gifts.

www.kraftwurx.com RP/AM service bureau. Also provides a service whereby you can offer your designs for sale.

http://i.materialise.com RP/AM result of using the online service offered by Materialise.

www.sculpteo.com/en RP/AM service bureau.

www.shapeways.com RP/AM service bureau. Also provides a service whereby you are able to offer your designs for others to buy.

RP/AM bureaus

www.protoshape.ch Service bureau for additive manufacturing in metals using the selective laser melting (SLM) process.

http://wohlersassociates.com/service-providers.html List of rapid product development service providers worldwide.

Metal plating for RP/AM parts

http://www.morganicmetalsolutions.com/applications.htm
www.3ddc.eu

RP/AM machine manufacturers and developers

Agilista www.keyence.co.jp
Arcam www.arcam.com
Asiga www.asiga.com
Aspect www.aspect-rp.co.jp
BluePrinter www.blueprinter.dk
Carima www.carima.com
CMET www.cmet.co.jp
Concept Laser www.concept-laser.de
DM3D Technology www.pomgroup.com
DWS www.dwssystems.com
EnvisionTEC www.envisiontec.de
EOS www.eos.info
Evonik http://corporate.evonik.com
ExOne www.prometal.com
Fabrisonic www.fabrisonic.com
HP http://www.hp3dprinting.co.uk
InssTek www.insstek.com
Irepa Laser www.beam-machines.com
Lithoz www.lithoz.com
Luxexcel www.luxexcel.com
Mcor Technologies www.mcortechnologies.com
MicroFab Technologies www.microfab.com
Microfabrica www.microfabrica.com
Optomec www.optomec.com
Phenix Systems www.phenix-systems.com/en
Realizer www.realizer.com
Renishaw www.renishaw.com
Sciaky www.sciaky.com
Shaanxi Hengtong Intelligent Machine Co. Ltd. www.china-rpm.com
Sintermask www.sintermask.com
SLM Solutions www.slm-solutions.com
Solidscape www.solid-scape.com
Stratasys www.stratasys.com
3D Systems www.3dsystems.com
3Geometry www.3geometry.com
Trumpsystem Precision Machinery www.trumpsystem.com
Voxeljet www.voxeljet.de

Low-cost RP machines

3T RPD Ltd www.3trpd.co.uk
Bits from Bytes www.bitsfrombytes.com
Cubify http://cubify.com
Desktop Factory http://desktopfactory.com
Fabbster www.fabbster.com
MakerBot www.makerbot.com
PP3DP http://pp3dp.com

Opensource RP machines

RepRap http://reprappro.com
Fab@Home www.fabathome.org

Materials for use in RP machines

DSM www.dsm.com
RepRap http://reprap.org/wiki/Printing_Material_Suppliers

Index

Page numbers in *italics* refer to illustrations;
page numbers in **bold** refer to Case Studies.

A

acceleration (G3) continuity 17, 18
additive manufacturing (AM) 68–69, 88, **140–157**
    definition 164
    designing for manufacture 137–139
    economic considerations 129–131
    the future 134–137, 158–161
    materials 131–132
    technology 135–137, 160–161
Additive Manufacturing Research Group
    (AMRG) **144–145**
additive rapid prototyping 68, 88–117, **100–117**
    direct light processing (DLP) 91–92, 164
    direct metal laser sintering (DMLS) 94–96, 118,
        133, 164
    fused metal deposition 96–97, 165
    jetting systems 89–90, 165
    selective mask sintering (SMS) 93–94, 166
    see also 3D printing (3DP); fused deposition
        modelling (FDM); selective laser sintering
        (SLS); stereolithography apparatus (SLA)
add-on software 40, 168
advanced materials 132
Airbike **156–157**
aircraft seating **36–37**
AlessiPhone and AlessiTab **50–51**
AM *see* additive manufacturing (AM)
ambience maps 47
ambient light (rendering) 44
angle (triangular mesh) 124, *125*
animation 56–58
    creating natural movement 58
    product models 57–58
    software 169
    using NURBS or solid models 56–57
anti-aliasing 48, 164
appearance prototype 164
area lights 42
aspect ratio (mesh) 124
assembly models 19, 164
attenuation (lighting) 43

B

back light 43
background 11, 164
Bathsheba Grossman **116–117**
Bespoke Innovations **150–151**
bicycle design **156–157**
bill of materials (BOM) 14, 164
biomimicry **146–147**
Bone Chair 8–9
bottle opener **116–117**
bump maps 47, 164

C

CAD *see* computer-aided design (CAD)
CAD/CAM software 168
CAE *see* computer-aided engineering (CAE)
CAM *see* computer-aided manufacture (CAM)
camera settings (rendering) 42, 164
carbon footprint 133
Catalyzer **34–35**
caustics (rendering) 45

ceramic designs **110–115**
CFD (computational fluid dynamics) 64–65, 164
chair design **100–101**
chord height (triangular mesh) 124, *125*
Class A surfaces 15, 164
closed polysurfaces 16, 164
closed surfaces 16, 164
cloud-based services 135, 136
CNC (computer numerical control) 18, 164
Colander Table **84–85**
colour maps *see* diffuse maps
coloured finishes 119
composite materials 131, 132
computational fluid dynamics (CFD) 64–65, 164
computer numerical control (CNC) 18, 164
computer-aided design (CAD) 11–65, **20–39,**
    50–55
    considerations for CAD models destined for
        RP 121–127
    definition 164
    drawings to 3D models 16–19
    modelling approaches 13–14, 15–16
    software 59–65, 167–169
    solid modelling 11, 13, *14*, 18, 166
    surface modelling 11, 13, *15*, 16–18, 121–127,
        166
    see also animation; rendering
computer-aided engineering (CAE) 18, 164
    software 64–65, 168
computer-aided manufacture (CAM) 18, 164, 168
construction planes 19, 164
consumer-led design 134–135, 138–139
continuity 17–18, 164
control points (NURBS) 13, 16, 164
cordless telephone **50–51**
cost considerations 129–131
curvature (G2) continuity 17, 18
customized products 68, 134–135, 138, **144–145,**
    150–153, 160–161
Customized Sprinting Spikes **144–145**

D

Daniel Rohr **84–85**
data *see* file
David Trubridge **80–83**
DCA Design **24–27**
decay (lighting) 43
decentralized design and production 130–131
dedicated CAE software 168
degree (NURBS) 13, 164
democratization of design 138
design history 19, 164
Design Partners **20–23**
design tree *see* design history
designing for manufacture 137–139
DesignLine television/home cinema **52–53**
development costs 129
diffuse maps 47, 164
digital scanning 16, **20**, 68, **110–111**
direct laser forming 94
direct light processing (DLP) 91–92, 164
direct lighting 43–44
direct manipulation 13, 164
direct metal deposition (DMD) 96
direct metal laser sintering (DMLS) 94–96, 118,
    133, 164

displacement maps 47
distance fall-off 43
DLP (direct light processing) 91–92, 164
DMD (direct metal deposition) 96
DMLS (direct metal laser sintering) 94–96, 118,
    133, 164
draft angle 138, 164
drawings 164
    conversion to 3D models 15–19
    production 14, 60–61
Dream Space **80–83**
dry sanding 119
dyes 119

E

EADS **156–157**
'ease-in/ease-out' 58
EBM (electron beam melting) 95, 133
economic considerations 129–131
Eden, Michael **112–115**
edge length (triangular mesh) 124, *125*
electrical discharge machining (EDM) 73, *74,*
    75, 166
electroforming 120–121
electron beam melting (EBM) 95, 133
energy-storage unit **38–39**
Entropia lamp **148–149**
environmental considerations 131, 132–134
Erich Ginder **110–111**
ExoVasc **152–153**
export (files) 121, 123, 127, 164
Exstent **152–153**

F

Fab@Home **142–143**
facet deviation 124
faceting 122–124
Factory Design **36–37**
FDM *see* fused deposition modelling (FDM)
FEA (finite element analysis) 64, 165
FGMs (functionally graded materials) 131, 138
file conversion software 168
file export 121, 123, 127, 164
file format 127
file size 127
file types 170
fill light 43
fillets 18, 127, 164
finishing processes 118, 121
finite element analysis (FEA) 64, 165
food production 134
fractal patterns **108–109,** **146–147**
Fractal.MGX Table **108–109**
frames (images) 56, 57–58, 165
Freedom Of Creation **102–103**
freeware software 168, 169
function curves 58
functionally graded materials (FGMs) 131, 138
fused deposition modelling (FDM) 98–99,
    100–101, 146–147, 165
    manufacturing machines **140–143**
    removing support material 118, *120*
fused metal deposition 96–97, 165
Fuseproject **100–101**
Future Factories **148–149**

G

gaps 126
garden gazebo **80–83**
Geometric Structure Cushion **78–79**
Ginder, Erich **110–111**
Giovannoni, Stefano **50–51**
global ambience (rendering) 44
global illumination (GI) 44–45, 165
Grossman, Bathsheba **116–117**
ground surface (rendering) 41, 47, 165
Growthobjects **146–147**

H

haptic modelling 165, 168
high dynamic range (HDR) images 44, 165
hobby sector 135
hollow metal parts 121
home cinema system **52–53**
hot-wire cutting 73, 74, 165

I

IK (inverse kinematics) 57
image maps 45, 165
image resolution see resolution
image-based lighting (IBL) 44, 165
image-based materials 45
implants (surgical) **152–153**
incandescence maps 47
indeterminate edges 125
indirect metal laser sintering 94
individualized products see personalized
    products
in-house production 136
initial grid quads 124
inkjet-based technologies 89–90
    see also 3D printing (3DP)
Insect Cage **104–105**
intellectual property protection 139
internal component modelling **29**
internet
    and CAD consumers 134, 138
    useful websites 171
invalid models 127
inverse decay 43
inverse kinematics (IK) 57

J

Jewellery modelling 97, 98, 107
Joris Laarman Lab 8–9

K

key light 43
keyframe 56, 165
Kina light **80**, 83
Klein Bottle Opener **116–117**

L

lacquer finish 120
laminated object manufacturing (LOM) 9
Laarman, Joris 8–9
laser cutting 70, 71, **76–79**, 165
laser engineered net shaping (LENS) 96
laser scanning 16, **20**, 68, **110–111**
Laser Sintered Aircraft **154–155**
LaserCusing 94
Lauren Moriarty **78–79**

LENS (laser engineered net shaping) 96
lens length 42
lighting (rendering) 42–45
lighting design **102–103**, **106–107**, **148–149**
living materials 132
local design and manufacturing 130–131
Loebach, Paul **86–87**
Loughborough University **144–145**
luminosity maps 47
Lunchbox **32–33**, **35**

M

machine technology 135–137, 160–161
machine tooling 129
manufacturability 137–139
manufacturing economics 129–131
material wastage 133
Materialized Vase **110–111**
materials (rendering) 45–47
materials (types) 131–132
maximum distance 124
Memento Rug **76–77**
mesh density 121–124
metal coating 120–121
metal encapsulation 120–121
metals 132
Michael Eden **112–115**
Michaella Janse van Vuuren **106–107**
milling 72, 73, **84–85**
MJM (multi-jet modelling) 90
model position 127
model tree see design history
Moriarty, Lauren **78–79**
Moving Platforms **54–55**
multi-jet modelling (MJM) 90
Mylo Pushchair **24–27**

N

Nakamura, Ryuji **104–105**
'naked' edges 125
non-uniform rational basis spline (NURBS) 12,
    13, 165
Noodle Block Cube **78–79**

O

office chair **100–101**
open edges 125
open organic form for the 3D model
open surfaces 16, 165
organic materials 132
organic shapes **146–147**

P

paint finishes 119–120
parameters 14, 134, 165
parametric modellers 14, 19, 165
parting lines 69, 165
patents 135
Paul Loebach **86–87**
personal navigational devices (PNDs) **28–31**
personalized products 68, 134–135, 138,
    150–153, 160–161
Philips Design **52–53**
photographs as underlays 16–17
pixels 48–49, 165
plasma cutting 70–71, 72, 73, 165

plastics see polymers
PLM (product lifecycle management) 59, 165
plotter cutter 165
plug-ins 40, 165
PNDs (personal navigational devices) **28–31**
polygon mesh models 12, 13–14, 165
    animation 56–57
    designing for manufacture 121–127
    software 167–168
polymers 131–132, 165
polysurfaces 16, 165
portable machines 135–136
positional (G0) continuity 17
positioning models 127
post curing 119
post processing 165
    see also finishing processes
Priestmangoode **54–55**
procedural materials 45
product lifecycle management (PLM) 59, 165
production costs 129–131
production drawings 14, 60–61, 165
production technology 135–137
prostheses **150–151**
prototyping bureaux 136

R

rapid manufacturing (RM) 68–69, 165
    see also additive manufacturing (AM)
rapid prototyping (RP) 67–127, 165–166
    CAD models destined for 121–127
    finishing processes 118–121
    software 168
    see also additive rapid prototyping;
        subtractive RP processes
ray tracing 45, 166
recycling and reuse of materials 131, 133
reflective surfaces 47
rendering 40–55, **50–55**
    anti-aliasing 48
    background 41
    camera settings 42
    definition 166
    ground surface 41
    image resolution 48–49
    lighting 42–45
    materials 45–47
    volume 48, 166
RepRap **140–141**
resolution 40–49, 166
retailing 130
reverse engineering **20**, **111**, 166, 168
ribs 166
rim light 43
RM see rapid manufacturing (RM)
Rohr, Daniel **84–85**
routing 72, 73, **80–83**, **86–87**
RP see rapid prototyping (RP)
rug design **76–77**
Ryuji Nakamura & Associates **104–105**

S

sand blasting 119
sanding 119
SAYL Office Chair **100–101**
screw bosses 166

selective laser melting (SLM) 94
selective laser sintering (SLS) 92–93, **102–103,
    106–107, 112–115, 144–157**
    definition 166
    material wastage 133
    removing excess build material 118
selective mask sintering (SMS) 93–94, 166
self-replicating manufacturing machines
    140–141
service bureaux 136
shaders (rendering) 47, 166
shadows (rendering) 45
Shelf Space **86–87**
simulation software 169
sketches as underlays 16–17
sky dome 42
skylight 42
SLM (selective laser melting) 94
SLS see selective laser sintering (SLS)
smoothing 119
smoothness 13, 18, 119, *123*
SMS (selective mask sintering) 93–94, 166
software 167–169
    computer-aided design (CAD) 59–65,
        121–122
    computer-aided engineering (CAE) 64–65
    future developments 134–135, 136–137
    products 167–169
solid freeform fabrication see additive
    manufacturing (AM)
solid modelling *11, 13, 14,* 18, 166
SolidWorks *19*
Southampton University **154–155**
specular maps 47
splines *12, 13, 15,* 16, 17, 166
sports shoes **144–145**
spotlights 42
stair-stepping 118, 166
standard triangulation language (STL) see
    surface triangulation language (STL)
Stefano Giovannoni **50–51**

stereolithography apparatus (SLA) 88–89,
    100–101, 104–105, 108–111, 146–147, 166
    removing excess build material 118
Stitch Studies **78–79**
STL see surface triangulation language (STL)
Studio Aisslinger **38–39**
subdivision 166
subtractive RP processes 67–68, 70–75, **76–87**
supply chains 130–131, 133, 160
support material 166
    removal 118, *119*
surface appearance 47, 119–120
surface continuity see continuity
surface finishing 119–121
surface gaps 126
surface modelling *11, 13, 15,* 16–18, 121–127, 166
surface normals 126, *127,* 166
surface overlaps 125, *126*
surface smoothness 13, 18, 119, *123*
surface triangulation language (STL) 18, 121,
    127, 166
surgical implants **152–153**

T

table design **84–85, 108–109**
tactile feedback see haptic modelling
tangential (G1) continuity 17
technology 135–137
telephone design **50–51**
television **52–53**
texture maps 45, 47
Therefore **28–31**
thermoplastics 166
3D CAD software 61–63, 167–168
3D file types 170
3D printing (3DP) 97–98, **112–117,** 164
    manufacturing machines **140–143**
    see also additive manufacturing (AM)
3D scanning 16, **20,** 68, **110–111**
tiling 47
time to market 129

tooling 129
Tools Design **32–35**
transparency maps 47
triangular meshes 121–124
triangulation tolerance 124
Trubridge, David **80–83**
tureen design **112–115**
2D CAD software 60–61, 167
2Form **76–77**

U

undercuts 121, 166
unmanned aerial vehicle (UAV) **154–155**

V

vacuum metallization 120, *121*
van Vuuren, Michaella Janse **106–107**
varnish finish 120
vase design **110–111**
visualization software 168–169
voxel based modelling 91–92, 168
voxels 166

W

wastage of material 133
water-jet cutting 70, *71,* 166
watertight 126, 166
Wedgwoodn't Tureen **112–115**
WertelOberfell Platform **108–109**
wet sanding 119
wire electrical discharge machining (wire EDM)
    73, *74,* 75, 166
Wireless Gaming Headset **20–23**
working prototype 166

Y

YILL energy-storage unit **38–39**

Z

Zebra Analysis 18, *18,* 166

Picture credits

Front cover
1597 wall light designed by Janne Kyttanen, manufacturer Freedom Of Creation.

Back cover
DCA Design International Ltd.

Pages 2–3 photo provided by QisDesign. Design by QisDesign/Qisda Creative Design Center, Taiwan, manufacturer Qisda Corporation, Taiwan.

Introduction
Page 6, figs. 1–3 courtesy Joris Laarman.

Chapter 1
Opener Ingo Aurin; figs. 1–3 Ingo Aurin; figs. 4 and 5 Ryan Chessar, 42 Technology Ltd; figs. 6–8 Ingo Aurin; fig. 9 Douglas Bryden; figs. 10 and 11 Ingo Aurin; fig. 12 Ryan Chessar, 42 Technology Ltd; figs. 13–19 James Lynch, Eugene Canavan, Andreas Connellan, all from Design Partners; Alex Danielson and Melissa Yale from Logitech ME team; figs. 20–26 DCA Design International Ltd; figs. 27–33 TomTom mechanical engineering team Amsterdam, freehand sketches: Martin Riddiford, CAD renders and photography: Rachael Roberts, final product picture: TomTom; figs. 34–40 Tools Design/Eva Solo; figs. 41–46 Factory Design; figs. 47–53 Photos: Younicos, Design: Studio Aisslinger, Company: Younicos; fig. 54 Ingo Aurin. fig. 55 Client: Philips, Agency: Stink Digital, 3D production: PK3D Studio www.pk3d.com; figs. 56–59 Ingo Aurin; fig. 60 Optos plc, i4 Product Design Ltd; figs. 61 and 62 Husqvarna Group, i4 Product Design Ltd; figs. 63 and 64 Ingo Aurin; fig. 65 Alfa Smyrna-Pixela, www.pixela-3d.com; fig. 66 SA6 in-ear monitors by Sleek Audio. Designed in collaboration with Robrady Design; figs. 67 and 68 Ingo Aurin; figs. 69–71 Tom Vack (AlessiPhone), Santi Caleca (AlessiTab); figs. 72–76 DesignLine TV and Home Theatre System designed by Philips Design in 2010; figs. 77–82 Moving Platforms by Priestmangoode; figs. 83–85 Ingo Aurin, avars by Alexandru Nechifor; figs. 86 and 87 Ingo Aurin; fig. 88 Ryan Chessar, 42 Technology Ltd; figs. 89 and 90 Ingo Aurin; fig. 91 Franke Product Line Color, Falkirk, United Kingdom, Cramasie Product Design Consultants, Edinburgh; figs. 92 and 93 Ingo Aurin; fig. 94 Franke Product Line Color, Falkirk, United Kingdom, Cramasie Product Design Consultants, Edinburgh; fig. 95 Ingo Aurin.

Chapter 2
Page 66 Maelstrom preparatory sketch, Rhino CAD rendering. Michael Eden 2011; fig. 1 Stratasys Ltd; fig. 2 courtesy Cappellini; fig. 3 Stratasys Ltd; fig. 4 Liquid Lattice Engine Block, designed by Within, manufactured by 3TRPD; fig. 5 hearing aid shells printed on a Perfactory® Digital Shell Printer from EnvisionTEC, Inc. using E-Shell 200 material; figs. 6–11 Fionn Tynan-O'Mahony; fig. 12 Optos plc, i4 Product Design Ltd; figs. 13–15 Ksenia Stanishevski, 2Form; fig. 16 photograph Lauren Moriarty; fig. 17 CAD file for 3D textile piece from the Stitch Studies series – reinterpreting fabric structures as CAD cut and layered pieces. Digital file Lauren Moriarty; fig. 18 photograph Lauren Moriarty; fig. 19 photography by David Trubridge. Designed by David

Trubridge with assistance from Madeleine Knight; figs. 20, 21 and 23 Design and photography by David Trubridge; figs. 22, 24 and 25 photography by David Trubridge. Designed by David Trubridge with assistance from Madeleine Knight; figs. 26–32 Daniel Rohr, www.danielrohr.com; figs. 33–38 courtesy Paul Loebach; figs. 33 and 37 photographs Jeremy Frechette; fig. 39 (diagram) Fionn Tynan-O'Mahony; (photograph) courtesy WertelOberfell Platform; fig. 40 produced by Ogle Models & Prototypes Ltd; fig. 41 (diagram) Fionn Tynan-O'Mahony; (photograph) one of ten 3D printers owned by 3D Creationlab; fig. 42 Fionn Tynan-O'Mahony; fig. 43 (diagram) Fionn Tynan-O'Mahony; (photograph) © Freedom Of Creation; figs. 44–46 Fionn Tynan-O'Mahony; fig. 47 (diagram) Fionn Tynan-O'Mahony (photograph) full-colour 3D concept model courtesy of 3D Systems; fig. 48 (diagram) Fionn Tynan-O'Mahony, (photograph) Stratasys Ltd; fig. 49 Stratasys Ltd; figs. 50–53 courtesy of Fuseproject; figs. 54–60 © Freedom Of Creation; figs. 61–65 Design: Ryuji Nakamura & Associates, Planning: Eizo Okada, Photo: Ryuji Nakamura & Associates, Takumi Ota; figs. 66–68 courtesy Dr Michaella Janse van Vuuren; figs. 69–74 WertelOberfell in collaboration with Matthias Bär, produced by Materialise.MGX; figs. 75–77 courtesy Erich Ginder; fig. 78 courtesy Adrian Sassoon; figs. 79 and 80 Michael Eden 2008; fig. 81 courtesy Adrian Sassoon; fig. 82 Maelstrom preparatory sketch, Michael Eden 2011; fig. 83 Michael Eden 2010; fig. 84 courtesy Adrian Sassoon; figs. 85–88 courtesy Bathsheba Grossman; fig. 89 © Freedom Of Creation; fig. 90 Fionn Tynan-O'Mahony; fig. 91 Fionn Tynan-O'Mahony and Kathrine Pelosi; figs. 92–94 Fionn Tynan-O'Mahony, (photograph) models: 3DDC Ltd, Hurst End Farm, Unit 4b, North Crawley, MK16 9HS, UK. 'Nigella' figurine designed by Phil Champ, LAPD Consultants Ltd; figs. 96 and 97 Fionn Tynan-O'Mahony; figs. 98 and 99 Douglas Bryden; figs. 100–102 Fionn Tynan-O'Mahony.

Chapter 3
Page 128 Scott Summit, Bespoke Innovations; fig. 1 Rael San Fratello / Emerging Objects. Design Ronald Rael, Virginia San Fratello, Emily Licht. Fabrication Emily Licht. Photo Kent Wilson; fig. 2 Defne Koz Design studio team; fig. 3 Rael San Fratello / Emerging Objects. Photo Ronald Rael, Design Ronald Rael, Virginia San Fratello, Emily Licht. Assembly and fabrication: Emily Licht, Nick Duccelli, Kent Wilson; fig. 4 top acetabular cup and tibial tray designed using Within Medical Software, manufactured using an EOS M280 in Titanium alloy, bottom finger implants designed by Within, manufactured by EOS; fig. 5 Rael San Fratello / Emerging Objects, photo Kent Wilson; fig. 6 Rael San Fratello / Emerging Objects, wood blocks designed by Anthony Gianini, photo Kent Wilson; fig. 7 Rael San Fratello / Emerging Objects, photo Kent Wilson; fig. 8 designers Jesse Louis-Rosenberg and Jessica Rosenkrantz, photo Jessica Rosenkrantz; fig. 9 left a 3D printer creating a kidney prototype, right prototype tissues and organs printed on a 3D printer; fig. 10 design for metal laser sintered airline seat buckle by Mike Ayre of Crucible Industrial Design Ltd, developed as part of the SAVING project funded by the Technology Strategy Board and built by

3T RPD Ltd; fig. 11 bio-inspired Heat Exchanger, designed by Within, manufactured by 3T RPD Ltd; fig. 12 prototype of a machine that can create custom chocolate candies, Marcelo Coelho; fig. 13. concept for digital gastronomy fabricator, Marcelo Coelho and Amit Zoran; fig. 14 N12 bikini designed by Jenna Fizel and Mary Huang, photograph by Mary Huang; fig. 15 STRVCT shoe designed by Mary Huang and Jenna Fizel, rendering by Jenna Fizel; fig. 16 produced by Materialise.MGX, photo Materialise.MGX; fig. 17 cell cycle generative design tool, designers Jesse Louis-Rosenberg and Jessica Rosenkrantz; fig. 18 bone cuff (left) and porous cuff (right), designers Jesse Louis-Rosenberg and Jessica Rosenkrantz, photo Jessica Rosenkrantz; fig. 19 Bethany Weeks; fig. 20 Roy Mwangi Ombatti and his friend and colleague Harris Mwambeo Nyali for his invaluable help in designing the shoes; figs. 21–23 courtesy of reprap.org; fig. 24 photo Floris van Breugel, design Fab@Home team, Cornell University; fig. 25 Fab@Home team, Cornell University; fig. 26 Evan Malone, Fab@Home team, Cornell University; figs. 27–29 Andrea Vinet, Loughborough University; figs. 30–35 Growthobjects (www.growthobjects.com); fig. 36 Kundalini S.r.l. (www.kundalini.it); figs. 37–40 Lionel Dean; fig. 41 Kundalini S.r.l. (www.kundalini.it); fig. 42 Lionel Dean; figs. 43–45 Scott Summit, Bespoke Innovations; figs. 46–49 SLS former and textile sleeve courtesy of Tal Golesworthy of Exstent. SLS former produced by CRDM Ltd, photographs Douglas Bryden; figs. 50–55 Jeroen van Schaik, University of Southampton; figs. 56–58 EADS; fig. 59 Jan Torgersen, Vienna University of Technology; fig. 60 Centre for Rapid Automated Fabrication Technologies (CRAFT), University of Southern California; fig. 61 Biomed Research Institute at the University of Hasselt, Belgium (Professor Dr Jules Poukens, Professor Dr Ivo Lambrichts, Dr Ingeborg van Kroonenburgh) in cooperation with engineers from Xios University College (Michäel Daenen), SIRRIS (Carsten Engel), Xilloc Medical BV, Maastricht, The Netherlands (Maikel Beerens), the Department of Medical Engineering at the University of Leuven, Belgium (Professor Dr Jos Vander Sloten), and the Department of Cranio-, Maxillo-Facial surgery at Orbis Medical Centre Sittard-Geleen, The Netherlands. Additive manufacturing by LayerWise (Ludwig Dehandschutter, Ruben Wauthle), fig. 62 above Markus Kayser working with the Solar Sinter, below printing a tile, photographs Amos Field Reid, Egypt, 2011.

Acknowledgements

I would like to thank all of the designers and researchers who contributed material for this book for their valuable time and generosity. I regret that not all of the material supplied to me could be used.

I would like to express my gratitude to Alex Milton for his encouragement to write this book; to my colleagues in the Product Design department and within the School of Design at Edinburgh College of Art for their encouragement and support; to my students, designers of the future, for their inspirational responses to my teaching; to Anna Hammond, for her assistance with initial research; and to Fionn Tynan O'Mahony, for his assistance with creating images and illustrations. Special thanks go to my colleague Ingo Aurin, for his invaluable work sourcing and creating images and illustrations.

I would like to thank Sophie Drysdale, my commissioning editor at Laurence King Publishing, without whom this book would not have existed and who provided me with helpful guidance from the outset. I would also like to thank Susan George for her patience and thoroughness and for her valuable input during the development of the text; Clare Double for her patience, attention to detail and management of the editorial and design process; Angela Koo the copy editor and Mark Ralph the proof-reader for their help refining the text; Fredrika Lökholm for her enthusiastic picture research; Srijana Gurung for her guidance on images; and Patrick Morrissey for his hard work designing this book.

Finally, I would like to thank and dedicate this book to my wife Preeya and my family for their unfaltering love, understanding and support.